Credits

Footprint credits
Editor: Alan Murphy
Production and Layout: Patrick Dawson, Elysia Alim, Danielle Bricker
Maps: Kevin Feeney

Managing Director: Andy Riddle
Commercial Director: Patrick Dawson
Publisher: Alan Murphy
Publishing Managers: Felicity Laughton, Nicola Gibbs
Digital Editors: Jo Williams, Tom Mellors
Marketing and PR: Liz Harper
Sales: Diane McEntee
Advertising: Renu Sibal
Finance and Administration: Elizabeth Taylor

Photography credits
Front cover: Ragne Kabanova/Shutterstock
Back cover: Philip Lange/Shutterstock

Printed in Great Britain by CPI Antony Rowe Chippenham, Wiltshire

Every effort has been made to ensure that the facts in this guidebook are accurate. However, travellers should still obtain advice from consulates, airlines etc about travel and visa requirements before travelling. The authors and publishers cannot accept responsibility for any loss, injury or inconvenience however caused.

Publishing information
Footprint *Focus Fès & Northern Morocco*
1st edition
© Footprint Handbooks Ltd
July 2011

ISBN: 978 1 908206 09 1
CIP DATA: A catalogue record for this book is available from the British Library

® Footprint Handbooks and the Footprint mark are a registered trademark of Footprint Handbooks Ltd

Published by Footprint
6 Riverside Court
Lower Bristol Road
Bath BA2 3DZ, UK
T +44 (0)1225 469141
F +44 (0)1225 469461
discover@footprintbooks.com
www.footprintbooks.com

Distributed in the USA by Globe Pequot Press, Guilford, Connecticut

The content of Footprint *Focus Fès & Northern Morocco* has been taken directly from Footprint's *Morocco Handbook*, which was researched and written by Julius Honnor.

Contents

Introduction
- 4 *Map: Fès and Northern Morocco*

Planning your trip
- 6 Getting there
- 6 Getting around
- 12 Sleeping
- 14 Eating & drinking
- 21 Essentials A-Z

28 Fès, Meknès, Middle Atlas
- 28 **Fès**
- 29 *Map: Fès: three cities*
- 32 Sights
- 34 *Map: Fès el Bali*
- 40 *Map: Fès el Jedid*
- 43 *Map: Fès Ville Nouvelle*
- 45 Listings
- 54 **Meknès**
- 56 *Map: Meknès*
- 58 Sights
- 59 *Map: Meknès Médina*
- 62 Moulay Idriss and Volubilis
- 65 *Map: Volubilis*
- 66 Listings
- 71 **Middle Atlas**
- 71 Azrou
- 73 Ifrane and the lakes
- 74 Khénifra and around
- 74 Midelt
- 75 Around Midelt
- 76 Listings
- 80 **Taza**
- 81 Sights
- 81 *Map: Taza Médina*
- 83 *Map: Jbel Tazzeka National Park*
- 87 Listings

90 Tangier & the North
- 92 **Tangier**
- 92 *Map: Tangier*
- 96 Sights
- 97 *Map: Tangier Médina*
- 101 Listings
- 108 **North Atlantic coast**
- 109 Asilah
- 108 *Map: Asilah*
- 110 El Utad, the stone circle at Mzoura
- 111 Larache
- 112 *Map: Larache*
- 113 *Map: Lixus*
- 114 Listings
- 118 **Ceuta**
- 119 Sights
- 120 *Map: Ceuta*
- 122 Listings
- 124 **Tetouan**
- 125 Sights
- 126 *Map: Tetouan*
- 128 Beach resorts around Tetouan
- 129 Listings
- 132 **Chefchaouen, the Rif and Al Hoceïma**
- 132 Chefchaouen
- 133 *Map: Chefchaouen*
- 135 Northern Rif
- 136 Ouezzane and Southern Rif
- 137 Al Hoceïma
- 139 Listings

Footnotes
- 146 Language in Morocco
- 150 Index

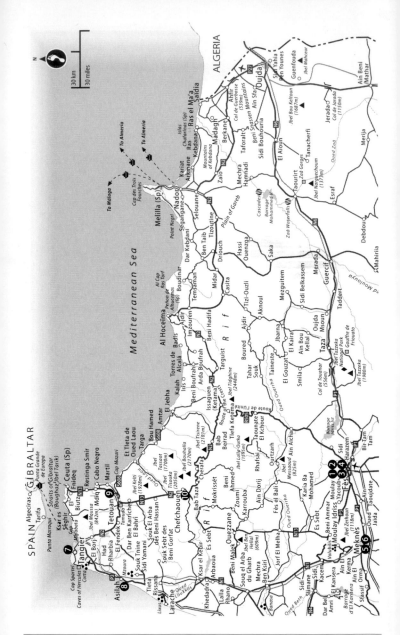

The area of central Morocco around the Jbel Zerhoun and the Saïss Plain was important even in ancient times, a strategic, fertile region on the trade routes leading from eastern North Africa to the Atlantic coast. Power has often been concentrated in this region – witness the ancient Roman city of Volubilis, and the imperial cities of Fès and Meknès.

Volubilis is one of the finest Roman sites in North Africa, and its ruins still manage to evoke life in a prosperous frontier town in the second and third centuries AD. Nearby, Moulay Idriss, the father of the Moroccan state, is honoured in the pilgrimage town of the same name, a memorable settlement, with houses cascading down hills on either side of a large mosque.

High on the plateau lands between Middle and High Atlas, the former mining town of Midelt is another useful base in the region. From here, there are plenty of interesting day trips into the hill country.

At the top of Morocco Africa is at its nearest to Europe, a short hop across the Straits of Gibraltar, yet a world away. Tangier, one-time international city, is the most obvious example: despite its geographical closeness and ferry connections, it is a place characterized more by stasis than dynamic crossover; its most potent image that of young African men standing for hours gazing across the sea at a hazy Spain. The city's seafront and kasbah are full of the decadent ghosts of writers along with a great museum and people-watching cafés. Inland from Tangier, Chefchaouen is a beautiful white- and blue-washed hill town, which, along with Ouezzane and Tetouan, reflects its links with Andalucía, long lost to the Moors.

Planning your trip

Getting there

Air

Major European airlines run frequent scheduled flights to Morocco's main airports at Casablanca-Mohamed V, Marrakech and Agadir, with most flights operating from France and Spain. National carrier **Royal Air Maroc (RAM)** (www.royalairmaroc.com) is reliable. Prices are similar to Air France and British Airways. The cheapest flights are usually with budget airlines **EasyJet, Ryanair** and **Atlas Blue**. Charter flights are another possible cheap option. Run by package holiday companies, they fly mainly to Agadir.

Aéroport Casablanca Mohammed V

Casablanca's main airport is at Nouasseur, 30 km southeast of Casablanca, T022-339100. The airport terminal has cafés, post boxes, bureaux de change and agencies for car hire companies. There are also ATMs on the main concourse, just after you pass customs. There is no hotel at this airport. Following the 2003 Casablanca bomb attacks, the airport was put off-limits to all but travellers with tickets. Those meeting travellers wait outside.

Onward travel is by train or taxi. The station is under the main airport concourse, and the Bidhaoui blue regional express train runs services on the hour to Casablanca Voyageurs (30dh), the main station for intercity trains. From here, you can take another train for the short ride to Casa-Port station, close to the hotels and the CTM bus terminal. You can also do this run in a red petit taxi, for around 10-15dh. Just outside the main door of the airport is the taxi rank. A grand taxi is 200dh to Casablanca city centre, 400dh to Rabat. Mercedes taxis for the airport may be found at the CTM bus station or close to the Place des Nations Unies, on Avenue Moulay Hassan I.

Aéroport Tangier Boukhalef

Situated 15 km from Tangier, the Aéroport Boukhalef, T039-935720, has a couple of banks with bureaux de change but at the time of writing no ATM. Travel into Tangier either by bus or grand taxi. The taxi should cost 70dh for up to six people. Make arrangements with other travellers inside the terminal regarding payment. There is a bus for the town centre.

Other airports

There are also some international flights to **Aéroport Charif Al Idrissi**, at Al Hoceïma, **Aéroport Fès Saïss**, at Fès, and **Aéroport Rabat-Salé**, 10 km from Rabat. All are well connected by buses or grand taxis.

Airport tax

There are no airport taxes.

Getting around

When planning a trip in Morocco, remember that the distances are great, and that long trips on buses can be tiring. Bus journeys are often excruciatingly slow, even over

Don't miss ...

1   Talaâ Kbira, page 32.
2   Bou Inania Medersa, page 33.
3   Chouara tanneries, page 38.
4   Festival de Fès, page 51.
5   Bab Mansour, page 61.
6   Moulay Ismaïl, page 61.
7   Tangier kasbah, page 96.
8   Asilah's seafood, page 116.
9   Tetouan médina, page 125.
10 Chefchaouen, page 132.

These numbers refer to the numbers on the map on page 4.

relatively short distances. To make maximum use of your time, especially if you don't mind dozing on a bus, take night buses to cover the longer distances. If you have sufficient funds, then there is always the option of internal flights – although these may not always fit in with your schedule. Public transport is very reasonably priced and the train network is good, and being heavily invested in, although it doesn't cover the whole country. Car hire can be expensive: although you may be able to get a small car for 1800-2500dh a week, you still have petrol or diesel costs on top of this. In many places, however, a car enables you to reach places which are otherwise inaccessible.

Air
Royal Air Maroc (www.royailairmaroc.com), operates domestic flights, most routed via Casablanca and requiring waits in the airport. Cities served include Tangier, Marrakech, Ouarzazate, Laâyoune, and Dakhla. There are limited direct flights between Marrakech and Fès. There are flights to and from Laâyoune on most days. A flight from Oujda to Casablanca (one a week) cuts out a 10-hour train journey.

Road
Bus Domestic bus services are plentiful. Price variations are small while the quality of service varies enormously. Broadly speaking, if the train, a **Supratours** bus or grands taxi run to your destination, don't bother with the small bus companies. For early morning services it's worth getting your ticket in advance, also at peak times when many Moroccans are travelling, like the end of Ramadan and around Aïd el Kebir (two months after the end of Ramadhan). You will find that there is a man who helps stow luggage on the roof or in the hold, so have a couple of dirham coins handy for him. Interailers note: the pass is not valid with Supratours.

In southern Morocco, the safest and most comfortable service is also with Supratours. Next best is the CTM, Compagnie de transport marocain (white buses with blue and red stripes). Often (but not always) their services run from stations away from the main gare routière (inter-city bus station). This is the case in Casablanca, Fès and Marrakech, for example. For Tangier, the CTM station is just outside the port zone gates. For information (renseignements) on CTM services try T022-458881. Both Supratours and CTM buses usually run on time. As an example of prices, a single Marrakech to Essaouira costs 65dh with Supratours. The CTM's quadrilingual website, www.ctm.co.ma, may one day be updated to give schedules.

Safety Vehicles used by many private bus companies do not conform to high safety standards. Drivers are severely underpaid, and, to make up for their low wages, may leave half-full, aiming to pick up extra passengers (whom they won't have to declare to their employers) en route. This makes for a slow, stop/go service. On routes worked by several companies, drivers race each other to be first to pick up passengers in the next settlement. Given the poor condition of the vehicles and the often narrow roads, accidents are inevitable.

Although inter-city buses can be very slow, (and you may even see the road surface under your feet), for many of the people who use them speed is not an issue. Pack mules link mountain villages to the rest of the world, while on the coastal plains, mule and donkey drawn buggies provide transport to the weekly souk.

City buses Most towns have city buses which provide great opportunities for local pickpockets when crowded. Casablanca buses are terrible, so have 20dh notes ready for short red-taxi runs. The orange Alsa buses in Marrakech are fine.

Car hire As distances are great having a car makes a huge difference to the amount you can cover. All the main hire car companies are represented and there are numerous small companies which vary hugely in reliability. The smallest car available is generally a Fiat Uno, more rarely a Renault 4. A large number of agencies now have Fiat Palios in their fleets. The Peugeot 205 is felt to be a more reliable small car, with slightly higher clearance and better road holding. A good deal would give you an Uno for 500dh a day, unlimited mileage, although some Marrakech agencies can be cheaper. Four-wheel drives available in Morocco include the Suzuki Gemini (two persons) and the Vitara (four persons), at around 800dh per day; long-base Mitsubishi Pajeros (6 persons) are hired at 900-1,000dh per day. Toyotas are said to be the best desert 4WDs. Landrovers are very uncomfortable for long cross-country runs on road, especially in summer without air conditioning. There is huge demand for hire cars during the Christmas and Easter breaks. Always try to have the mobile phone number of an agency representative in case of emergency. Most cars do not as yet use unleaded petrol – if you have one that does, you will find that not all petrol stations have unleaded, especially in the south. Always drive more slowly than you would in Europe.

Remember that you are responsible for damage if you take a car unsuited to the piste into areas suitable only for 4WDs. Regarding insurance, the best agencies will provide all risk insurance. Check for scratches and especially tyre condition (this includes spare tyre), presence of jack and warning triangle, working lights and safety belts. When hiring an all-terrain vehicle, try to ascertain that the agency you are hiring from has a reliable, well-maintained fleet. Make sure that the vehicle will go into four-wheel drive easily.

In general, you will need dirhams to pay, as only the larger agencies take credit cards. They will take an imprint of your credit card as a guarantee. See individual city and town directories for details of companies.

Car insurance In terms of car insurance and damage to vehicle, there are several possibilities. A good agency will have agreements with garages across Morocco for repairs. The garage will talk to the agency about the nature of the repairs, and the matter will be handled. If the damage is your fault (eg because you have taken the car onto rough tracks in breach of contract), you will be responsible for covering the cost of repairs. In the case of accidents, you have to get a constat de police (a police report), which is a document drawn up by the police stating whose fault the accident is. Depending on the type of insurance, the client pays a percentage of the cost of repairs. You can have a sans franchise (rental contract) which means that you will have nothing to pay, or with a franchise set at a certain level, that is a 50% franchise means that you pay 50% more than rental cost, so that in a case of an accident, you pay only 50% cost of repairs.

Petrol and other costs You may have to pay for the petrol already in the tank of your hire car. Usually, the car will be almost empty, and you fill up yourself. At the time of writing, diesel in Morocco is around 7.5dh per litre, petrol 10.5dh. Hire cars in Morocco generally run on petrol (super) rather than diesel. Lead-free petrol is sans plomb. A fill-up (le plein) for a Fiat Uno or a Clio costs around 400dh. In such a car, 250dh does the four-hour trip on winding mountain roads from Marrakech to Ouarzazate. A fill-up with diesel for a Pajero 4WD costs around 600dh, and on this the vehicle will do the 800 km trip Marrakech to Zagora and back.

In remote areas, remember to fill up whenever possible, preferably at one of the larger petrol stations (Shell, Mobil, CMH, in most cities, Ziz in the South). There have been cases of petrol being watered down, with unfortunate results, in certain places. New looking service stations in towns are best.

Should you need tyre repairs, prices vary. Expect to pay upwards of 50dh as a foreigner in a hurry in a small town, rather less if you have time to wait in some rural outpost.

Risky roads There are a number of dangerous stretches of road which you may have to deal with in your hire car. Much concentration is needed on the four-hour drive on the winding, mountainous N9, Marrakech to Ouarzazate, via the Tizi-n-Tichka. Fog and icy surfaces are possible in winter. There are roads which seem excellent, you drive fast, and then meet sudden dips and turns, such as Ouarzazate to Skoura, Agdz to Nekob. The new N11, the Casablanca to Marrakech motorway, has much improved road transport between the two cities but care must be taken on the Rabat to Fès N1, especially as there are few crash barriers. In the Middle and High Atlas barriers are put across the road on routes to Azrou, Ifrane, Midelt and over the Tizi-n-Tichka and Tizi-n-Test when snow blocks roads.

Road accidents cost the State about US$1.2 billion a year, according to official figures. In one week in July 2008, 23 people were killed and 1309 injured, including 87 seriously, in 1001 traffic accidents.

Highway code The Moroccan highway code follows the international model. Speeds are limited to 120 kph on the autoroute, 100 kph on main roads, 60 kph on approaches to urban areas and 40 kph in urban areas. Speed restriction signs do not always follow a logical sequence. There are two types of police to be met on the roads: the blue-uniformed urban police and the grey-uniformed gendarmes in rural areas. The latter are generally stationed outside large villages, at busy junctions, or under shady eucalyptus trees near bends with no-overtaking marks.

The wearing of seat belts is compulsory outside the cities, and the gendarmes will be watching to see you're wearing them. (Many Moroccans who know the checkpoint locations well seem to think that seat-belts are worn just for the gendarmes.) It is traditional to slow down for the gendarmes, although as a foreigner driving a hire car you will generally be waved through. They will not, on the whole, ask for 'coffee money' from you. Note, however, that the police are empowered to levy on the spot fines for contravention of traffic regulations. Fines are now quite severe in response to the high number of fatal accidents due to careless driving.

Other highway code tips: red and white curb markings mean no parking; warning triangles are not compulsory – but highly useful; in the case of an accident, report to nearest gendarmerie or police post to obtain a written report, otherwise the insurance will be invalid.

Car parking In towns, parking is fairly easy. Parking meters rarely function and instead a sort of watchman, identified by blue overalls and a metal badge will pop up. Give him some spare change, say 10dh, when you return to your undamaged vehicle. At night, it is essential to leave your vehicle in a place where there is a night watchman (le gardien de nuit). All good hotels and streets with restaurants will have such a figure who will keep an eye out.

Hitchhiking
It is possible to hitchhike in Morocco. There are lorries which go to and from Europe, and drivers can sometimes be persuaded to take a passenger. In remote areas, vans and lorries may pick up passengers for a bargained price. However, don't count on hitching, as vehicles out in the sticks are generally packed with locals. Landrover taxis (jeeps) and Mercedes Transit are not run for hitchers – they are public transport with a price. Hitching is unadvisable for women travelling on their own.

Taxi
Long distance grands taxis, generally Mercedes 200 saloon cars, run over fixed routes between cities, or within urban areas between centre and outlying suburbs. There is a fixed price for each route and passengers pay for a place, six in a Mercedes, nine in a Peugeot 504 estate car. Taxis wait until they are full. You may, however, feel rich enough to pay for two places in order to be comfortable at the front (and be able to wear a safety belt). In a Peugeot estate, the best places are undoubtedly at the front, or, if you are quite small, right at the back. The middle place in the middle row is probably the worst.

Between towns, grands taxis are quicker than trains or buses, and normally only a little more expensive. Each town has a grand taxi rank, generally, although not always, next to the main bus station. The drivers cry out the name of their destination, and as you near the taxi station, you may be approached by touts eager to help you find a taxi.

In mountain areas, the same system applies, although the vehicles are Mercedes transit vans (where there is tarmac) or landrovers, which have two people next to the driver and ten in the back.

Petits taxis are used within towns, and are generally Fiat Unos and Palios. They are colour-coded by town (blue for Rabat, red for Casa, khaki for Marrakech, tasteful pistachio green in Mohammedia). Officially they are metered, with an initial minimum fare, followed by increments of time and distance. There is a 50% surcharge after 2100. A petit taxi may take up to three passengers. In Marrakech, Rabat and Casablanca, drivers generally use the meters, in Tangier they try to charge what they like. In some cities (notably Rabat and Casablanca, where taxis are in short supply) drivers allow themselves to pick up other passengers en route if they are going the same way, thus earning a double fee for part of the route. Taxi drivers welcome a tip – many of them are not driving their own vehicles, and make little more than 100dh a day. In terms of price, a short run between old and new town in Marrakech will set you back 12dh. Casa Port station to Casa Voyageurs is about 12dh too.

Train
The **ONCF** (Office national des chemins de fer) runs an efficient though generally slowish service between major cities. There is 1900 km of railway line, the central node being at railway town Sidi Kacem, some 46 km north of Meknès. Coming into Casablanca airport, you can take the blue Bidhaoui shuttle train to Casa-Voyageurs station on the main north-south line. This line runs from Tangier to Marrakech with significant stations being Kénitra, Sidi Kacem, Salé, Rabat, Casa-Voyageurs, Settat, and Benguerir. The ONCF's main west-east route does Casa-Voyageurs to Oujda, the main stations on this route being Rabat, Sidi Kacem, Meknès and Fès. A new fast double decker service connects Casablanca with Fès in three hours 20 minutes. There are also frequent trains from Marrakech to Fès. ONCF timetables are available at all main stations and can be accessed at www.oncf.ma.

Prices and journey times Prices are reasonable. A first-class single ticket, Marrakech to Fès, is 276dh, or 180dh in second class. Services between Casablanca and Rabat, depending on station and class, range form 32dh to 55dh. Casa-Voyageurs to Tangier is 175dh first class. In terms of time, Casablanca to Marrakech generally takes three hours, Casablanca to Rabat just under one hour, Rabat to Fès nearly four hours. Fès to Oujda is another 5½ hours, while Rabat to Tangier is 4¾ hours. Marrakech to Fès is around seven hours.

Train-bus link **Supratours** run buses to connect with trains from a number of stations. Routes covered include Tnine Sidi el Yamami, just south of Asilah, to Tetoutan; Taourirt to Nador and Khouribga to Beni Mellal. From outside Marrakech station, Supratours has connecting buses to Ouarzazate, Essaouira, Agadir, Laâyoune and Dakhla. Sample prices as follows: Marrakech to Agadir 95dh, Agadir to Laâyoune 210dh, Marrakech to Ouarzazate 80dh.

Train classes On the trains, first-class compartments are spacious and generally quieter than second class. Second-class rail fares are slightly more expensive than the CTM buses. You gain, however, in time saved, reliability and safety. Trains normally have a snack trolley.

Sleeping

Morocco has a good range of accommodation to suit all budgets. There are several well-appointed business hotels in the main cities, luxurious places for the discerning visitor and clean basic hotels to suit those with limited funds. Independent travellers appreciate the growing number of maisons d'hôte or guesthouses (generally referred to as riads), some very swish indeed, while in the mountain areas walkers and climbers will find rooms available in local people's homes. Modern self-catering accommodation is also sometimes available.

There is an official star rating system, although few hotels will boast about their membership of the one-, two- or even three-star categories. There does not appear to be very tight central control on how prices reflect facilities on offer. There are considerable variations in standards, and surprises are possible. Note too that breakfast is generally not included in the room price – except in riads.

Cheap
At the budget end of the market are simple hotels, often close to bus or train stations. There may be a washbasin, sometimes a bidet. Loos and showers will usually be shared and you may have to pay for a hot shower. The worst of this sort of accommodation will be little better than a concrete cell, stifling in summer. The best is often quite pleasant outside summer, with helpful staff and lots of clean, bright tiling. Rooms often open on to a central courtyard, limiting privacy and meaning you have to leave your room closed when out. Outside the big tourist cities, such hotels have almost exclusively Moroccan customers. Although such hotels are generally clean, it may be best to bring a sheet with you if you're planning to use them a lot. Water, especially in the southern desert towns, can be a problem. Generally, there will be a public bath (hammam) close by for you to take a shower after a long bus journey.

Mid-range
More expensive one-star type hotels, generally in the new part of town (ville nouvelle neighbourhoods). Showers may be en suite, breakfast (coffee, bread and jam, a croissant, orange juice) should be available, possibly at the café on the groundfloor, for around 20dh. Next up are the two and three star-ish places. Most will be in the ville nouvelle areas of towns. Rooms will have high ceilings and en suite shower and loo. Light sleepers need to watch out for noisy, street-facing rooms. Some of these hotels are being revamped, not always very effectively. Still in this price bracket, are a number of establishments with a personal, family-run feel.

Expensive
Top hotels are generally run by international groups such as Accor and Le Méridien. Upmarket hotels in Morocco can either be vast and brash, revamped and nouveau riche, or solid but tasteful and even discrete with a touch of old-fashioned elegance. The main cities also have large business hotels.

Riads and guesthouses
The big phenomenon of the late 1990s and 2000s in the Moroccan tourist industry has

Sleeping and eating price codes

Sleeping

€€€€	over €140	€€€	€71-140
€€	€35-70	€	Under €35

Price codes refer to the cost of two people sharing a double room in the high season.

Eating

¶¶¶	Expensive over €8	¶¶	Mid-range €4-8
¶	Cheap under €4		

Prices refer to the average cost of a two-course meal for one person, not including ·
drinks or service charge.

been the development of the maison d'hôte. Wealthy Europeans have bought old property in the médinas of Marrakech, Fès and Essaouira as second homes. Rather than leave the property closed for much of the year, the solution was to rent it out. A number of agencies specializing in the rental of riads (as these properties are generally called, after their garden courtyards or riads) were set up. Some riads are occupied for most of the year by their owners and so are more like guesthouses. If thinking of staying in a riad, you could make your first approach via a reliable agency like **Riads au Maroc**, Rue Mahjoub Rmiza, Marrakech, T024-431900, www.riadomaroc.com. Certain UK travel companies now have riads in their brochures. Basically, they satisfy a growing demand for spacious accommodation with a personal touch. The service in a riad should be far better than in a four-star hotel. Generally, riad charges cover accommodation and breakfast. Meals can be laid on at extra charge, and as they are prepared to order for a small number of people, will be of excellent quality. In a place like Marrakech, hygiene in a riad should also be far better than in one of the city's jaded four-star establishments. There is now guesthouse accommodation to suit medium to large holiday budgets.

When reserving riad accommodation, you need to be clear on how you will be met (finding such houses in complicated médina streets is generally impossible for taxi drivers). Also check whether your accommodation is ground floor (damper in winter) or top floor (hot in summer) and the nature of the heating. Moroccan nights can be very chilly in winter. Another consideration, if you have small children, is the presence of small pools without fencing.

For more on riads check www.marrakech-medina.com, www.marrakech-riads.net or www.essaouiramedina.com.

Youth hostels (Auberges de jeunesse)

There are 11 hostels in all affiliated to the IYHA, located in the cities (Casablanca, Rabat, Fès, Meknès and Marrakech, Oujda and Laâyoune) as well as Azrou (Middle Atlas) and Asni (High Atlas). The HQ is in Meknès, on Av Oqba ibn Nafi. Overnight charge 20-40dh, use of kitchen 2dh, maximum stay of three nights and priority to the under-30s. Summer opening hours are 0800-1300, 1830-2400, winter 0800-1000, 1200-15000, 1800-2230. For information try the **Moroccan Youth Hostel Federation**, Parc de la Ligue arabe, Casablanca, T022-220551. It is better to go for cheap hotels, more conveniently located and with better loos and showers. The Fès hostel has had good reviews but is in the Ville nouvelle, convenient for the train station, but a long way from sights and old-town atmosphere.

Mountain accommodation

In the mountains, you can easily bivouac out in summer or, in the high mountains, kip in a stone *azib* (shepherd's shelter). There are three main options for paying accommodation: floor space in someone's home, a gîte of some kind, or a refuge run by the CAF (Club Alpin Français, see www.cafmaroc.co.ma). The refuges are shelters with basic dormitory and kitchen facilities. Rates depend on category and season but about 15-50dh per night per person is usual. The CAF can also be contacted via BP 6178, Casablanca, T022-270090, and BP 4437 Rabat, T037-734442.

In remote villages, there are gîtes d'étape, simple dormitory accommodation, marked with the colourful GTAM (Grande traversée de l'Atlas marocain) logo. The warden generally lives in the house next door. Prices here are set by the ONMT (tourist board), and the gîte will be clean if spartan. The board also publishes an annual guide listing people authorized to provide gîte type accommodation.

In mountain villages where there is no gîte, you will usually find space in people's homes, provided you have a sleeping bag. Many houses have large living rooms with room for people to bed down on thin foam mattresses. It is the custom to leave a small sum in payment for this sort of service. On the whole, you will be made very welcome.

Camping

There are campsites all over Morocco – the ONMT quotes 87 sites in well-chosen locations. Few sites, however, respect basic international standards. Security is a problem close to large towns, even if the site is surrounded by a wall with broken glass on top. Never leave anything valuable in your tent. Many campsites also lack shade, can be noisy and the ground tends to be hard and stony, requiring tough tent pegs. As campsites are really not much cheaper than basic hotels, and as even simple things like clean toilets and running water can be problematic, hotel accommodation is usually preferable. There are some notable exceptions however (see listings throughout the book).

Eating and drinking

The finest of the Moroccan arts is undoubtedly its cuisine. There are the basics: harira and bessera soups, kebabs, couscous, tagine and the famous pastilla, pigeon, egg and almonds in layers of filo pastry. And there are other dishes, less well known, gazelle's horns, coiling m'hencha and other fabulous pâtisseries. The Moroccans consider their traditional cooking to be on a par with Indian, Chinese and French cuisine – though the finest dishes are probably to be found in private homes. Today, however, upmarket restaurants, notably in Marrakech, will give you an idea of how good fine Moroccan food can be. Moroccan cuisine is beginning to get the international respect it deserves, with new restaurants opening in European capitals. However, the spices and vegetables, meat and fish, fresh from the markets of Morocco, undoubtedly give the edge to cooks in old médina houses.

The climate and soils of Morocco mean that magnificent vegetables can be produced all year round, thanks to assiduous irrigation. Although there is industrial chicken production, in many smaller restaurants, the chicken you eat is as likely to have been reared by a small-holder. Beef and lamb come straight from the local farms.

In addition to the basic products, Moroccan cooking gets its characteristic flavours from a range of spices and minor ingredients. Saffron (*zaâfrane*), though expensive, is widely used, turmeric (*kurkum*) is also much in evidence. Other widely used condiments include a mixed all spice, referred to as *ra's el hanout* ('head of the shop'), cumin (*kamoun*), black pepper, oregano and rosemary (*yazir*). Prominent greens in use include broad-leaved parsley (*ma'dnous*), coriander (*kuzbur*) and, in some variations of couscous, a sort of celery called *klefs*. Preserved lemons (modestly called *bouserra*, 'navels', despite their breast-like shape) can be found in fish and chicken tajines. Bay leaves (*warqa Sidna Moussa*, 'the leaf of our lord Moses') are also commonly employed. Almonds, much used in pâtisserie, are used in tajines too, while powdered cinnamon (Arabic karfa, cannelle in French) provides the finishing touch for pastilla. In pâtisserie, orange-flower water and rose water (*ma ouarda*) are essential to achieve a refined taste.

Eating times vary widely in Morocco. Marrakech gets up early – and goes to bed early, too, so people tend to sit down to dine around about 2000. Casa-Rabat have a more reasonable rhythm, while Tangier takes a Spanish line, rising late, taking a siesta, and eating late. Across the country, the big meal of the week is Friday lunch, a time for people to gather in their families. The main meal of the day tends to be lunch, although this varies according to work and lifestyle. As anywhere, eating out in plush eateries is a popular upper-income occupation. Locals will tend to favour restaurants with French or southern European cuisine, while Moroccan 'palace' restaurants are patronized almost exclusively by tourists.

Starters

Harira is a basic Moroccan soup, ingredients vary but include chick peas, lentils, veg and a little meat. Often eaten accompanied with hard-boiled eggs. *Bissara* is a pea soup, a cheap and filling winter breakfast. *Briouat* are tiny envelopes of filo pastry, something akin to the Indian samosa, with a variety of savoury fillings. Also come with an almond filling for dessert.

Snacks

Cheaper restaurants serve kebabs (aka *brochettes*), with tiny pieces of beef, lamb and fat. Also popular is *kefta*, mince-meat brochettes, served in sandwiches with chips, mustard and *harissa* (red-pepper spicey sauce). Tiny bowls of finely chopped tomato and onion are another popular accompaniment. On Jemaâ el Fna in Marrakech, strong stomachs may want to snack on the local *babouche* (snails).

Main dishes

Seksou (couscous) is the great North African speciality. Granules of semolina are steamed over a pot filled with a rich meat and vegetable stew. Unlike Tunisian couscous, which tends to be flavoured with a tomato sauce, Moroccan couscous is pale yellow. In some families, couscous is the big Friday lunch, an approximate equivalent of old-fashioned English Sunday lunch.

Tagines are stews, the basic Moroccan dish. It is actually the term for the two-part terracotta dish (base and conical lid) in which meat or fish are cooked with a variety of vegetables, essentially, carrots, potato, onion and turnip. *Tajine* is everywhere in Morocco. Simmered in front of you on a *brasero* at a roadside café, it is always good and safe to eat. Out trekking and in the South, it is the staple of life. For tajines, there are four main sauce preparations: *m'qalli*, a yellow sauce created using olive oil, ginger and saffron; *m'hammer*, a red sauce which includes butter, paprika (*felfla hlwa*) and cumin; *qudra*, another yellow sauce, slightly lighter than *m'qalli*, made using butter, onions, pepper and saffron, and finally *m'chermel*, made using ingredients from the other sauces. Variations on these base sauces are obtained using a range of ingredients, including parsley and coriander, garlic and lemon juice, *boussera*, eggs, sugar, honey and cinammon (*karfa*).

In the better restaurants, look out for *djaj bil-hamid* (chicken with preserved lemons and olives), sweet and sour *tajine barkouk* (lamb with plums), *djaj qudra* (chicken with almonds and caramelized onion) and *tajine maqfoul*. Another pleasant dish is *tajine kefta*, basically fried minced meat balls cooked with eggs and chopped parsley. In eateries next to food markets, delicacies such as *ra's embekhar* (steamed sheep's head) and *kourayn* (animal feet) are a popular feed.

A dish rarely prepared in restaurants is *djaj souiri*, aka *djaj mqeddem*, the only *plat gratiné* in Moroccan cuisine. Here, at the very last minute, a sauce of beaten eggs and chopped parsley is added to the chicken, already slow-cooked in olives, diced preserved lemon, olive oil, and various spices.

All over Morocco, lamb is much appreciated, and connoisseurs reckon they can tell what the sheep has been eating (rosemary, mountain pasture, straw, or mixed rubbish at the vast Mediouna tip near Casablanca). Lamb is cheaper in drought years when farmers have to reduce their flocks, expensive when the grazing is good, and is often best eaten at roadside restaurants where the lorry drivers pull in for a feed.

Desserts

A limited selection of desserts is served in Moroccan restaurants. In the palace restaurants, there will be a choice between *orange à la cannelle* (slices of orange with cinammon) or some sort of marzipan pâtisserie like *cornes de gazelle* or *ghrayeb*, rather like round short-cake. *El jaouhar*, also onomatopoeically known as *tchak-tchouka*, is served as a pile of crunchy, fried filo pastry discs topped with a sweet custardy sauce with almonds. Also on offer you may find *m'hencha*, coils of almond paste wrapped in filo pastry, served crisp from the oven and sprinkled with icing sugar and cinammon, and *bechkito*, little crackly biscuits.

Most large towns will have a couple of large pâtisseries, providing French pastries and the petits fours essential for proper entertaining. See Pâtisserie Hilton, Rue de Yougoslavie, Marrakech. Here you will find *slilou* (aka *masfouf*), a richly flavoured nutty powder served in tiny saucers to accompany tea but you won't find *maâjoun*, the Moroccan equivalent of hash brownies, made to liven up dull guests at wedding parties. (On the more disastrous effects of *maâjoun*, see the 1952 Paul Bowles' thriller, *Let It Come Down*.)

In local laiteries, try a glass of yoghurt. Oranges (*limoun*) and mandarins (*tchina*) are cheap, as are prickly pears, sold off barrows. In winter in the mountains, look out for kids selling tiny red arbutus berries (*sasnou*) carefully packaged in little wicker cones. Fresh hazelnuts are charmingly known as *tigerguist*.

Dishes for Ramadan

At sunset the fast is broken with a rich and savoury *harira* (see above), *beghrira* (little honeycombed pancakes served with melted butter and honey) and *shebbakia* (lace-work pastry basted in oil and covered in honey). Distinctive too are the sticky pastry whorls with sesame seeds on top.

Cafés and restaurants

Cafés offer croissants, petit-pain and cake (Madeleine), occasionally soup and basic snacks. Restaurants basically divide into four types: snack eateries, in the médina and ville nouvelle, generally cheap and basic. Some are modelled on international themed fast-food restaurants (Taki Chicken in Rabat). Then you have the laiteries, which sell yoghurt, fruit juices and will make up sandwiches with processed cheese, salad and kacher (processed meat). Full blown restaurants are generally found only in larger towns, and some are very good indeed – 'vaut le détour' as the French guides say. And finally, in cities like Fès and Meknès, Marrakech and Rabat, you have the great palaces of Moroccan cuisine, restaurants set in old, often beautifully restored private homes. These can set you back 500dh or even more. Some of these restaurants allow you to eat à la carte (El Fassia in Marrakech, La Zitouna in Meknes), rather than giving you the full banquet menu (and late night indigestion).

Eating out cheaply

If you're on a very tight budget, try the ubiquitous food stalls and open air restaurants serving various types of soup, normally the standard broth (*harira*), snacks and grilled meat. The best place for the adventurous open air eater is the Jemaâ el Fna square in Marrakech. Another good place is the fish market in the centre of Essaouira. Obviously there is a greater risk of food poisoning at street eateries, so go for food that is cooked as you wait, or that is on the boil. Avoid fried fish in the médina of Casablanca.

Vegetarian food

Moroccan food is not terribly interesting for vegetarians, and in many places 'vegetarian cuisine' means taking the meat off the top of the couscous or tajine. The concept is really quite alien to most Moroccans, as receiving someone well for dinner means serving them a tajine with good chunk of meat. There are some excellent salads, however. Be prepared to eat lots of processed cheese and omelettes.

Food markets

Each city will have a colourful central market, generally dating back to the early years of this century, stuffed with high quality fresh produce. Try the one of Avenue Mohammed V at Casablanca (which has some good basket work stalls), the markets on the Avenue Hassan II in Rabat (to your left off the Avenue Mohammed V as you enter the médina) and the Guéliz market in Marrakech, again, on the Avenue Mohammed V, on your left after the intersection with Rue de la Liberté as you head for the town centre.

Eating in people's homes

Moroccan families may eat from a communal dish, often with spoons, sometimes with the hands. If invited to a home, you may well be something of a guest of honour.

Depending on your hosts, it's a good idea to take some fruit or pâtisseries along. If spoons or cutlery are not provided, you eat using bread, using your right hand, not the left hand since it is ritually unclean. If the dishes with the food are placed at floor level, keep your feet tucked under your body away from the food. In a poorer home, there will only be a small amount of meat, so wait until a share is offered. Basically, good manners are the same anywhere. Let common sense guide you.

Drinks

Tea All over Morocco the main drink apart from water is mint tea (*thé à la menthe/attay*) a cheap, refreshing drink which is made with green tea, fresh mint and masses of white sugar. The latter two ingredients predominate in the taste. If you want a reduced sugar tea, ask for *attay msous* or *bila sukar/sans sucre*). In cafés, tea is served in mini-metal tea pots. In homes it is poured from high above the glass to generate a froth (*attay bi-rizatou*, 'tea with a turban') to use the local expression. Generally, tradition has it that you drink three glasses. To avoid burning your fingers, hold the glass with thumb under the base and index finger on rim. In some homes, various other herbs are added to make a more interesting brew, including *flayou* (peppermint), *louiza* (verbena) and even *sheeba* (absinthe). If you want a herb tea, ask for a *verveine* or *louiza*, which may be with either hot water or hot milk (*bil-halib*).

Coffee Coffee is commonly drunk black and strong (*kahwa kahla/un exprès*). For a weak milky coffee, ask for a *café au lait/kahwa halib*. A stronger milky coffee is called a *café cassé/ kahwa mherza*.

Other soft drinks All the usual soft drinks are available in Morocco. If you want still mineral water (*eau plate*) ask for Sidi Harazem, Sidi Ali or Ciel. The main brands of fizzy mineral water (*eau pétillante*), are Oulmès and Bonacqua, a new water produced by Coca Cola.

The better cafés and local laiteries (milk-product shops) do milkshakes, combinations of avocado, banana, apple and orange, made to measure. Ask for a jus d'avocat or a jus de banane, for example.

Wines and spirits For a Muslim country, Morocco is fairly relaxed about alcohol. In the top hotels, imported spirits are available, although at a price. The main locally made lager **beers** are Flag, Flag Spécial, Stork, Castel and Heineken. In the spring, look out for the extremely pleasant Bière de Mars, made only in March with Fès spring water.

Morocco produces **wine**, the main growing areas being Guerrouane and Meknès. Reds tend to prevail. Celliers de Meknès (CdM) and Sincomar are the main producers. At the top of the scale (off licence prices in brackets), are Médaillon (90dh) and Beau Vallon (CdM, 90dh, anything up to 185dh in a restaurant). A CdM Merlot will set you back 45dh. Another reliable red is Domaine de Sahari, Aït Yazem. A pleasant claret, best drunk chilled in summer (30dh). The whites include Coquillages and Sémillant, probably the best (40dh). At the very bottom of the scale is rough and ready Rabbi Jacob, or, cheaper and still cheerful, Chaud Soleil. The local fig fire-water is Mahia la Gazelle.

If you want to buy alcohol outside a restaurant, every major town will have a few licensed sales point. Often they are very well stocked with local and imported wines. The Marjane hypermarket chain, now represented in all major cities, also has an off licence

Festivals

Morocco has a number of regional and local festivals, often focusing around a local saint or harvest time of a particular product, and are fairly recent in origin. The main Moroccan festivals come in three categories: firstly, the more religious festivals, the timing of which relates to the lunar Islamic year; secondly the annual semi-commercial regional or town festivals with relatively fixed dates; and thirdly, the new generation of arts and film festivals.

Regional or town festivals

February Festival of the Almond Blossom, Tafraoute, near Agadir.

April Honey Festival, Immouzer des Ida Outanane.

May Rose Festival, El Kelaâ des Mgouna, Dadès Valley.

Moussem de Sid Ahmed Ben Mansour, Moulay Bousselham, north of Kenitra.

June Cherry Festival, Sefrou.

Festival of Folk Art and Music, Marrakech.

Moussem de Moulay Abdeslam ben M'chich, Larache.

Moussem de Sidi Mohammed Ma El Ainin, Tan Tan.

July Festival of Sea Produce, Al Hoceïma.

August Moussem of Moulay Abdallah, El Jadida.

Festival des Pommes, Immouzer du Kandar.

Moussem of Moulay Idris Zerhoun, Moulay Idriss.

Moussem of Setti Fatma, Setti Fatma, Ourika Valley near Marrakech.

Moussem of Sidi Ahmed ou Moussa, Tiznit.

September Marriage Festival, Imilchil in the last week of September/first week of October).

Horse Festival, Tissa near Fès.

Moussem of Moulay Idris al Azhar, Fès.

October Date Festival, Erfoud.

Arts festivals

February Salon du livre, Casablanca. Morocco's biggest annual bookfair. Prix du Grand Atlas, literary events.

May Les Alizés, Essaouira. Small classical music festival in early May, www.alizesfestival.com. **Festival des Musiques Sacrées**, Fès – generally late May running into June. Attracts a strange mixture of the spiritual, the hippy and the wealthy. Accompanied by popular music concerts open to all. See www.fesfestival.com.

Mawazine Festival, Rabat. The capital comes alive with world music and pop concerts held in various venues. Whitney Houston closed the 2008 festival.

May/June Tanjazz Tangier jazz festival, mixture of free and paying concerts, www.tanjazz.org.

June L'Boulevard, Casablanca. Annual urban music (hip-hop, electro, fusion, rock etc) festival, www.boulevard.ma. **Festival Gnaoua**, Essaouira. One of Morocco's most successful music festivals, www.festival-gnaoua.co.ma.

Festival Rawafld des créateurs marocains de l'étranger, Casablanca. Late July. Focusing on work by Moroccan creative artists abroad. Music and film.

August Arts Festival, Asilah. Paintings of the médina, festival now in its 30th year.

September Festival international du film méditerranéen, Tetouan. Long-established but slightly erratic small film festival.

October Festival cinématographique de Marrakech, Marrakech. Established annual film fest. festivalmarrakech.info.

section. Asouak Essalam, the main competitor, does not stock alcohol, however. In Ramadan, alcohol is on sale to non Muslim foreigners only and many of the off licences shut down for the month. At Marjane, towards the end of Ramadan, you may well be asked by locals to buy a few bottles for their end of fasting booze-up.

Essentials A-Z

Accident and emergency

Police: T19. **Fire brigade**: T15. Larger towns will have an **SOS Médecins** (private doctor on call service), and almost all towns of any size have a pharmacy on duty at night, the pharmacie de garde. Any large hotel should be able to give you the telephone/address of these. For most ailments, a médecin généraliste (general practitioner) will be sufficient.

Dress

In coastal resorts, you can wear shorts and expose arms and shoulders. However, when wandering round médinas and going to city centres, both men and women should cover shoulders. Sandals are fine but shorts should be baggy not skimpy. Expect lots of remarks and attention if you do go wandering round the souks in your brief running shorts. I have some smart but cool tops with you for summer travelling. Inland, winter is cold. Night temperatures in the desert and at altitude are low all the year – a fleece is handy, even as a pillow.

Electricity

Morocco has a fairly reliable electricity supply of 220V, using continental European round two-pin plugs. In some more remote areas, however, there is no mains electricity.

Health

Diarrhoea and intestinal upset

Diarrhoea can refer either to loose stools or an increased frequency of bowel movement, both of which can be a nuisance. Symptoms should be relatively short-lived but if they persist beyond two weeks specialist medical attention should be sought. Also seek medical help if there is blood in the stools and/or fever.

Adults can use an antidiarrhoeal medication such as loperamide to control the symptoms but only for up to 24 hours. In addition keep well hydrated by drinking plenty of fluids and eat bland foods. Oral rehydration sachets taken after each loose stool are a useful way to keep well hydrated. These should always be used when treating children and the elderly.

Bacterial traveller's diarrhoea is the most common form. Ciproxin (Ciprofloxacin) is a useful antibiotic and can be obtained by private prescription in the UK. You need to take one 500 mg tablet when the diarrhoea starts. If there are so signs of improvement after 24 hours the diarrhoea is likely to be viral and not bacterial. If it is due to other organisms such as those causing giardia or amoebic dysentery, different antibiotics will be required.

The standard advice to prevent problems is to be careful with water and ice for drinking. Ask yourself where the water came from. If you have any doubts then boil it or filter and treat it. There are many filter/treatment devices now available on the market. Food can also transmit disease. Be wary of salads (what were they washed in, who handled them), re-heated foods or food that has been left out in the sun having been cooked earlier in the day. There is a simple adage that says wash it, peel it, boil it or forget it. Also be wary of unpasteurized dairy products as these can transmit a range of diseases.

Sun

Overexposure to the sun can lead to sunburn and, in the longer term, skin cancers and premature skin aging. The best advice is simply to avoid exposure to the sun by covering exposed skin, wearing a hat and staying out of the sun if possible, particularly between late morning and early afternoon. Apply a high factor sunscreen (greater than SPF15) and also make sure it screens against UVB. A further danger in tropical climates is heat exhaustion or more seriously heatstroke. This can be avoided by good hydration, which means drinking water past the point of simply quenching thirst. Also when first exposed to tropical heat take time to acclimatize by avoiding strenuous activity in the middle of the day. If you cannot avoid heavy exercise it is also a good idea to increase salt intake.

Vaccinations

None required unless travelling from a country where yellow fever and/or cholera frequently occurs. You should be up to date with polio, tetanus, and typhoid protection. If you are going to be travelling in rural areas where hygiene is often a bit rough and ready, then having a hepatitis B shot is a good thing. You could also have a cholera shot, although there is no agreement among medics on how effective this is.

Water

In major cities, tap water should be fine to drink, though many visitors stick to bottled water to make sure. Out in the sticks you should definitely only drink the bottled variety.

Further information

Foreign and Commonwealth Office (FCO) (UK), www.fco.gov.uk
The National Travel Health Network and Centre (NaTHNaC) www.nathnac.org/
World Health Organisation, www.who.int
Fit for Travel (UK), www.fitfortravel.scot. nhs.uk. A-Z of vaccine and travel health advice requirements for each country.

Language

Arabic is the official language of Morocco, but nearly all Moroccans with a secondary education have enough French to communicate with, and a smattering of English. In the North, Spanish maintains a presence thanks to TV and radio. Outside education, however, Moroccan Arabic in the cities and Amazigh in the mountains are the languages of everyday life, and attempts to use a few words and phrases, no matter how stumblingly, will be appreciated. Those with some Arabic learned elsewhere often find the Moroccan Arabic difficult. It is characterized by a clipped quality (the vowels just seem to disappear), and the words taken from classical Arabic are often very different from those used in the Middle East. In addition, there is the influence of the Berber languages and a mixture of French and Spanish terms, often heavily 'Moroccanized'. In many situations French is more or less understood. However, you will come across plenty of people who have had little opportunity to go to school and whose French may be limited to a very small number of phrases.

If you wish to learn Arabic, ALIF (Arabic Language Institute in Fès, T035-624850, www.alif-fes.com), an offshoot of the American Language Centre, has a very good reputation. They organize a range of long and short courses in both classical and Moroccan Arabic. Courses in Amazigh languages can be set up, too.

Money
Currency

The major unit of currency in Morocco is the dirham (dh). In 1 dirham there are 100 centimes. There are coins for 1 centime (very rare), 5, 10, 20 and 50 centimes, and for 1, 2, 5 and 10 dirhams, as well as notes for 20, 50, 100 and 200 dirhams. The coins can be a little confusing. There are two sorts of 5 dirham coin: the older and larger cupro-nickel ('silver coloured' version), being phased out, and the new bi-metal version, brass colour on the inside. There is a brownish 20 dirham note, easily confused with the 100 dirham note.

The 50 dirham note is green, the 100 dirhams brown and sand colour, and the 200 dirham note is in shades of blue and turquoise. Currency is labelled in Arabic and French.

You can sometimes buy Moroccan dirhams at bureaux de change at the London airports but dirhams may not be taken out of Morocco. If you have excess dirhams, you can exchange them back into euros at a bank on production of exchange receipts. However, as European cash and Visa cards function in Moroccan ATMs (guichets automatiques), in major towns it is possible to withdraw more or less exactly the amount you need on a daily basis. At weekends and during big public holidays, airport and city-centre ATMs can be temperamental. The most reliable ATMs are those of the **Wafa Bank** (green and yellow livery) and the **BMCI**.

Moroccans among themselves count in older currency units. To the complete confusion of travellers, many Moroccans refer to francs, which equal 1 centime, and reals, though both these units only exist in speech. Even more confusingly, the value of a real varies from region to region. A dirham equals 20 reals in most regions. However, around Tangier and in most of the North, 1 dirham equals 2 reals. Alf franc (1000 francs) is 10 dirhams. Unless you are good at calculations, it's easiest to stick to dirhams.

Exchange rate → US$1 = 8.02dh, UK £1 = 12.93dh, €1 = 11.28dh (May 2011). There is a fixed rate for changing notes and no commission ought to be charged for this.

Credit cards
Credit cards are widely accepted at banks, top hotels, restaurants and big tourist shops. For restaurants, check first before splashing out. Remember to keep all credit card receipts – and before you sign, check where the decimal marker (a comma in Morocco rather than a dot), has been placed, and that there

isn't a zero too many. You don't want to be paying thousands rather than hundreds of dirhams. To reduce problems with card fraud, it makes sense to use a credit card for payments of large items like carpets and hotel bills. If a payment is not legitimate, it is a lot less painful if the transaction is on the credit card rather than drawn from your current account.

Traveller's cheques
Although somewhat time consuming to change, traveller's cheques (TCs) are still useful (though a small commission will be charged for changing them). Take TCs from a well known bank or company, preferably in euros. Some hotels and shops will exchange TCs.

Banking hours
Main banks include the **BMCE**, **Crédit du Maroc**, **Wafabank**, and **Banque Populaire** all widespread. The **BMCE** and the **Crédit du Maroc** seem to have the best change facilities, while the **Banque Populaire** is often the only bank in southern towns. Banking in Morocco can be a slow, tortuous process. The easiest way to get money is thus to use your Visa or cash card at a cash dispenser. See Opening hours below for banking hours.

Cost of travelling
As a budget traveller, it is possible to get by in Morocco for £30-35/US$60-70 a day. Your costs can be reduced by having yoghurt and bread and cheese for lunch and staying in an 80dh a night hotel (you can often find even cheaper options in small towns).

Accommodation, food and transport are all relatively cheap compared to Europe and America, and there is a lot to see and do for free. However, this budget does not allow much room for unexpected costs like the frequent small tips expected for minor services. If you start buying imported goods, notably cosmetics and toiletries, foods and electrical goods, things can get expensive. Allowing £40/US$80 is more realistic.

In top-quality hotels, restaurants, nightclubs and bars, prices are similar to Europe. Rabat, Casablanca and Agadir are the most expensive places while manufactured goods in remote rural areas tend to cost more. Around the 200dh mark, you can get a much better feed in a restaurant than you can in western Europe. Shopaholics will be more than satisfied with the gifty goodies on sale (prices negotiable). Prices for food and drink are non-negotiable.

Cost of living
Although prices for many basics can seem very low indeed to those used to prices in European capitals, the cost of living is high for most Moroccans. At one end of the scale, in the mountainous rural areas, there is Morocco's fourth world, still on the margins of the cash economy. In these regions, families produce much of their own food, and are badly hit in drought years when there is nothing to sell in the souk to generate cash to buy oil, extra flour and sugar. This precariousness means much 'hidden' malnutrition.

Conditions are improving for the city shanty-town dwellers. Here families will be getting by on 2000dh a month, sometimes much less. The urban middle classes, those with salaried jobs in the public and private sectors, are doing fairly well. A primary school teacher may be on 3000dh a month, a private company employee at the start of their career will make around 3000dh a month, too. This category has access to loans and is seeing a general improvement in living standards. Morocco's top-flight IT technicians, doctors, and business people have a plush lifestyle with villas and servants available to few Europeans. And finally, a very small group of plutocrats has long been doing very, very well, thank you.

To put the contrasts in perspective, there are parents for whom the best option is to place their pre-adolescent girls as maids with city families in exchange for 300dh a month. The Amazigh-speaking boy who serves you in the corner shop may be given 50dh a week, plus food and lodging (of a sort). His horizons will be limited to the shop, there will be a trip back to the home village once a year. He may never learn to read. At the other, distant end of the scale, there are couples who can easily spend 40,000dh a semester to purchase an English-language higher education for one of their offspring at the private Al Akhawayn University in Ifrane.

Opening hours
The working week for businesses is Monday to Friday, with half day working Saturday. On Fridays, the lunch break tends to be longer, as the main weekly prayers with sermon are on that day. Official business takes considerably longer in Ramadan.

Banks: 0830-1130 and 1430-1600 in winter, afternoons 1500-1700 in summer, 0930-1400 during Ramadan.

Post offices: 0830-1230 and 1430-1830, shorter hours in Ramadan.

Shops: Generally from 0900-1200 and from 1500-1900, although this varies in the big towns.

Museums: Most close on a Tuesday. Hours generally 0900-1200 and 1500-1700, although this can vary considerably.

Public holidays
1 January New Year's Day.
1 May Fête du Travail (Labour Day).
9 July Fête de la Jeunesse.
30 July Fête du Trône. Commemorates the present king Mohamed VI's accession.
20 August Anniversaire de la Révolution.
6 November Marche Verte/El Massira el Khadhra. Commemorates a march by Moroccan civilians to retake the Spanish- held Saharan territories of Río de Oro and Saguiet El Hamra.

18 November Independence Day. Commemorates independence and Mohammed V's return from exile.

Religious holidays

Religious holidays are scheduled according to the Hijna calendar, a lunar-based calendar. The lunar year is shorter than the solar year, so the Muslim year moves forward by 11 days every Christian year.

1 Muharram First day of the Muslim year.
Mouloud Celebration of the Prophet Mohammed's birthday.
Ramadan A month of fasting and sexual abstinence during daylight hours.
Aïd el Fitr (the Lesser Aïd) Two-day holiday ending the month of Ramadan.
Aïd el Kebir (the Great Aïd) One-day holiday which comes 70 days after Aïd el Fitr. Commemorates how God rewarded Ibrahim's faith by sending down a lamb for him to sacrifice instead of his son. When possible, every family sacrifices a sheep on this occasion.

During **Ramadan**, the whole country switches to a different rhythm. Public offices go on to half-time, and the general pace slows down during the daytime. No Moroccan would be caught eating in public during the day, and the vast majority of cafés and restaurants, except those frequented by resident Europeans and tourists, are closed. At night, the ambiance is almost palpable. There is a sense of collective effort, shared with millions of other Muslims worldwide. People who never go out all year are out visiting friends and family, strolling the streets in Ramadhan. Shops stay open late, especially during the second half of the month. Ramadan is an interesting time to visit Morocco as a tourist, but probably to be avoided if possible if you need to do business.

Safety

Morocco is basically a very safe country, although there is occasional violent street crime in Casablanca and (very rarely) Marrakech. Travelling on public transport, you need to watch your pockets. Do not carry all your money and cards, etc in the same place. A money belt is a very good idea. Never have more money than you can afford to lose in the pockets of your jeans. Thieves operate best in crowds getting on and off trains and at bus and taxi stations where they can quickly disappear into an anonymous mass of people.

Be aware of the various skilled con-artists in operation in certain places. Hasslers of various kinds are active at the gates of Tangier port, and to a lesser extent in Tetouan. There are all sorts of ruses used by hasslers to extract a little money from tourists: 'the sick relative story', 'the grand taxi fare to Rabat to start university story', 'the supplement for the onward reservation to Chaouen story'. You need to be polite and confident, distant and sceptical – even a little bored by the whole thing. Some of the ruses, however, are pretty good, ie at Marrakech airport, 'would you like to make a contribution to the taxi drivers' football team fund?' Learn the values of the banknotes quickly (the yellow-brown 100dhs and the blue 200dhs are the big ones, a red 10dh is no great loss). Keep your wits about you. Remember, you are especially vulnerable stumbling bleary eyed off that overnight bus.

Should you be robbed, reporting it to the police will take time – but may alert them to the fact that there are thieves operating in a given place. For safety matters with regard to women travelling alone.

Security and terrorism

On the night of 14 May 2003, Casablanca was shaken by co-ordinated kamikaze bomb attacks targeting a Jewish social club and a major hotel. Over 40 Moroccans were murdered. Salafiya-Jihadiya fundamentalist groups organized these murders and the national security forces reacted with a wave of arrests. Summer 2003 saw the men responsible, including some of the suicide-bombers who survived, on trial. Some were condemned to the death penalty, which is not likely to be applied, however. The speedy trials were widely criticized as being more a vengeful reaction to the attacks than an attempt to apply justice. Nine of those found guilty escaped from prison in Kénitra in 2008.

Morocco's tourist industry suffered further setback on 28 April 2011, when a terrorist bomb exploded in a café overlooking the Jamaa el-Fnaa square in the tourist centre of Marrakech, killing 16, including a British travel writer. The attack adds to the challenges facing the country's ruler, King Mohammed VI, as he tries to prevent the uprisings across the Arab world from reaching his kingdom. The king has promised to reform the constitution in order to placate pro-democracy protesters and had recently pardoned political prisoners, including alleged militant Islamists.

Time
Morocco follows GMT all year round. Summer is 1 hour behind the UK and 2 hours behind Spain. Ceuta and Melilla work on Spanish time.

Tipping
This can be a bit of a 'hidden cost' during your stay in Morocco. Tipping is expected in restaurants and cafés, by guides, porters and car park attendants, and others who render small services. Make sure you have small change at the ready. Tipping taxi drivers is optional. Do not tip for journeys when the meter has not been used, because the negotiated price will be generous anyway. For porters in hotels, tip around 3dh, on buses 3dh-5dh, and 5dh on trains and in airports.

Visas
No visas are required for full passport holders of the UK, USA, Canada, Australia, New Zealand/Aotearoa, Canada, Ireland and most EU countries. Benelux passport holders require visas at the present time. On the aeroplane or boat, or at the border, travellers will be required to fill in a form with standard personal and passport details, an exercise to be repeated in almost all hotels and guesthouses throughout the country. From the point of entry travellers can stay in Morocco for three months.

Visa extensions
These require a visit to the Immigration or Bureau des Etrangers department at the police station of a larger town, as well as considerable patience. An easier option is to leave Morocco for a few days, preferably to Spain or the Canary Islands, or to one of the two Spanish enclaves, either Ceuta, close to Tangier, or Melilla, rather more remote in northeastern Morocco. People coming into Morocco from either of these Spanish enclaves for a second or third time have on occasion run into problems with the Moroccan customs. With numerous foreigners resident in Agadir and Marrakech, it may be easiest to arrange visa extensions in these cities. Approval of the extension has to come from Rabat and may take a few days.

Weights and measures
Morocco uses the metric system.

Contents

28 Fès

28	Ins and outs
29	Background
32	Sights
32	Fès el Bali: Adoua el Quaraouiyine
38	Fès el Bali: Adoua el Andalus
40	Fès el Jedid
41	Around Fès
45	Listings

54 Meknès

54	Ins and outs
55	Background
58	Sights
62	Moulay Idriss and Volubilis
66	Listings

71 Middle Atlas

71	Azrou
73	Ifrane and the lakes
74	Khénifra and around
74	Midelt
75	Around Midelt
76	Listings

80 Taza

80	Ins and outs
80	Background
81	Sights
82	Jbel Tazzeka National Park
84	East of Taza
87	Listings

Footprint features

39	Bathtime blues

Fès, Meknès, Middle Atlas

At a glance

◉ **Getting around** Fès and Meknès are both spread-out cities – use buses or petits taxis to get around. There are buses to towns in the Middle Atlas but you'll need a car to explore further.

↻ **Time required** Ideally allow at least couple of days for each city.

❈ **Weather** The winters are very cold and the summers very hot. Spring (May or even June) is the best time to visit.

Fès

Fès (also spelt Fez in English) is a fascinating city – perhaps as near to the Middle Ages as you can get in a couple of hours by air from Europe. It is not an easy city to get to know, but repays time and effort spent on it. With three main sections, the city has numerous historic buildings, centred around the Qaraouiyine Mosque and some memorable souks. Fès is also a base from which to explore nearby regions, Bhalil and Sefrou to the south and the spa towns of Sidi Harazem and Moulay Yacoub, as well as sites further afield, the Middle Atlas resorts of Azrou and Ifrane. Also nearby is the other central Moroccan imperial city of Meknès, with Volubilis and Moulay Idriss close by. **»** *For listings, see pages 45-53.*

Ins and outs

Getting there
Fès is accessible by train, bus and grand taxi. There are direct train services from Marrakech, Rabat and Casablanca, all via Meknès, taking respectively around four hours, five hours and eight hours. Coming by train from Tangier (nearly six hours), you will change at Sidi Kacem or Sidi Slimane. There are plenty of bus services to main cities, with some useful late-night services for points south; Marrakech and Er Rachidia are around nine hours away, for example, Tangier six hours. There are two bus stations: the main one is outside the city walls near Bab Mahrouk, while the CTM station is on Av Mohammed V in the ville nouvelle. If you come in from Taza and all points east, you will probably arrive at yet another bus terminus, at Bab Ftouh.

Fès has a small airport, with flights to Casablanca. There are fewer scheduled flights to Marrakech. **Atlas Blue** fly to Marseille and Lyon, **Jet4you** fly to Paris and **Ryanair** fly to Frankfurt, Brussels, Milan, Gerona and Marseille. Ryanair also ran a direct flight from London to Fès for a while but, at the time of writing, had stopped these flights. The **Aéroport de Fès-Saïss**, 15 km south of town, is a grand taxi ride out of town. **»** *See Transport, page 52.*

Getting around
Fès is a spread out sort of place, and distances are greater than they may at first seem, so look forward to some considerable hikes from one place to another, or petit taxi rides. If you are based in a ville nouvelle hotel – probably the best bet – you can get a taxi from the Pl Mohammed V or the main PTT on the Av Hassan II. Getting around the historic neighbourhoods of Fès, which divide into Fès el Bali (the Old) and Fès el Jedid (the New), is another matter. You will be dealing with a complex network of lanes and alleys. Especially if your time is limited, it may be better to engage an official guide – rather than get lost and have (possibly unpleasant) dealings with an unofficial guide. From the tourist

information office on Place de la Résistance in the ville nouvelle to Bab Boujeloud, effectively the beginning of Old Fès, is a 3-km trot. The train station is a similar distance from Fès el Bali, the CTM terminus roughly 4 km.

Tourist information Office du Tourisme ⓘ *Pl de la Résistance, T035-623460.* Syndicat d'Initiative ⓘ *Av Mohammed V, T035-625301.*

Background

Spiritual capital
Fès has a highly strategic location. The city is situated in the Oued Sebou basin, astride the traditional trade route from the Sahara to the Mediterranean, as well as on the path from Algeria and the Islamic heartland beyond into Morocco. For centuries the dominant axis within Morocco was between Fès and Marrakech, two cities linked by their immense power as well as by their rivalry. Even today, while the coastal belt centred on Rabat and Casablanca dominates the country in demographic, political and economic terms, Fès continues to fascinate, for it has another characteristic, perhaps its dominant feature: Fès is a religious place, and is felt to be the spiritual capital of Morocco.

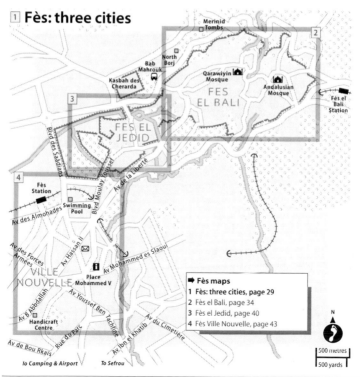

1 Fès: three cities

➡ **Fès maps**
1 Fès: three cities, page 29
2 Fès el Bali, page 34
3 Fès el Jedid, page 40
4 Fès Ville Nouvelle, page 43

500 metres
500 yards

The influence of a saintly person, the *baraka* or blessing of a protector, was felt to be essential for a Moroccan city in times gone by. Fès, founded by Idriss II, El Azhar, 'the Splendid', had its patron, too and the life of the city once gravitated around the cathedral-mosque where Moulay Idriss and his descendants are buried. In recent memory, the end of each summer saw great celebrations for the moussem of Moulay Idriss. The craftsmen's corporations would take part in great processions to the shrine of the city's founder, a sacrificial bull, horns and head decorated with henna, the heart of every procession.

The people of Fès were deeply religious. Some early European writers saw the city as a great Mont-St-Michel, a prayer-saturated place with its mosques, zaouïas and oratories. Dr Edmond Secret, writing in the 1930s, said that "the majority do their five daily prayers. Draped in modesty in the enveloping folds of their cloaks, the bourgeois, prayer carpets under their arms, recall monks in their dignity." This air of religiosity still clings to the city, especially during Ramadan. And on every night of the year, in the hours which precede the dawn, a time hard for those who are sick and in pain, a company of muezzins maintains a vigil in the minaret of the Andalucían Mosque, praying for those asleep and those awake.

Intellectual heritage
The city's religious life was closely tied to education. "If learning was born in Médina, maintained in Mecca and milled in Egypt, then it was sieved in Fès," went the adage. In the early Middle Ages, it was a centre of cultural exchange. One Gerbert d'Aurillac, later to become Pope Sylvester II, from 999 to 1003, studied in Fès in his youth, and brought Arabic numerals back to Europe. Famous names to have studied or taught in Fès include Maimonides, the Jewish philosopher and doctor, Ibn' Arabi (died 1240) the mystic, Ibn Khaldoun (died 1282), and the mathematician, Ibn el Banna (died 1321).

Thus Fès supplied the intellectual élite of the country, along with many of its leading merchants, and you will find Fassis (the people of Fès) in most towns and cities. They are rightly proud of their city; their self-confidence, verging at times on self-satisfaction, is a distinctive trait, making them rather different from most other Moroccans. Fès does not have the immediate friendliness of the villages, the mountains or the desert but it is a city well worth spending time in – like it or not, it will not leave you indifferent. Driss Chraïbi, for one, in his 1954 breakthrough novel *Le Passé Simple*, certainly did not mince his words: "I do not like this city. It is my past and I don't like my past. I have grown up, I have pruned myself back. Fès has quite simply shrivelled up. However, I know that as I go deeper into the city it seizes me and makes me entity, quantum, brick among bricks, lizard, dust – without me needing to be aware of it. Is it not the city of the Lords?"

Settlers from Andalucía and Kairouan
The first settlement here was the village Medinat Fès founded in 789/90 by Moulay Idriss. However the town proper was founded by his son Idriss II as Al Aliya in 808/9. Muslim families, refugees from Cordoba and surrounding areas of Andalucía soon took up residence in the Adwa al Andalusiyin quarter. Later 300 families from Kairouan (in contemporary Tunisia), then one of the largest Muslim towns in North Africa, settled on the opposite bank, forming Adwa al Qaraouiyine. The Qaraouiyine Mosque, perhaps the foremost religious centre of Morocco, is the centre of a university founded in 859, one of

the most prestigious in the Arab World. The influence of the university grew a few centuries later under the Merinids with the construction of colleges or medersas. On the right bank of the Oued Boukhrareb, the Jamaâ Madlous or Andalusian Mosque was also founded in the ninth century and remains the main mosque of Adoua el Andalus.

Almoravids and Almohads
The two parts of Fès el Bali were united by the Almoravids in the 11th century, and Fès became one of the major cities of Islam. In the 12th century the Qaraouiyine mosque was enlarged to its present form; one of the largest in North Africa, it can take up to 22,000 worshippers. The Almohads strengthened the fortifications of the great city. Under both dynasties Fès was in competition with the southern capital of Marrakech.

Growth of Fès under the Merinids
Fès reached its peak in the Merinid period, when the dynasty built the new capital of Fès el Jedid containing the green-roofed Dar al Makhzen still occupied by the monarch, the Grand Mosque with its distinctive polychrome minaret dating from 1279, and the mellah, to which the Jews of Fès el Bali were moved in 1438. The Merinid sultans Abu Said Uthman and Abu Inan left a particularly notable legacy of public buildings, including the Medersa Bou Inania, several mosques and the Merinid Tombs. The Zaouïa of Moulay Idriss, housing the tomb of Idriss II, was rebuilt in 1437. In the 15th century Fès consolidated its position as a major centre for craft industries and trade.

From Saâdian Fès to the present
Under the Saâdians (15th to 16th centuries) Fès declined, with a degree of antagonism between the authorities and the people. The Saâdians did however refortify the city, adding the Borj Sud and Borj Nord fortresses on the hills to the south and north of the city.

Under the Alaouites, Fès lost ground to the expanding coastal towns, which were far better located to benefit from trade with Europe. The occupation of Algeria also meant Fès was out of phase with the huge changes taking place to the east. In 1889 the French writer Pierre Loti described it as a dead city. However, the dynasty had added a number of new medersa and mosques, and reconstructed other important buildings.

The French entered Fès in 1911, but proved unable to gain full control of the city and its hinterland. Plans to make it the Protectorate's capital were thus abandoned. In any case, Rabat on the coast was better located with respect to fertile farmlands and ports. Although the ville nouvelle, also often referred to as Dar Dbibagh, was founded in 1916, it dates principally from the late 1920s. French policy was to leave the historic quarters intact, preserved in their traditional form. Since the early 1990s, the city has exploded beyond its former limits, with huge new areas of low rise housing on the hills behind the Borj Sud at Sahrij Gnaoua and to the north at Dhar Khemis and Bab Siffer.

Sights

Fès is spectacular, but not as immediately attractive as Marrakech. Unlike the capital of the South, a crossroads for caravans and peoples, Fès is more secretive, its old ways hidden behind the cliff-like walls of its alleyways. Its sights are not easily discovered and several days are really necessary to take in the city's atmosphere. Essentially, there are three main areas to visit: **Fès el Bali**, the oldest part of the city, a médina divided by the river into Adwa al Andalusiyin (the Andalucían quarter on the east bank) and Adwa al Qaraouiyine (the Qaraouiyine quarter on the west bank); **Fès el Jedid**, containing the royal palace and the mellah and founded under the Merinids, you need half a day; and the **ville nouvelle**, the city built by the French which has taken over many of the political, administrative and commercial functions of old Fès. You'd be well advised to save some energy to get up to the Borj Nord/Merinid tombs for views across Fès el Bali at sundown. While Fès el Jedid is fairly flat, Fès el Bali has long sloping streets. In the winter it can rain heavily, turning Talaâ Sghira and Talaâ Kbira into minor torrents. Many of the main sites are decayed and maintenance works to the monuments of Fès seem to last forever.

Fès el Bali: Adoua el Quaraouiyine

On the left bank of the Oued Boukhrareb, the Adoua el Quaraouiyine is a rewarding place to visit, as long as you don't expect too many well structured heritage sites. If time is very short, then the minimum half-day circuit will allow you to get down the main street, Talaâ Kbira, to the central souks and main religious monuments, the Moulay Idriss Zaouïa and the Qaraouiyine Mosque (closed to non-Muslim visitors). Either at the start or the end of the tour, you should take a look in at the the Dar Batha, a 19th-century Hispano-Moorish palace and now home to a Museum of Moroccan Arts and Handicrafts. With more time, you could visit the Fondouk Nejjarine, now a museum of wood and carpentry, and head up to the right bank, Adoua el Andalus. A couple of days in Fès will give you time to get to know the souks thoroughly and explore the higher, upscale neighbourhoods of Douh, Zerbtana and Ziat, where some of the largest of the city's palaces are located.

Fès el Bali can only be explored on foot. The layout is complex and it may save time to engage the services of an official guide, as long as the balance between sites of interest and expensive shops is agreed in advance. Avoid unofficial guides and 'students' offering their services. So saying, sometimes you do get lost and need someone to guide you out (10dh is a reasonable tip). The points from which you can get taxis are Errecif, down at the bottom, between the two halves of Fès el Bali, and Batha (pronounced 'bat-Ha'), up at the top.

Boujeloud Gardens and the Batha Museum

Approaching Fès el Bali from the **Boujeloud Gardens** (Jnène Sbil or Jardins de la Marche Verte) ① *Tue-Sun 0900-1800*, you could follow Rue de l'UNESCO right round past the **Dar el Beida**, a late 19th-century palace, on your left. The road continues past a line of early 20th-century buildings (Pension Campini, police station), then the Préfecture on your right, before you reach the rather undistinguished entrance to the **Musée Dar Batha** ① *T035-634116, Wed-Mon 0830-1630*, on your left almost opposite the Préfecture. The most important displays are the carpets and the distinctive Fès pottery. A 10th-century technique enabled by the use of cobalt produced the famous 'Fès blue'. (On Talaâ Kbira there are a couple of shops stocking this traditional pottery.) In the museum also look out for the minbar or preacher's chair from the Medersa Bou Inania.

Bab Boujeloud and around

If you're staying in a cheap hotel, it's likely that you'll be somewhere near Bab Boujeloud. The neighbourhood takes its name from the striking gate which marks the main western entrance to Fès el Bali. With blue *zellige* tiles on the outside and green on the inside, Bab Boujeloud makes a fittingly stylish access point to the city – and was revamped under the French in 1913. Just to the right of the gate as you arrive from the Place Boujeloud, there is a small gate in the wall, generally kept closed, which leads into the restored **brick water collector**. Though this may not sound very exciting, it is a good piece of late mediaeval hydraulic engineering, channelling the waters of the Oued Fès into underground pipes which supplied the distributors of each neighbourhood. The whole system was still in operation in the late 19th century. The two minarets visible from the gate are those of the 14th-century **Medersa Bou Inania** and the simpler ninth-century **Sidi Lazzaz Mosque**.

On your left as you arrive at Bab Boujeloud, the impressive gate flanked by twin octagonal towers is **Bab Chorfa**, leading into Kasbah Nouar, or Kasbah Filala, so named because it was once occupied by people from the Tafilalet who arrived with the early Alaouite rulers.

There are two main thoroughfares in Fès el Bali. Talaâ Seghira leads to the right. Talaâ Kebira leads to the left, directly past the Sidi Lazzaz Mosque, and the next major building, the Bou Inania Medersa, one of the most important sites in Fès, and straight on down through the médina to the Qaraouiyine Mosque.

Bou Inania Medersa

ⓘ *0830-1730, 10dh. Open to non-Muslims.*

Fès's most spectacular sight, and one of Morocco's most beautiful buildings, the 14th-century Medersa Bou Inania is located handily close to Bab Boujeloud, the entrance near the top of Talaâ Kbira. Built by the Merinid Sultan Abu Inan between 1350-55, it was used to accommodate students until the 1960s and is now open to the public after a lengthy restoration. You enter through a highly decorated vestibule roofed by a stalactite dome. The building centres on a large, stone-flagged courtyard, at the far end of which a sort of dry moat, where water taken from the Oued Fès once flowed, separates the prayer hall from the square courtyard. The mosque area has a highly decorated minaret, indicating that it was far more important than most medersas, which normally do not have minarets or even pulpits for the Friday prayer. Indeed, the medersa has the status of a Friday mosque, and for a time rivalled the Qaraouiyine Mosque. For the best view of the minaret, go for a coffee and a cake on the roof terrace of Café Clock, opposite (see page 50). The courtyard is decorated with ceramic mosaic, Koranic inscriptions, and some fine carved woodwork. On ground and first floors are the students' cell-like rooms, some with decorated ceilings.

There used to be a complex 14th-century *clepsydra* (**water clock**) built in the wall opposite the medersa. Using brass bowls and the dripping of water, and complete with chimes, it is said to have been used to allow the Medersa Bou Inania, visible from both the Qaraouiyine Mosque and the Mosque of Fès el Jedid, to signal the correct time for prayer.

The wooden structure has been restored, and at some point the clock may actually be made to work again.

Down Talaâ Kebira to the Qaraouiyine, the souks and medersas

The narrow Talaâ Kebira, the principal street in Adoua el Qaraouiyine, descends steeply towards the spiritual and commercial heart of the city, a tangle of streets and alleys

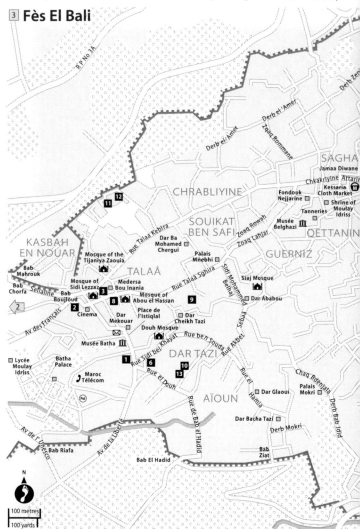

3 Fès El Bali

around the shrine (*zaouïa*) of Moulay Idriss and the Qaraouiyine Mosque. The 20-minute walk from Bab Boujeloud is many people's most memorable experience of Fès, an extraordinary wander through noises, smells, sights and a mass of humanity, from camels' heads on display at the butchers to aged mint sellers to heavily laden mules carrying goods across the city, guided by muleteers crying out 'Balak!' to warn pedestrians. Once you get to the bottom of Talaâ Kebira, the main religious monuments

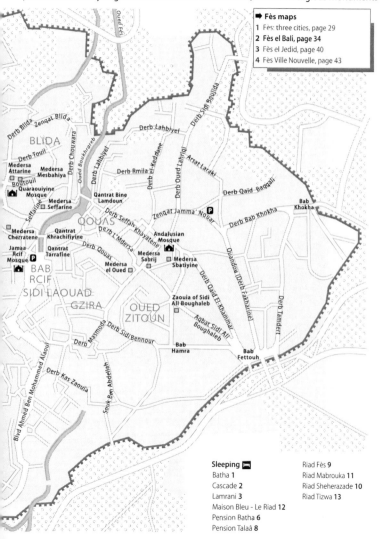

➡ **Fès maps**
1 Fès: three cities, page 29
2 **Fès el Bali, page 34**
3 Fès el Jedid, page 40
4 Fès Ville Nouvelle, page 43

Sleeping 🛏
Batha **1**
Cascade **2**
Lamrani **3**
Maison Bleu - Le Riad **12**
Pension Batha **6**
Pension Talaâ **8**

Riad Fès **9**
Riad Mabrouka **11**
Riad Sheherazade **10**
Riad Tizwa **13**

are off limits to non-Muslims, though the doors to the Qaraouiyine Mosque are often open, allowing a quick glimpse of the interior. It may be possible, depending on restoration works, to get into one of the medersas which ring the Qaraouiyine Mosque. Try to see the Medersa el Attarine and don't miss the restored Foundouk Nejjarine, the Carpenters' Fondouk and the main accessible historic building in the central part of Fès el Bali. The other don't-miss sight is the main tannery, Dar Debbagh, located quite close to the well-signed Musée Belghazi.

As Talaâ Kebira descends, it goes through frequent identity changes, taking on the name of the different crafts which are (or were) practised along different sections of the street. First it becomes Rue Cherabliyine (slippermakers) where each afternoon except Friday people hawk second-hand shoes and slippers. The **Cherabliyine Mosque** dates from 1342, the reign of Sultan Abul Hassan, and has a small and attractive minaret tiled in green and white including the *darj w ktaf* motif. On the right is the **Palais des Merinides**, one of the more impressive of the palace restaurants, and worth a look inside even if you cannot afford the food. Further on, Rue Cherabliyin is called **Aïn Allou**, where leather articles are auctioned every day except Friday. After Aïn Allou, the street is named for the basket weavers (Msamriyine) and bag makers (Chakakyrine), before becoming the **Souk el Attarine**, the former perfumers' souk, the most prestigious in the médina. Between Attarine and the Zaouïa of Moulay Idriss is the lively main **kissaria**, the place to buy traditional clothing.

Before getting tangled up in Souk el Attarine, you should take a right and then a left down some steps off Chrabliyine to get to the square in front of the 18th-century **Fondouk Nejjarine**, an impressive building now home to the **Musée du Bois** ① *38 Rue Abdelazuz Boutaleb, T035-621706, 1000-1700, 20dh*, an interesting museum of wooden crafts and tools. A professionally run museum, this beautiful space is filled with some interesting pieces, including carved doors and windows, handsome coffers and musical instruments. There's also a nice door knocker carved from one piece of wood. Apart from taking a look at the traditional woodwork for which Fès was famous, the fondouk is definitely worth a visit for its roof terrace, where there's a good, if rather pricey, café. Back on the square, the **Nejjarine Fountain**, also carefully restored, is reputed for the fever-curing properties of its waters. On the far side of the square from the fondouk is **Hammam Laraïs**, the wedding baths, once much used by grooms and brides before a pre-marriage trip to the Zaouïa of Moulay Idriss. At Nejjarine, you are close to the tanneries or **Dar Debbagh**. To get there, go right at the far end of the Nejjarine Square and follow the street round.

Surrounded by narrow streets, the 18th-century **Zaouïa of Moulay Idriss**, last resting place of the 9th-century ruler Idriss II, is off-limits to non-Muslim visitors – although parts of the interior can be seen by tactful glances through the large unscreened doorways. Shops around the zaouïa sell candles and other artefacts for pilgrims, the distinctive chewy sweets which are taken home as souvenirs of a pilgrimage, and silverware. Each entrance to the precinct is crossed by a wooden bar, ensuring no pack animals go wandering into the sacred area. On your way round, note a circular porthole through which offerings can be discretely passed.

The Qaraouiyine Mosque (see below) is also surrounded by narrow streets on all sides. In the immediate vicinity of the mosque are four medersas: going clockwise, **Medersa Attarine** (the most important, visitable, see below), **Medersa Mishbahiya** (partly ruined),

Medersa Seffarine (the Coppersmiths' Medersa, recently restored), and **Medersa Cherratène** (more modern, three storeys). All were in use well within living memory.

Dating from 1323, the **Medersa Attarine** (currently undergoing restoration) was built by Merinid Sultan Abu Said. It used to accommodate students studying at the nearby Qaraouiyine University. The courtyard is one of the most elaborately decorated in Morocco, with the usual carved stucco and cedar wood, and *zellige* tiling. The courtyard has a solid, white marble fountain bowl. In the dark prayer hall, a chandelier bears the name of the medersa's founder and the date. As with most medersas, the second floor has a succession of students' cells. From the roof (if accessible) there is a good view of the minaret and courtyard of the Qaraouiyine Mosque.

Qaraouiyine Mosque

ⓘ *Inaccessible to non-Muslims. From the narrow streets, you may be able to take diplomatic glances through unscreened entrances.*

At the end of Souk el Attarine, the Quaraouiyine Mosque, the focal point of Fès el Bali, is probably the most important religious building in Morocco and was once a major centre of medieval learning, with professors in law, theology, algebra, mathematics, philosophy, and astronomy. With space for some 20,000 worshippers it is one of the biggest mosques in North Africa. Original funding to build this mosque was provided in 857 by a wealthy immigrant family from Kairouan (in present day Tunisia), hence the name. The building was enlarged in 956 and again – most importantly – under the Almoravids between 1135 and 1144. The Almohads added a large ablution hall, the Merinids rebuilt the courtyard and minaret. The twin pavilions in the courtyard are 17th-century Saâdian additions. While the minaret goes back to 956, the 'Trumpeters' Tower or Borj an-Naffara, is later and used during Ramadan to signal time to begin fasting again. Built under Sultan Abou Inan in the second half of the 14th century, the tower originally functioned as an observatory. There are said to be plans to convert the tower into a museum dedicated to astrolabes and astrology – an important science in the Muslim world given the religion's use of a lunar calendar and the need to calculate the precise direction of Mecca for prayer. The Qaraouiyine has 14 doors, 275 pillars and three areas for ablutions. Features include elaborate Almohad carving and a venerable wooden pulpit. Some of the chandeliers were made from church bells. Women have a separate worship area, on a mezzanine floor, behind the men.

A minor sight on the Derb Bou Touil, the street running along the eastern side of the mosque, is the 14th-century three-storey **Fondouk Titouani**, originally built to accommodate merchants from Tetouan, and today used by artisans and a carpet shop. Both this and the nearby Palais de Fès restaurant have good views of the Quaraouiyine's courtyard.

Place Seffarine

On the southeast side of the Qaraouiyine, the triangular Place Seffarine (Brassworkers' Square) is marked by a tree visible from the north or south Borj. On the right is the **Qaraouiyine Library**, founded in 1349 and still operational. You can usually enter the courtyard and entrance hall; non-Muslims are not allowed in the library itself. Of passing interest, behind the tree on Hyadriyine are two of the oldest **hammams** in Fès.

The **Medersa Seffarine**, built in 1271, was the first in the city and much simpler in style than the later medersas. It continues to be used by students and for a 10dh tip to the man on the door you can have a quick guided tour – it's interesting to see a working medersa but it's a little like looking around a youth hostel, albeit a very ancient one.

If you head left of the tree on Seffarine, you can follow through to one of the bridges over the Oued Boukhrareb, either Qantarat Kharchifiyine or after Sebbaghine, Qantarat Terrafine. Here you come out onto Rcif, where there are buses and taxis.

Chouara tanneries
The most colourful sight in Fès, the Chouara tanneries have not really changed since medieval times. At the bottom of the valley, they use the water of the Oued Boukhrareb, as well as a smelly mix of urine and guano to turn animal hides into dyed, usable leather. To get there from the Medersa Seffarine, follow Derb Mechattine (the narrow right-hand street of the two at the top of the square) around to the left onto Zanka Chouara. The best views of the tanneries are from leather shops that have terraces from where you can view the work going on below. Afterwards you'll be expected to have a look at the handiwork for sale. There's no obligation to buy anything, although the quality is high, and you could do much worse for a souvenir of the city.

Fès el Bali: Adoua el Andalus

Probably the poorest area of the médina, the Andalus quarter, the south bank of Fès el Bali, has fewer obvious sights than the north bank. However, the Medersa Essahrij, next to the Mosque al Andalus, is worth a visit. You can approach the neighbourhood from the southeast, taking a petit taxi to Bab Fettouh, or by climbing up out of Bab Rcif, losing yourself in the maze of streets of the Qouas neighbourhood.

With its green and white minaret, the **Mosque al Andalus** is a distinctive building dating from the same period as the great Qaraouiyine Mosque. The minaret dates from the 10th century, and the mosque was enlarged in the 13th century, with an architect from Toledo designing the grand main doorway, particularly impressive if you approach the mosque coming up the steps from below. If interested in a relic of the city's commercial life, take a look in at the **Fondouk el Madlous**, a few steps down from the mosque entrance on the left. Restored under Moulay Hassan I in the 19th century, this fondouk is still used for accommodation and storage.

As you face the main door of the mosque, go right along Derb Yasmina to reach the entrance of the nearby **Medersa Essahrij** ('School of the Reflecting Pool'), built 1321-1323 to house students studying at the mosque. There has been no major restoration campaign here yet and cats snooze on the weathered wood screens topped with scallop designs. The white marble basin, after which the medersa was named, has been removed from the courtyard. The large prayer hall contained the library against the qibla wall at either side of the mihrab. Try to get up onto the roof for the view. In between the mosque and the medersa is the **Medersa Sebbayine**, now closed. After visiting the Medersa Essahrij, you could carry along the same street, past the unmarked Medersa el Oued on your right. A few metres further on, a sharp right will take you onto Derb Gzira. Just after the turn is a house which bears the strange name of **Dar Gdam Nbi**, the 'house of the Prophet's foot', so called because a sandal which supposedly once belonged to the Prophet Mohamed was conserved there. Once a year, just before the Prophet's birthday

Bathtime blues

Early in the 19th century, Fès was visited by the Spaniard Domingo Badia y Leblich, travelling under the pseudonym Ali Bey el Abbassi. He noted the importance of the public baths or *hammams* of Fès: "The baths are open to the public all day. The men go in the morning, the women in the afternoon. I generally used to go in the evening, taking the whole bathhouse for myself so that there would be no outsiders … The first time I went there, I noted that there were buckets of water placed symmetrically in the corner of each room and each cubicle. I asked what they were for. 'Do not touch them, sir,' the personnel of the hammam replied in haste. 'Why?' 'These are buckets for the people down below.' 'Who are they?' 'The demons who come to wash during the night'."

A few centuries earlier, Leo Africanus described the traditions of the hammams of Fès: "The companions and the owners of the steam-baths hold festivities once a year, celebrating in the following way. First of all they invite all their friends, and go through the city to fife, tambourine and trumpets, then they take a hyacinth bulb, placing it in a fine copper container which they cover with a white cloth. Then they go back through the city, accompanied by music, to the door of the hammam. There they put the bulb in a basket which they hang over the door, saying, 'This will bring seed to the hammam, because of it there will be many visitors'."

Traditions related to the hammam seem to have died away today. But, even in the 1920s and 1930s, superstitions were very much alive. Dr Edmond Secret, a French doctor working in Fès, noted how those who went to the hammam very early, washing alone, were considered courageous and genies were held to live in damp corners and the water pipes.

or Mouloud, the Tahiri family would open their home to allow the faithful to approach the semi-sacred item of footwear. Unfortunately, the owners have sold up and the property has been divided. Continue therefore on Derb Gzira which winds down to Er Recif where you could find a bus (No 18) to take you back up to Place de la Résistance in the ville nouvelle. There will be red taxis here as well.

Fès vantage points

The **Borj nord**, built by the Saâdian Sultan Ahmad al Mansour in 1582, is a small but interesting example of 16th-century fortress architecture. There are good views of parts of Fès el Bali from the roof. Inside, the **Arms Museum** ① *T035-645241, closed Tue,* has displays of weapons and military paraphernalia from all periods, including European cannon. The collections have been built up mainly as a result of royal donations and include a number of rare pieces. Many of these killing tools have a certain splendour as crafted items. Look out for the largest weapon of all, a 5-m-long cannon weighing 12 tonnes used during the Battle of the Three Kings. From the Borj nord, you can head along the hillside to the 14th-century **Merinid Tombs**. The tombs are ruins, and much of the ornamentation described by earlier visitors has not survived. (Note that this is not a safe place to go alone at night.) In the late afternoon, the garden promenade behind the Borj nord and tombs is busy with locals out for a stroll. The views over Fès el Bali are splendid. Nearby is Restaurant Palais des Merinides, also with an excellent view.

From the 13th-century **Borj sud**, occupied by the military, you can look north over Fès. The nearby son et lumière auditorium bathes Fès el Bali in white light. Unfortunately there are no lasers to pick out the parts of the city being described in the commentary. Until the late 1990s, this southern military outpost of the city stood in isolation but nowadays the low-rise flats of the sprawling Sahrij Gnaoua neighbourhood have marched up the hills, threatening to engulf it.

Fès el Jedid

The one-time Merinid capital, containing Royal Palace and the old Jewish quarter, is now a pleasant haven between the hustle and bustle of Fès el Bali and the ville nouvelle. Allow half a day, perhaps in the late afternoon, before heading for the Borj Nord at sunset.

The best place to start is probably at the **Place des Alaouites**, close to the Royal Palace, and instantly recognisable by its spectacular doors giving onto a vast esplanade, used essentially on ceremonial occasions – or, in the early 1990s, during urban riots. Over on the right, at the edge of a small garden terrace, is the elegant **Bab Lamar**. Between this and the Rue Bou Kssissat, opt for the small gate which takes you into Rue des Mérinides in the **mellah**. The term, used throughout Morocco, probably derives from the Oued Melah, literally 'salty river' which once ran close to this part of Fès, but which, like so many of the watercourses in the region, has disappeared. Off Rue des Mérinides, the streets once had

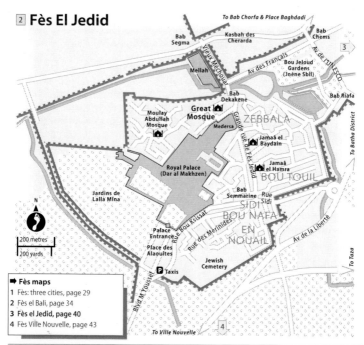

② **Fès El Jedid**

➡ **Fès maps**
1 Fès: three cities, page 29
2 Fès el Bali, page 34
3 Fès el Jedid, page 40
4 Fès Ville Nouvelle, page 43

names which reflected the area's Jewish past. Take the fourth street on the right, Rue de Temara, which will take you to the **Synagogue Aben-Danan**. (There used to be two other synagogues, the Em Habbanim and the Mansour.) In fact, until the 13th century, the Jews lived in Fès el Bali in the Bab Guissa area, still referred to as Fondouq el Yahoudi. In the main hall of the synagogue, there is a collection of objects which will give some idea of the material context of Fassi Jewish life. After the synagogue, past a small square, head across to the **Nouaïl** area. Next to the Jewish cemetery, a new museum of Jewish life is scheduled to open soon. (If you go right here, the street leads down to a door which will take you down to the American animal hospital or **Fondouk el Amerikan**.) From the Nouaïl area try to cut through to the continuation of Rue des Mérinides, Rue Sekkakine and the imposing Bab Semmarine which leads you to Fès el Jedid proper. (If you double back on Rue des Mérinides, you'll find Bab Magana, the 'clock gate', whose scruffy timepiece stopped a while ago.) All along the street are the elegant façades of the houses built by prosperous Jewish families in the early 20th century.

Bab Semmarine, a chunky structure characterized by a double horseshoe arch and lozenge motifs, takes you through into the wide main street of **Fès el Jedid**, often referred to as Avenue Moulay Slimane. This divides the madina al bayda, the white city founded by the Merinids in 1276, in two and takes you through to **Bab Dekakene**. On the right, **Jamaâ el Hamra** 'the red mosque' is the first of the two mosques, so called because it was founded by a red woman from the Tafilalelt. The second mosque on your right is the **Jamaâ el Bayda**. Continue straight ahead and at the end of the avenue you can cut through an arched gate in the walls to your right which will take you past the dry course of the Oued Chrachar to a decrepit waterwheel and a small café-restaurant. Double back, cut through left, and you are at **Bab Dekakene**. Here you want to go through to the right to the walled square referred to as the Vieux Mechouar. On the left are the Italianate entrance gates to the **Makina**, originally built in the 19th century to house an arms factory. It now handles various functions including rug factory and youth club. Going straight ahead, you come to **Bab Sba'**, which takes you through onto the main road running along the north side of the city, linking the ville nouvelle to Fès el Bali. You might take a look at the unusual twin octagonal towers of **Bab Segma**, flanking the ring road. The fortified structure to the north is the **Kasbah des Cherarda**, built 1670 by Sultan Moulay Rachid and today housing a branch of the university and a hospital.

For those with plenty of time, the trail through Fès el Jedid should include a dawdle through Moulay Abdallah neighbourhood, north of the palace. There are a couple of mosques for non-Muslims to look at from the exterior here. Those with plenty of energy should head through the Boujeloud gardens and along Avenue des Français to **Bab Boujeloud**, the western end of Fès el Bali.

Around Fès

Moulay Yacoub

Every bit a country spa-town, Moulay Yacoub, 20 km northwest of Fès, is a short 45-minute journey through rolling countryside and some interesting capital-intensive irrigated farming. Taxis from Bab Boujeloud stop near the car park above the village. Steep flights of steps lead down into the village. There are plenty of hammams, small shops, cafés and a number of cheap lodging houses, some with rudimentary self-catering facilities.

Moulay Yacoub is a destination for local tourists, and a visit to one of the **hammams** can be quite an experience. There are baths for both men and women. The buildings date from the 1930s, and could do with some maintenance, but at the price, you can't complain. The men's hammam has a pool of extremely hot sulphurous water – a bucket of Moulay Yacoub water poured on your head is guaranteed to boil your brains. There are few foreigners; beware the masseur, who may well delight in making an exhibition of you with a poolside pummel and stretching designed for Olympic athletes. Merely bathing in the hot spring water will leave you exhausted – and hopefully rejuvenated. There is also a luxury spa down in the valley.

Sidi Harazem

In restaurants all over Morocco, Sidi Ali and Sidi Harazem are the most widely available mineral waters, along with sparkling Oulmès. The saintly Sidi Harazem is said to have died in Fès in 1164. He taught at the Qaraouiyin Mosque, and it is said his classes and lectures were so interesting that even the djinn, the 'other ones', attended. The village of Sidi Harazem, with its spring and spa centre, is only 4 km along the N6 from Fès, with buses leaving from the CTM bus station and Bab Boujeloud, and other buses and grands taxis from Bab Ftouh. The area around the thermal baths is still very popular for swimming and picnics. There is a 17th-century koubba, dating from the time of the village's establishment as a resort under Sultan Moulay Rachid.

If you want to stay there is the pricey (for what it is) **Hotel Sidi Harazem** (T035-690135, www.sogatour.ma), with 62 air-conditioned rooms, health facilities, restaurant and bar (**€€**).

Bhalil

En route to Sefrou, 5 km before the town off the N8, is Bhalil. This small hill village may have had a Christian population before the coming of Islam. Behind the picturesque village are several **troglodyte dwellings**, with people still inhabiting the caves. The road takes you round the town, giving excellent views on all sides, and two good, clean cafés on the outskirts when approaching from the east.

Sefrou

Sefrou is 32 km south of Fès along the R503. It is not the sort of place you would visit if travelling south, as the N8/N13, via Ifrane and Azrou, is a better route from Fès to Er Rachidia and the South. However, Sefrou is certainly worth visiting as a side trip from Fès or even for an overnight stay, as it is one of the most appealing towns in Morocco, a poor but relatively unspoilt historic walled town lying in a beautiful wooded valley, with a calm and genuinely friendly atmosphere.

Ins and outs Both buses and taxis arrive and leave from Place Moulay Hassan, by Bab Taksebt and Bab M'kam, where the road from Fès meets the old town. Buses from Fès leave from Bab Boujeloud and many go on to Er Rachidia. Grands taxis from Fès leave from Bab Ftouh. **Syndicat d'Initiative** ① *past the Jardin publique, T035-660380.*

Background Although now bypassed by new roads, Sefrou once lay astride the major caravan routes from Fès and the north, to the south and the Sahara beyond. It does, however, remain an important market place for the surrounding agricultural region. Like

4 Fès Ville Nouvelle

To Meknès & Rabat (RP 1)   *To Fès El Jedid*

To Fès El Bali

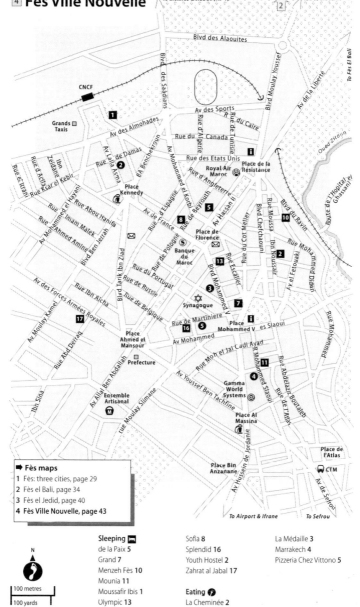

➡ Fès maps
1 Fès: three cities, page 29
2 Fès el Bali, page 34
3 Fès el Jedid, page 40
4 Fès Ville Nouvelle, page 43

N

100 metres
100 yards

Sleeping 🛏
de la Paix **5**
Grand **7**
Menzeh Fès **10**
Mounia **11**
Moussafir Ibis **1**
Olympic **13**

Sofia **8**
Splendid **16**
Youth Hostel **2**
Zahrat al Jabal **17**

Eating 🍴
La Cheminée **2**

La Médaille **3**
Marrakech **4**
Pizzeria Chez Vittono **5**

Debdou and Demnate, Sefrou was one of those small inland Moroccan towns which had a distinctive character because of its large Jewish population which predated the Islamic conquest. Although many Berbers and Jews were converted to Islam by Moulay Idriss, Sefrou's Jewish element was reinforced with the migration of Jews from Tafilalet and Algeria in the 13th century. After the Second World War, large numbers of Jews emigrated to Morocco's large cities, Europe and Israel. The 1967 Arab-Israeli War was the final blow. Sefrou has fascinated American academics, with the likes of anthropologists Geertz, Rosen and Rabinow carrying out research here. Recently Sefrou was created capital of a new province, receiving new and badly needed investment. A town declining into shabby anonymity, it may yet rescue something of its heritage and find a place on the tourist map.

Sights The market place below and east of Avenue Mohammed V is a relaxed area to wander, best during the Thursday **market**. The town, which is known for olive and cherry production, has a large Fête des Cerises in June, and other smaller fêtes during the year. There is a moussem, or religious gathering, for Sidi Lahcen Lyoussi.

Entering from the north the road curves down to the Oued Aggaï, past the **Centre Artisanal** ① *Mon-Sat 0800-1200 and 1400-1900*, into the busy Place Moulay Hassan. From here **Bab M'kam** is the main entrance to the médina which lies north of the river and **Bab Taksebt** the main entrance, over the bridge, into the mellah. Both are small, maze-like quarters, but it is difficult to get seriously lost. The **mellah** can also be entered from the covered marketplace through **Bab M'Rabja**. Beside a mosque built into the wall, bend right and down the main street, beside small restaurants, butchers, shops and craftsmen, and then left to reach one of several small bridges over the Oued Aggaï. Alternatively, take one of the small side turnings to discover the cramped design of the mellah, now mainly occupied by poor rural migrants, with houses often built over the narrow streets.

In the médina, the **Grand Mosque**, restored in the 19th century, lies beside the river, and the souks just upstream. Past the souks is the **Zaouïa of Sidi Lahcen ben Ahmed**. In the médina there is a clearly discernible difference in the design of the quarter, reflecting the strict regulations and conditions under which Jews in the mellah lived. Sefrou is quite remarkable, however, in that the mellah is as large as the médina.

Avenue Moulay Hassan crosses the Oued Aggaï, where there is a Syndicat d'Initiative which has a **swimming pool** and continues as Avenue Mohammed V, the main street of the unexciting new town, with the post office, and a few shops and simple café-restaurants. Turn into Rue Ziad by the post office, past Hotel Sidi Lahcen Lyoussi and continue uphill on the black top road. Camping is signed to the left but continue up to the **koubba of Sidi Bou Ali**, with its white walls and distinctive green-tiled roof. There is a café, a few stalls and a magnificent view. Another small excursion beginning south of the river leads west to a small **waterfall** (les cascades).

Fès listings

For Sleeping and Eating price codes and other relevant information, see pages 12-20.

🛏 Sleeping

There are hotels and riads in Fès to suit all budgets, including some very luxurious ones in and around the tangled lanes of the médina – certainly the best place to stay if you want to get a real feel of old Fès. If you want to stay in a riad, a reservation is essential and someone will be sent to meet you. New riads are opening all the time, and they tend to be owned by a slightly younger crowd than in Marrakech. Fès also has a disproportionate number of British riad owners compared to other Moroccan cities. **Fez Riads**, T035-637713, www.fez-riads.com, is an excellent agency offering luxury accommodation in the médina.

Fès médina riads *p32, map 34*
€€€€ Maison Bleue – Le Riad, 33 Derb el Miter, Talaâ Kbira, T035-741873, T061-196851 (mob), www.maisonbleue.com. Much more atmospheric than its over-priced sibling near Place Batha, Riad Maison Bleue has a good pool, 12 connected suites and a hammam. Rooms have a/c, TVs, and 4-poster beds on old *zellige* floors. At the edge of the médina, the roof terrace is not as quiet as those in the centre of the médina but there's a bar and a fitness room to compensate.
€€€€ Riad Fès, 5 Derb Ben Sliman Zerbtana, T035-741206, www.riadfes.com. This vast house, originally built in 1900, was one of the first in Fès to be transformed into upscale accommodation, and it remains one of the city's most luxurious places to stay. Particularly at night its poolside bar is spectacular, and seriously hip. The 26 rooms are a little more dated, but no less elegant and the roof terrace has fantastic views.
€€€€ Riad Laroussa, 3 Derb Bechara, T074-187639 (mob), www.riad-laaroussa.com.

Passing what may be the world's largest visitors' book, Riad Laroussa opens out around a grassy courtyard with fountains and orange trees. As well as 4-poster beds and a *tadelakt* roof terrace, there are inventive touches such as kettles for taps. The dining room has black and white photos and jazz playing, while the 7 bedrooms are all themed around a colour. There's an elegant hammam and spa and copious amounts of intricately carved plaster.
€€€€ Riad 9, 9 Derb Lamsside, Souiket Ben Safi, Zkak el Ma, T035-634045, www.riad9.com. Sophisticated and elegant, Riad 9 has everything necessary to make a stay in Fès unusually stylish, from books, jazz, Chinese lanterns and panoramic views to a hyperactive cat. Run by a French designer, Riad 9 has the rugs and pouffes but also goes a step further, with great touches like tree trunk underwear drawers, dentists' chairs in bathrooms and turtle doves on the roof. Old antiques mix with inventive contemporary design to create something very special. The 3 rooms will soon become 5, and look out for a pan-Arab restaurant at some point too. The 5000dh price tag includes some very good wine.
€€€ Dar Attajali, 2 Derb Qettana, Zqaq Rommane, T035-637728, T077-081192 (mob), www.attajalli.com. Run by a yoga teacher, Attajali has a feminine feel, with lots of pinks, purples and silky fabrics. There are 5 individually decorated rooms with wooden ceilings, old tiles, antiques, comfortable mattresses and imported German duvets. And the 'purple suite' has a spectacular draped 4-poster bed. The high quality food is organic where possible and predominantly vegetarian. The roof terrace has great views right across the médina. One room also has a kitchenette, which would be good for families. Welcoming and homely.
€€€ Dar Bennis, just off Talaâ Sghira, T061-564364, www.houseinfez.com. Available only

to rent in its entirety, Dar Bennis sleeps 2-4 very comfortably and 5 at a push. Owned by the Director of the American Language Centre, it is a simple but beautiful house, on 4 levels around a small courtyard, this would make a great base for a couple or a family. Along with the house, you also get Hafid, the manager, to make you breakfast and be around if and when you need him. €80 per night for one person, plus an extra €20 for each extra person.

€€€ Dar Roumana, 30 Derb el Amer, Zkak Roumane, T035-741637, www.darroumana. com. A big riad with some amazingly beautiful Moroccan detailing, Dar Roumana is one of the friendliest places you could hope to stay. It also has some of the best food around and Jennifer, one of the owners, can impart culinary wisdom in cookery lessons. Inventive ingredients feature in the tagines, such as sherry, garlic and saffron, or you could go for swordfish with pomegranate. As well as breakfast, the price includes afternoon tea, and fresh bread is made in the house. The roof terrace has great views of the médina and the Merenid tombs, and, should you tire of looking at the intricate carved plaster, tiles and coloured glass, there's an excellent library, Wi-Fi and a TV room too.

€€€ Dar Seffarine, 14 Sbaa Louyate, T035-635205, www.darseffarine.com. One of Fès's most beautiful riads is run by a Norwegian graphic designer and an Iraqi architect. Just around the corner from the Qaraouiyine Mosque, Seffarine has a spectacular courtyard, with high arches. Rooms have a restrained but elegant style and you're sure to be very well looked after.

€€€ Riad Louna, 21 Derb Serraj, T035-741985, riadlouna.com. On a street linking Talaâ Sghira with the Batha, Louna has a greenery-filled courtyard with trees and blue and white tiles. Rooms have 4-poster beds and there are nice old baths with feet. There are 2 terraces, one where you can eat, one with good views over the médina.

€€€ Riad Mabrouka, 25 Derb el Miter, T035-636345, www.ryadmabrouka.com. Despite its position at the edge of the médina, this is a quiet spot, with good high views and some well chosen art. There's a big white courtyard, and large windows overlook a garden and a pool which, unlike those in most riads, is big enough to swim in. There are 6 rooms, including a very smart royal suite. It's a family-run place and the owners' Burgundian origins show through in their wine selection. Guarded parking is available nearby.

€€€ Riad Tizwa, Derb Guebbas 15, Douh Batha, T07973-238444 (UK mob) or T068-190872 (Morocco mob), www.riadtizwa.com. Sibling to the more established Tizwa in Marrakech, Tizwa Fès has 9 chic double bedrooms and a big roof terrace which is great for breakfast. All rooms are generously big and include an ipod docking station, which is indicative of the attitude that makes the place so pleasurable – modern and accommodating, but without any pretensions. Bathrooms are all done out in *tadelakt* and the bathrobes are luxuriously thick. It only opened in 2007 and at the time of writing there were some rougher edges than in the slicker Tizwa in Marrakech, but expect these to be ironed out soon.

€€ Dar el Hana, 22 Rue Ferrane Couicha, Cherabliyene, T035-635854, T076-286584 (mob), www.darelhana.com. A homely little riad, you'll be fantastically well looked after here, whether you rent the whole place or just a room. Carefully restored, Dar el Hana has wooden beamed ceilings, shuttered windows and a 'secret' window just above the pillows. All rooms have private bathrooms but in the smaller rooms they are not en suite. Guests breakfast together in the courtyard or on the terrace. The whole place can be rented out for €215.

€€ Dar Imam, 6 Derb Ben Azahoum, T035-636528. A friendly and good value place, in a good position, just off Talaâ Kebira. The terrace has lots of shaded soft furnishings and rooms apparently have new *tadelakt* on the way.

Fès médina hotels *p32, map 34*
Budget accommodation in the médina, mostly in the Bab Boujeloud area, fills up very quickly in spring and summer.

€€€€ Hotel Le Méridien Mérinides, Borj nord, T035-646218. 107 rooms, 11 suites. Superb views over the médina. Pool, restaurant, bar, nightclub, modern, conference room. One of Fès' premier addresses. Recommended.

€€€€ Hotel Palais Jamaï, Bab el Guissa, T035- 634331/3. A former palace with superb views of the médina and a beautiful garden, Jamaï has 123 rooms, 19 suites, 2 restaurants, bar, hammam, sauna, tennis court and a pool that is heated in winter. Service can be slow, though, and breakfast disappointing.

€€ Hotel Batha, Rue de l'Unesco, T035-634860. Popular, priced hotel with 61 rooms, comfortable, a/c, handy for sites. Small pool, good bar, reception sometimes a bit miserable and reservations notoriously flaky, breakfast poor – go for a coffee over the road instead.

€€ Pension Dar Bou Inania, 21 Derb Ben Salem, Talaâ Kebira, T035-637282. A rarity in the médina, Dar Bouanania is a reasonably priced hotel with some style. Colourful, though not always that light, rooms have big rugs and ornate wood details. A good option if you can't stretch to a riad.

€ Hotel Cascade, 26 Rue Serrajine, T035-638442. A traveller's institution, the busy Cascade is in the very heart of the action, just inside the main gate of Bab Boujeloud. Rooms are OK for the price, good views over the comings and goings down below, and you can sleep cheaply on the roof terrace.

€ Hotel Lamrani, Talaâ Sghira, T035-634411. Next to the fountain on the left on your way down Talaâ Sgira, Lamrani is a decent budget option, with 16 light and impeccably clean rooms, some with up to 4

beds. Hot showers included. Manager friendly but a little eccentric.

€ Pension Batha, 8 Sid Lkhayat, T035-741150. Not to be confused with the nearby Hotel Batha, this is a basic but clean budget place just off the square in Batha. Big bed and good breakfast. Don't expect much in the way of customer service though.

€ Pension Talaâ, on your right as you head down Talaâ Sgira, T035-633359. Just 6 rooms with hard beds and without wash basin. Good roof terrace though, with view of Bou Inania Medersa.

Fès ville nouvelle *map p43*
€€€€ Hotel Jnan Palace, Av Ahmed Chaouki, behind the craft centre off Av Allal Ben Abdallah, T035-652230. Beautiful grounds, pool, 195 rooms and 51 suites and a disco.

€€€€ Royal Mirage Fès, Av des FAR, T035-625002. 271 rooms, modern, comfortable, extensive gardens, 2 restaurants, coffee shop, bar, tennis and pool, used by tour groups. There's even a car rental inside.

€€€ Hotel Menzeh Fès, 10 Rue Mohammed Diouri, T035-625531, menzeh.zalagh@iam. net.ma. Close to Pl de la Résistance in an odd residential neighbourhood. Gardens, good pool open to outsiders for a small fee, tennis courts. Go for upper rooms with fine views over the médina. Nightclub, restaurant, pizzeria and connecting tunnel between the two parts of the hotel. Not great service.

€€€ Hotel Sofia, 3 Rue Arabie Saoudite, just off Av Hassan II, in heart of city, T035-624265-67. Comfortable but fairly soulless, like most hotels in the ville nouvelle, the Sofia has 98 a/c rooms and 4 suites, 2 restaurants, a nightclub, a pool, safe parking and a pub Anglais. Balconies but no views.

€€ Grand Hotel, Blvd Chefchaouni, T035-932026, grandhotelfes@menara.co.ma. A big 1930s building in centre of the ville nouvelle. All rooms have bathrooms and high ceilings.

A new refurbishment is removing some of the retro styling but also adding a lift. Bar at the back of the restaurant. Helpful reception.

€€ Hotel de la Paix, 44 Av Hassan II, T035-625072. Reasonably stylish, almost funky in places, this is a professionally run hotel with English-speaking staff. Some floors are more staid than others and some of the attempts at modern styling aren't that successful, but some Protectorate-era atmosphere remains nevertheless. Bar and restaurant.

€€ Hotel Mounia, 60 Rue Cuny (Rue Asilah), T035-624838, www.hotelmouniafes.ma. Good, reasonably priced hotel with lots of glossy contemporary Moroccan styling and an Institut de Beauté, in a street parallel to Av Mohammed V, close to Pl Al Massira.

€€ Hotel Moussafir Ibis, Av des Almohades, T035-651902/08. Part of the Accor group. Very handy for the railway station. 122 rooms, small pool, conference room for up to 180 people, secure parking.

€€ Hotel Splendid, 9 Rue Abdelkarim el Khattabi (a block away from the pedestrian bit of Abd el Karim el Khattabi), T035- 622148. Not exactly splendid, but also not too bad, with 70 clean and modern a/c rooms. There's a good sunny pool, a restaurant and bar, TV and safe parking. There's nothing in the way of views or character but it's friendly and reliable.

€€ Zahrat al Jabal, Ave des FAR, T035-944646. A modern place that opened in 2006, with 62 rooms and a panoramic restaurant on the rooftop. It's friendly and competent and rooms are contemporary, with a/c and TV.

€ Hotel Amor, 31 Rue d'Arabie séoudite, coming from the train station, take a left as you come onto the Pl de Florence, T035-622724. 35 rooms, most with shower, no groups. Clean beds. Bar, café-pâtisserie in street below. Avoid street-facing rooms. Good value for money.

€ Hotel Central, 50 Rue du Nador, T035-622333. Big, clean rooms, with rather old,

sagging beds. En suite bathrooms are generous, though, and you also get a desk, chair and mirror. Not at all bad for the price.

€ Hotel Olympic, Av Mohammed V, almost opposite the Wafa Bank but entrance on side street, T035-932682. 31 small rooms, most with a/c and some 1930s style.

€ Hotel Nouzha, 7 Rue Hassan Dkhissi, off Pl Atlas, T035-640002. Handy for the CTM station but a good 20-min hike from the train station. Cybercafé on ground floor. Fairly clean, efficient staff, café, bar. A good option in this category for a night or two.

€ Renaissance, 29 Rue Abdelfrim et Khattabi, T035-622193. Reasonable for the price, pink clover bedspreads and plastic picnic chairs in rooms. Some also have balconies.

€ Youth hostel, 18 Rue Abdesslam Serghini, in the ville nouvelle, T035-624085, www.fesyouth-hostel.com. Widely considered to be Morocco's best youth hostel, this is a spotless and very professional outfit, worth considering even if you don't usually stay in youth hostels. There's a very pleasant courtyard and garden, with lilies, trees and birds and they have single-sex dorms as well as a range of smaller rooms for 2-7 people. You can do laundry on the roof and information and advice is freely given. Reception open 0800-2200 but rooms closed 1000-1200 and 1500-1800. 65dh per person for a double room, no card necessary.

Camping

Camping du Diamant vert, near Aïn Chkeff, right off the N6. Expensive but the site has a shop and snack restaurant. Can be reached by bus No 19 from Fès from outside the PTT. Shade trees but poorly maintained wash-blocks. If staying here, you can use the next door aqua-fun complex (out of use out of season). Packed in summer.

Camping international, on the Sefrou road, some 3 km from Fès, reached by bus No 38 from Pl Atlas, T035-731439. Well maintained but expensive site with pool and shops. Bars with alcohol make this a lively, even noisy, site.

Moulay Yacoub *p41*
At quiet times, there will be plenty of rooms in private homes on offer.

€€ Hotel Moulay Yacoub, T035-694035, www.sogatour.ma. Part of the Sogatour group. 60 rooms with TV, bath and terrace, 60 bungalows, restaurant with magnificent views, bar, tennis, pool. A new treelined road leads down to the medical treatment centre using thermal springs, with neat gardens, café and practice golf.

€ Hotel Lamrani, T035 694021. Perhaps the best of the cheap accommodation.

Sefrou *p42*
€€ Hotel Sidi Lahcen Lyoussi, off Av Moulay Hassan, T035-660497. Dated but comfortable with 22 rooms, a restaurant, bar and pool.

€ Hotel La Frenie, Route de Fès, T035-660030. A small but generally OK place.

Camping
Camping de Sefrou, 2 km from the town, follow Rue Ziad, by the post office on Av Mohammed V, T035-673340. In site of 4 ha, bar/snack, groceries, showers, laundry, petrol at 2 km.

Eating

Fès médina *p32, map 34*
The médina is not over-endowed with good places to eat and many of the médina restaurants are not licensed. One of the best places to eat in the médina is the British-run Café Clock (see cafés, below). Many of the 'traditional Moroccan' restaurants in converted médina premises are open for lunch only and much used by tour groups.

¶¶¶ Al Fassia, in the Hotel Palais Jamaï, Bab el Guissa, T035-634331. Reservations advisable,

one of the best Moroccan restaurants with a vast array of dishes including quail tagine, plus traditional music. Extra charge when there is floorshow with Oriental dancers.

¶¶¶ Palais Tijani, 51-53 Derb Ben Chekroune Lablida, T035-741128. A full-on palace restaurant, intricate ornamentation and drummers, low tables, a range of set menus.

¶¶¶ Restaurant Palais des Merinides, 99 Zkak Roah, T035-634028. Serves lunch and dinner, splendid setting, around 110dh per course.

¶¶ Café Médina, just outside Bab Boujeloud. Despite the name, more upmarket than the surrounding options, and with some more interesting tagines too. The roof terrace is a peaceful spot, especially considering the location, with climbing clematis.

¶¶ Mezzanine, 17 Kasbat Chams, in front of the entrance to the Jnan Sbil Gardens, near Bab Boujloud, T011-078336. A new, British-run place that opened in 2008, Mezzanine is a chic bar and restaurant with Moroccan styling that serves food from 1100 until 2300 and stays open until 0100. The menu is a French/ Moroccan tapas hybrid, with sardines, brochettes, chorizo, marinated aubergines and tapenade, or just go for a mixed plate of tapas.

¶ Zohra, 3 Derb Aïn Nass Blida, T035-637699. Near the Medersa el Attarine, Zohra is smaller than most of the other palace restaurants in the médina, but with the same, slightly over-the-top decor. It is used by some small tour groups but feels more homely than most. Low Moroccan tables and good-value set menu.

There is no shortage of cheap restaurants in Fès el Bali, particularly just inside Bab Boujloud, where there is a busy row of cheap places with outdoor tables, all of which are good for an evening meal. Of these, Thami, under the tree, is perhaps the most often recommended, though there's not much to choose between them.

¶ Bouyard, underneath Hotel Cascade, Bab

Boujeloud. A surprisingly comfortable place, with candles and lace tablecloths and rifles on the wall. Good mixed salad and fish tagine, but avoid the pizzas.

Ṭ Café Restaurant Benyamina, Toute Tannery, Chaoura, T035-638291. A small, 1st floor place with low and comfy chairs. Obviously placed to catch tourists returning from the tanneries, but it has a good-value set menu and is not used by tour groups like many of the other places around here.

Ṭ La Kasbah, 18 Bab Boujeloud, T035-741533. One of the better Bab Boujeloud options, with a cheap menu including excellent brochettes. The balcony facing Bab Boujeloud itself fills up quickly. Make sure that you know what you are paying when you order, otherwise prices can be a bit arbitrary.

Cafés

Café Clock, 7 Derb el Magana, Talaâ Knira, T035-637855, www.cafeclock.com. In a beautiful old building just off Talaâ Kbira, in the heart of the médina, Café Clock is so much more than just a café. It has become the epicenter of traveller and ex-pat Fès in a remarkably short time, and understandably so. Hip, young, and energetic, there always seems to be something going on, whether it's a 'knit for peace' art installation or French conversation classes or a concert of Saharan music. On top of all that there's a mouth-wateringly tasty menu (camel burgers are popular, as are the fishcakes), great coffee and cakes, and a stunning view of the minaret of the Medersa Bou Inania across the other side of Talaâ Kbira from the fantastic roof terrace. There's even free Wi-Fi, and if you want to find anything out about the city you'll probably find someone here who will be happy to tell you. It's more of a daytime than an evening place – they stop serving about 2030 – but that's not enough to stop it being probably the best café in Morocco.

Cremerie de Place, on the northern point of Place Seffarine, a little café that does excellent panache (mixed fruit juice).

Óuali's Café, Pl Bouros, Talaâ Kebira. An unmarked and unprepossessing café with a few rickety outdoor tables on the right as you head down Talaâ Kebira, the much-photographed and rather ancient Óuali will serve you an exquisitely spiced coffee with commendable panache. You even get a home-made leather holder to stop your hands from burning.

Fès ville nouvelle *map p43*

Fès is far from having the same variety and choice of International restaurants as Marrakech. Nevertheless, there are a few reasonable options and many of them are licensed.

ṬṬṬ Trois Sauces, an out-of-town complex with a pool, Trois Sauces is a Western-style restaurant with good (but not amazing) European and American food. Very good service, but you could be just about anywhere.

ṬṬ La Cheminée 6 Av Lalla Asma (ex-Blvd Chenguit), T035-624902. Under the arcades on your right as you head towards the station, about 250 m away. Licensed, Franco-Moroccan cooking and popular with Moroccans as well as tourists.

ṬṬ La Médaille 24 Rue Med el Hayani, T035-620183, near the central market, off Blvd Mohammed V to your right as you come from Pl de Florence. Reasonably smart Moroccan place. Licensed.

ṬṬ Marrakech, 11 Rue Omar el Mokhtar, just off Mohammed V, T035-930876. A fairly smart place, with shiny walls and pinky red tablecloths. English is spoken and it has a decent range of tagines as well as set-price menus. Warm bread and good appetizers add to its appeal.

ṬṬ Restaurant Pizzeria Chez Vittorio, 21 Rue Brahim Roudani/Rue Nador, T035-624730. Good Italian food, wine, no credit cards. Licensed, and does lots of meat dishes as well as pizzas, though these are not as good as at nearby Vesuvio.

Vesuvio, 9 Rue AbiHayane Taouhidi, T035-930747. A good licensed pizza place which comes reasonably close to Italian authenticity, with dark wooden beams and smart waiters. Pastas too.

There are several good cheap options along Av Chefchaouni selling brochettes, lentils and the like.

Sicilia, 4 Av Chefchaouni, T035 625265, pizzas and sandwiches.

Cafés

In the ville nouvelle, try the following: **L'Elysée**, 4 Rue de Paris; or **Café Les Ambassadeurs** on Pl de Florence; **Cremerie Skali**, Mohammed V, an enormous juice and shakes menu. Fruit piled high testifies to the imaginative concoctions they will rustle up for you.

Bars

Fès *p28*

A drink in the Hotel Palais Jamaï is a good break in the médina and the Hotel des Merinides has a good view of the city, but for the classiest bar, go to Riad Fès and sit by the pool. Many of Fès's ex-pats favour the bar in the Hotel Batha, or there's the newly opened Mezzanine.

In the ville nouvelle try: **Es Saada**, on Av Slaoui; and **Bar du Centre**, Av Mohammed V.

Festivals and events

Fès *p28*

Jun For 10 days Fès vibrates to the rhythmic drumming and soaring voices of the **Festival de Fès des musiques sacrées du monde.** From sufi to gospel, the range is wide, and there is a scattering of dance too. Free open air concerts take place in the square outside Bab Boujeloud, with other, ticketed events at locations such as the Batha Museum and Bab Makina. Prices for individual concerts range from around 150dh to 600dh, or you can buy a pass for all the concerts for 2900dh. Tickets are available online at www.fesfestival.com.

Shopping

Fès *p28*

Moroccan goods

Fès has for long been one of the great trading centres of Morocco. The souks, kissaria and boutiques offer a splendid selection for visitors. Many of the boutiques in the hotels, the ville nouvelle and near the important tourist attractions will try to charge inflated prices. As elsewhere, the large carpet shops have very experienced salesmen who work with guides to whom they pay a commission for sales completed. Best buy in Fès is probably the blue and white painted, quite rustic, pottery once typical of the city. For smaller gift items, slippers and traditional clothing wander in the kissaria (clothes market) area between the Zaouïa of Moulay Idriss and the Qaraouiyine Mosque.

Coopartim Centre Artisanal, Blvd Allal Ben Abdallah, T035-625654. 0900-1400, 1600-1900. A good selection of crafts in the ville nouvelle.

Activities and tours

Fès *p28*

Tour operators

Azur Voyage, 3 Blvd Lalla Meryem, T035-625115.

Fès Voyages, 9 Rue de Turquie, T035-621776.

Number One, 41 Av Slaoui, T035-621234.

Tak Voyages, 41 Av Mohammed V, T035-624550.

Wagons-Lits Tourisme, Immeuble Grand Hotel, T035-654464.

Fès *p28*
Air
Aéroport de Fès-Saiss is 15 km to the south of the city, off the N8, T035-624712. There are flights to **Casablanca** with connections to internal and international les destinations, 1 a week to **Er Rachidia**, as well as direct flights to **Marseille**, **Paris** and several other European cities with **Ryanair** and **Atlas Blue**. To get to the airport take Bus 16 from the train station. **RAM** office, T035-625516/7, reservations T035-620456/7, at 54 Av Hassan II in the ville nouvelle.

Bus
Local buses cost 2dh. No 1 runs from Pl des Alaouites to Dar Batha, No 3 from Pl des Alaouites to Pl de la Résistance, No 9 from Pl de la Résistance to Dar Batha, No 10 from Bab Guissa to Pl des Alaouites, No 18 from Pl de la Résistance to Bab Ftouh and No 20 from Pl de Florence to Hotel les Merinides.

    CTM buses depart from the station on Av Mohammed V, T035-622041, for **Beni Mellal**, **Marrakech** (early morning departure, 8 hrs), **Tetouan**, **Tangier** (in the small hours), **Taza**, **Oujda**, **Nador**. For **Casablanca**, 8 departures a day, 0700-1900, for **Rabat**, 7 a day, and for **Meknès**, 8 a day, 0700-1900. Most other private line buses leave from the new terminal off the Route du Tour de Fès, below the Borj Nord and not far from Bab Boujeloud. Buses for the **Middle Atlas** leave from the Laghzaoui terminal, Rue Ksar el Kebir.

Car hire
Fès lies at a crossroads in Morocco, and is an excellent base from which to plan and carry out the next stage of travels. Note that on the routes into the city, men on motorbikes often drive alongside motorists to tout for unofficial guide work: best to ignore them. Parking can be a problem approaching the médina, so it

is perhaps better not to use your own car. **Avis**, 50 Blvd Chefchaouni, T035-626746. **Budget**, adjacent Palais Jamaï Hotel, T035-620919. **Europcar-Inter-Rent**, 41 Av Hassan II, T035-626545. **Hertz**, Kissariat de la Foire No 1, Blvd Lalla Meryem, T035-622812; airport T035-651823. **Holiday Car**, 41 Av Mohammed V, T035-624550. **SAFLOC**, Hotel Sheraton, T035-931201. **Zeit**, 35 Av Mohammed Slaoui, T035-625510.

Taxi
Grands taxis leave from Pl Baghdadi, except for Sefrou and Azrou which leave from Rue de Normandie. Red, cheap and a quick way to get around Fès, petits taxis generally have meters. Sample fares, Bab Boujeloud to Pl Mohammed V, 10dh; Pl Mohammed V to Hotel Les Merinides, 15dh.

Train
The railway station is at the end of Blvd Chenguit, in the ville nouvelle, T035-622501. To get to the town centre (ville nouvelle), head down this road and slightly to the left into Av de la Liberté. This joins Av Hassan II at Pl de Florence. If you arrive by train, check your departure time at the station. Trains run east to **Taza** and **Oujda** and west to **Meknès**, **Tangier**, **Rabat** and **Casablanca**.

Fès *p28*
Banks Lots of banks in ville nouvelle on Pl Florence and Av Mohamed V. Most reliable ATM is the **Wafa Bank**, Av Mohammed V, T035-622591. Other banks with ATMs in the big Immeuble Mamda, Pl de Florence. ATMs in Fès el Bali difficult to locate but many shopkeepers will change euros. **Books and newspapers** English Bookshop, 68 Av Hassan II, near Pl de la Résistance. Newspapers from the stalls in Av Mohammed V. **Cultural and language centres** Institut Français, 33 Rue el Bahrein, T035-623921, library and films. **Alif** (Arabic Language in

Fès), in the ville nouvelle at 2 Rue Ahmed Hiba (close to the Hotel Zalagh), T035-624850. Has a good reputation for organizing courses in Arabic, both literary and spoken Moroccan. They can cater for specific language needs, and at any one time have around 30 or more students, from various backgrounds. See also Café Clock, above.

Medical services Chemists: there is an all-night chemist at the Municipalité de Fès, blvd Moulay Youssef, T035-623380 (2000-0800). During the day try **Bahja**, Av Mohammed V, T035-622441 or **Bab Ftouh** at Bab Ftouh, T035-649135. **Hospital**: Hôpital **Ghassani**, Quartier Dhar Mehraz, T035-622776. **Internet** Internet cafés can be found on Av Hassan II in the ville nouvelle and near the intersection of Rue Douh and the Batha in Fès el Bali. **Post/telephone** The **PTT Centrale** is at the junction of Av Hassan II and Av Mohammed V, phone section open 0800-2100. In the médina, main PO is on Pl Batha. **Useful addresses Fire**: T15. Police, Av Mohammed V, T19. **Garages** Try **Mécanique Générale**, 22 Av Cameroun. Fiat repairs at **Auto Maroc**, Av Mohammed V, T035-623435.

Meknès

Meknès never set out to be an 'imperial city'. But, as chance would have it, the inhabitants of Fès and Marrakech showed little enthusiasm for 17th-century ruler and builder Moulay Ismaïl, and so he turned his attentions towards Meknès. Strategically situated at the heart of Morocco, Meknès became his capital and he embarked on a massive building programme. Meknès is known as a city of minarets – gentle green or grey in colour, the tall, angular, linear towers dominate the old town, which, with its cream colour-washed houses and terraces sits above the narrow valley of the Oued Boufekrane. There are pleasant souks, a medersa – but, above all, an easy pace which is almost relaxing after the tension and press of Fès. The most famous monument is the great Bab Mansour el Aleuj, and although today little is left except for vast pisé walls, once upon a time this great gate to a palace complex was worthy of the Thousand and One Nights. Meknès also offers some rewarding side trips – to the Roman site of Volubilis, and to the pilgrimage centre of Moulay Idriss.

➡ *For listings, see pages 66-70.*

Ins and outs

Getting there
Meknès has direct rail links from Marrakech, Casablanca, Rabat and Fès, and plenty of buses and grands taxis to other destinations. There are buses to Meknès from Rabat (five hours), Tangier (seven hours) and Marrakech (nine hours), calling at Beni-Mellal. If driving up from Marrakech, there are some beautiful views on the Azrou to Meknès route (the N13), with the Belvédère d'Ito, or you can turn onto the R212, which will take you from Mrirt through fine landscapes to join the N13 north of El Hajeb. ➡ *See Transport, page 69, for further details.*

Getting around
Meknès is a fairly spread out place. The médina, along with the ruined palace complexes of the 17th century, is situated across the valley of the Oued Boufekrane, a good kilometre walk away from the train station. The new bus station (private buses), however, is at Bab el Khemis, on the far side of the médina from the ville nouvelle. The old CTM bus station is on Av Mohammed V in the ville nouvelle, and some grands taxis leave from nearby on ave des FAR.

When visiting Meknès in summer, it can get hot, and the distances between the different parts of the 17th-century palace city are considerable. You will probably need a full day, with most of a morning dedicated to the palace complex. In half a day, you could do the médina very nicely.

Tourist information Office du Tourisme (ONMT) ① *27 Pl Batha-l'Istiqlal, T035-521286.* Helpful, although not overly endowed with information.

Background

Coming up to Meknès by road from Rabat, you get a good idea of why Moulay Ismaïl chose the town as his capital. The N6 passes through the Mamora Forest and a belt of fertile, relatively prosperous countryside. Meknès was originally a kasbah from the eighth century, used by the Kharajite Berbers against the Arabs. The town itself was founded by the Zenata Amazigh tribe called Meknassa in the 10th century and then destroyed by the Almoravids in 1069. A later kasbah was destroyed by the Almohad Sultan Abd el Moumen in order to build a new grid-patterned médina, some features of which still remain. This city was ruined during the conflict between the Almohads and the Merinids, but was partially rebuilt and repopulated in 1276 under Sultan Moulay Youssef. A fine medersa was built under the Merinids as they sought to expand Sunni orthodoxy to reduce the influence of Soufi leaders.

The reign of Moulay Ismaïl

The reign of the Alaouite sultan, Moulay Ismaïl (1672-1727), saw Meknès raised to the status of imperial capital. Even before his succession to the imperial throne, Moulay Ismaïl developed the city. Meknès was chosen as his capital rather than the rebellious and self-important rivals of Fès and Marrakech. Moulay Ismaïl is renowned for his ruthless violence, but many of the stories recounted by the guides may be apocryphal. What is certain is that he made an impression on European visitors to the court. Meknès was described as a Moroccan Versailles. Indeed, some suggest that the sultan was trying to rival Louis XIV, then involved in building his palace complex outside Paris. Having conquered Morocco, Moulay Ismaïl left his mark all over the country. Kasbahs were built by his troops as they pacified the tribes, cities acquired mosques and public buildings.

Moulay Ismaïl's vision of Meknès was vast, and although much of the pisé and rubble walls are in ruins, those still standing are testimony to its original scale. The city was built by a massive army of slaves, both Muslim and Christian, and the sultan was in particular famed for his barbaric treatment of these people, supposedly having them buried in the walls. He built several palaces to accommodate his wives, concubines, children and court, as well as quarters for his army the Abid Bukhari, an élite praetorian guard of black slaves, the chief instrument of his power. The city contained within it all that was necessary for such a large military machine, with store houses, stables, armouries, gardens and reservoirs.

After Moulay Ismaïl

After Moulay Ismaïl's death, Meknès gradually declined. His huge court and army could not be held together without his immense ego, and his successors Moulay Abdallah and

Sidi Mohammed returned the emphasis to Fès and Marrakech. Furthermore, the earthquake of 1755 destroyed many of Moulay Ismaïl's creations. The French revitalized Meknès, appreciating its strategic position in the corridor linking eastern Morocco and Algeria with the coastal belt around Rabat and Casablanca. They built their ville nouvelle apart from the médina and the imperial city, on the east bank of the Oued Boufekrane, as part of their policy of separate development of Moroccan and European quarters. During the Protectorate, Meknès became the most important garrison town in Morocco, and continued as an important military town after independence.

1 Meknès

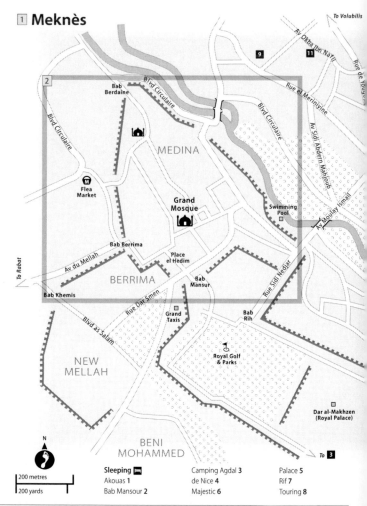

Sleeping 🛏
Akouas 1
Bab Mansour 2

Camping Agdal 3
de Nice 4
Majestic 6

Palace 5
Rif 7
Touring 8

Meknès today

Although Meknès is perhaps overshadowed by its near neighbour Fès, it is today the fifth largest city in Morocco with both tourism and industrial activities, and is the centre of a highly productive agricultural region. After a period of relative stagnation, Meknès is re-emerging as an important town. National planners made the city capital of the Meknès-Tafilalelt region which extends southeast to Er Rachidia, Erfoud and Rissani down one of the country's most strategic lines of communication. The late 1990s saw a spate of new building, not all of it in keeping with the city's character. Along with assorted

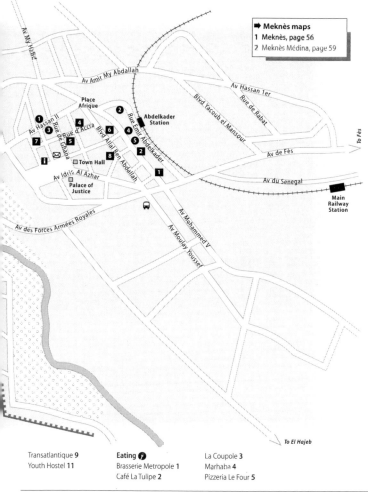

➡ **Meknès maps**
1 Meknès, page 56
2 Meknès Médina, page 59

Transatlantique 9
Youth Hostel 11

Eating 🍴
Brasserie Metropole 1
Café La Tulipe 2

La Coupole 3
Marhaba 4
Pizzeria Le Four 5

concrete blocks, a McDonald's has gone up on the corridor of parkland designed as a green lung for the heart of the city. And, horror of horrors, some philistine has put up a low-rise housing block in the heart of the médina, higher than some of the minarets.

Lovers of Moroccan red wines will find place names in the region south of Meknès familiar. The country's best vineyards are located here, near settlements like Aït Souala, Aït Yazm and Agouraï. Quality is improving with foreign investors putting money into improved vinification methods.

Sights

Meknès is a striking town, a fact accentuated by the distant backdrop views of the Jbel Zerhoun, which rises to over 1000 m to the north. The wooded foothills and orchards of olives, apples and pears below provide a green setting to the city for much of the year. One of the great historic cities of Morocco, its vast imperial city is now nevertheless more memorable for the impressive sense of scale and feeling of space than for any existing historic architecture. Another distinct part of Meknès is the médina which includes the intricately decorated Medersa Bou Inania, vibrant souks, the Dar Jamaï palace museum and numerous mosques. The cream-washed walls and daily life of the residential areas just behind rue Dar Smen still carry an antiquated 'Morocco that was' feel about them. To the east of the médina, on the opposite bank of the Oued Boufekrane, there stands the early 20th-century ville nouvelle. Carefully laid out by planner Henri Prost, the new town commands impressive (and as yet unspoiled) views over both médina and the imperial city. It has a relaxed atmosphere, and is a calm place to drink a coffee or tea and watch the evening promenade. Meknès is one of the easiest imperial cities to explore independently but there is no shortage of faux guides offering their services in Place el Hedim and nearby. If you need assistance, obtain an official guide from the tourist office or one of the larger hotels. About 150dh is a realistic fee.

Médina

Place el Hedim (the Square of Destruction), opposite Bab Mansour, is the centre of Meknès' old city, and the best starting point for exploration. The biggest open square in the city, it was once as busy as the Jemaâ el Fna in Marrakech, with acrobats, storytellers and snake charmers plying their trade. Despite its name, the square is now a quiet area with some cheap cafés at the far end opposite Bab Mansour. Renovation works are underway and hopefully the square will remain the central place to stroll on a Meknès evening rather than becoming a car park. To the left of the square is a crowded, covered **food market** with bright displays of fresh vegetables and pickles; definitely worth a look. On the right-hand corner of the square down a few steps is **Dar Jamaï**, a 19th-century palace, owned by officials at the court of Sultan Moulay Hassan, and now the **Museum of Moroccan Arts** ① *T035-530863, Wed-Mon 0900-1700, 10dh.* Built in 1882, it was the residence of the Jamaï family, two members of which were ministers to Moulay Hassan. It was used as a military hospital after 1912 and in 1920 became a museum. Exploring the house gives an insight into the lifestyle of the 19th-century Muslim élite. On display are wrought iron, carved wood, weaving, leather and metal work, and various antique household items. Look out for richly painted wooden chests and panels. Upstairs is a furnished reception room. The garden planted with cypress and fruit trees is a pleasant halt in the heat of the day.

The médina of Meknès has seven traditional **souks**, which while not quite of the order of those in Marrakech or Fès, are nevertheless well worth exploring. Immediately to the left of the Dar Jamaï a small entrance leads to the souks. The alley bends around to the right behind Dar Jamaï past some undistinguished clothes shops. Just before a carpet shop turn left. The passage, now covered, widens slightly, and continues past a range of shops selling modern goods, a bank, and various minor side turnings. At the junction, on the left, is **Souk Nejjarine**, which includes sellers of textiles, and carpenters, another entrance to the carpet souk, and a fondouk hardly changed since it was built. This route passes the Almoravid Nejjarine Mosque. At the end one can turn left towards the mellah or Place el Hedim or right into the dusty and noisy **Souk Sraira**, just inside the city walls, used by carpenters and metalworkers. At the very end, on the left, is the 12th-century Almohad Bab Jedid gate, around which are some interesting stalls selling musical instruments. **Souk Cherchira**, initially occupied by tentmakers, runs parallel to Souk Sraira but outside the city walls. **Souk Sebbat** is the right-hand turning opposite Souk Nejjarine and includes sellers of babouches, modern clothes and caftans, several tourist and handicraft shops, a fondouk on the right, and another on the left before the Bou Inania Medersa. A turning on the right opposite the medersa leads directly onto Rue Dar Smen, a good alternative route to remember.

2 Meknès Médina

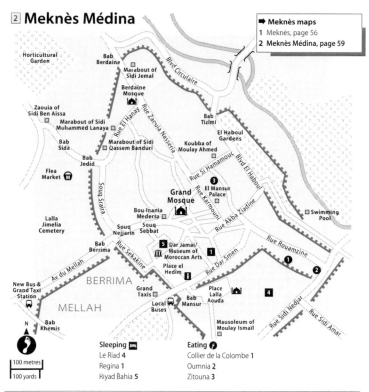

➡ **Meknès maps**
1 Meknès, page 56
2 Meknès Médina, page 59

Sleeping 🛏
Le Riad 4
Regina 1
Riyad Bahia 5

Eating 🍴
Collier de la Colombe 1
Oumnia 2
Zitouna 3

Best approached from Souk Sebbat is the **Bou Inania Medersa** ① *0900-1200, 1500-1800. Climb up onto the roof for a view of the médina, including the roofs of the Great Mosque, the minaret of the Nejjarine and other mosques.* Founded circa 1345 by Merinid Sultan Abou el Hassan this former college dispensing religious and legal instruction is a must-visit. The door to the medersa, part of a cedar screen, is just under a dome (notable for its ribbed design) at an intersection in the souk. Altogether, the college had 40 cells for its students, on both floors, around an oblong courtyard including a pool, with arcades surrounded by a screened passageway. As with many of the medersas, there is eye-catching *zellige* tiling and carved wood lintels. Take a look at the green-and-yellow tiled prayer hall. The doorway is ornamented with *zellige* tiling, as well as the customary and perhaps a little over-the-top stalactite-style plasterwork.

Nearby, the **Grand Mosque**, situated in the heart of the médina, is a 12th-century Almoravid foundation with 14th-century alterations. It is one of the oldest in Meknès and also the largest. Although non-Muslims are not permitted to enter the mosque, it is possible to view its lovely green-tiled roof and the minaret from the neighbouring Medersa Bou Inania (see above).

Mellah
To the west of Place el Hedim, through a street popular with hawkers of household goods, turn left into Avenue de Mellah. On the left is the mellah, a quarter built by Moulay Ismaïl in 1682 for his large Jewish community, which was walled off from the Muslim médina. The Bab Berrima Mosque dates from the 18th century, a time when the mellah was becoming increasingly Muslim. Few members of Meknès's once important Jewish community remain today, however.

Bab el Khemis
Heading southwest towards Rabat, the city wall is broken by Bab el Khemis, built by Moulay Ismaïl, with a range of different arches, decoration and calligraphy. This is the only remaining piece of the garden quarter attributed to Moulay Ismaïl. The rest has gone. It was destroyed by Moulay Abdallah, son of the great Moulay Ismaïl, who was not pleased by the reception he received from the inhabitants when he returned from an unsuccessful campaign. After this the Boulevard Circulaire leads past a cemetery containing the 18th-century tomb of Sidi Mohammed Ben Aissa, founder of the important religious brotherhood of the Aissoua. It's closed to non-Muslims but worth a look from a respectable distance. The Ben Aissa religious ceremonies are still held on the Mouloud (Prophet Mohamed's birthday). The Boulevard Circulaire continues round to Bab Berdaine, the entrance to the north médina.

Northern médina
Less frequented by tourists, the northern médina is reached by either weaving through the streets from the medersa or the souks, or, more easily, coming round on the Boulevard Circulaire. Bab Berdaine dates from the 17th century, a building decorated by Jamaâ el Rouah and flanked by two immense towers. Inside, on Place el Berdaine, is the Berdaine Mosque. Travelling south, the streets continue through an area of the traditional médina, only occasionally spoilt by insensitive new building. Here you are in traditional neighbourhoods where private and public space are clearly differentiated, each quarter having its own mosque, hammam and public oven.

Back on the Boulevard Circulaire, the next major gate around towards Oued Boufekrane is Bab Tizmi, near to Restaurant Zitouna. Opposite Bab Tizmi is the quiet Parc el Haboul, part of an area of gardens and recreational facilities in the valley dividing the médina and the ville nouvelle.

Bab Mansour

Claimed by some to be the finest gateway in North Africa, Meknès is dominated by this monumental gate at the top of the hill in the médina, opposite Place el Hedim. It dates from the reign of Sultan Moulay Ismaïl, and was completed by his son Moulay Mohammed Ben Abdallah in 1732, and marks the entrance to the huge grounds of his imperial city. The gate is named after one of the sultan's Christian slaves, Mansour the Infidel. The huge size is more of a testimony to its sultan than a reflection of defensive strength. The gate is clearly more about imperial splendour than anything else. The decorated flanking towers do not even have firing posts. The outrepassé arch is surrounded by a blind arch, including the usual lozenge network motif and *zellige* tiling. Between the arch and framing band is a black-tiled area with floral patterns. The overall effect of the main gate is exuberant and powerful. The gate has come to be a symbol of Meknès, even of Morocco as a whole.

Imperial city

The imperial city of Moulay Ismaïl is a massive area of crumbling walls and ruins, well worth taking a day to explore at leisure. Immediately through Bab Mansour from Place el Hedim there is Place Lalla Aouda, once the public meeting point during the period of Moulay Ismaïl and now a relaxing and pleasant area to rest. In the far corner is the **Lalla Aouda Mosque**, the story being that it was built by Princess Aouda as penance for eating a peach during the Ramadan fast.

Directly opposite Bab Mansour, in the right-hand corner of the square, a space in the walls leads through to a second square, the Mechouar. To the right note the domed **Koubat al Khayyatine** ① *on the left of the entrance to the building, tickets 10dh,* situated in a small park behind a fence; a plain building with pleasing simple decor. In the 18th century this was used to receive ambassadors, and later to make uniforms. Koubat el Khayyatine translates as 'the tailors' dome'. Inside is a display of photos of old Meknès. Outside, right of the entrance, a flight of stairs leads down to dank and vaulted underground chambers, said by guides to be the prison of the Christian slaves, although why one should want to keep a workforce down here is anyone's guess.

In the wall opposite the small park the right-hand gate leads to a golf course. This was originally to have been a lake, but was converted to its present use by the king. Behind the golf course is a later palace of Moulay Ismaïl, the **Royal Palace** or **Dar al Makhzen** ① *closed to visitors,* still in use and now heavily restored.

South of Place Lalla Aouda, the **Mausoleum of Moulay Ismaïl** ① *access via the monumental entrance in the cream wall opposite an arcade of craft shops (stock-up on film here), unusually for religious buildings in Morocco, the mausoleum is open to non-Muslims, and there is an entrance fee (sometimes),* contains the tombs of Moulay Ismaïl, his wife and Moulay Ahmed. Non-Muslim visitors can enter as far as an annex to the mosque section and admire from there the plaster stucco, *zellige* tiling and distinctive and exuberant colouring. The guardian normally allows visitors to take photos of the interior of the mosque from the annex.

Just past the mausoleum is an entrance to **Dar el Kebira** ('the big house'), Moulay Ismaïl's late 17th-century palace. The palace is in ruins, but the nature of the original structure of the building can be discerned. Since the 18th century, houses have been built into the walls of the palace. Back out on the road pass under the passage of the Bab ar Rih ('Gate of the Winds'), a long, arched structure. Follow the walled road, running between the Dar el Kebira and the Dar al Makhzen and turn right at the end. Carry straight ahead through another arch and after around 200 m you reach another chunky pisé wall, the Heri es Souani building.

Heri es-Souani
① *0830-1200, 1430-1830.*
Close to the city campsite and a hefty 35-minute walk from the médina, Heri es Souani, also called Dar el Ma ('the Water Palace'), is a large, impressive structure, also dating from the reign of Moulay Ismaïl, and used variously as granary, warehouse and water point, to provide for the court, army and followers in either the normal run of events or in case of emergencies such as conflict or drought. It is a good indication of the scale of Moulay Ismaïl's imperial ambitions. From the roof there would be a good view if one were allowed up. The nearby Agdal basin is now used for storing water for irrigation purposes. Once it was presumably a vital reserve in case of siege. Popular at weekends and summer evenings with strollers, the location is a little stark on a hot summer afternoon, so have a post-visit drink at the café in the nearby campsite.

Moulay Idriss and Volubilis

The shrine town of Moulay Idriss and the Roman ruins at Volubilis are an easy day trip from Meknès, although there is a hotel at Volubilis and more at Moulay Idriss for those who want to stay over and get a really early start, a good idea in summer when the heat can be oppressive. Volubilis, set in open fields, is a delight in spring, with wild flowers abounding. The ruins, covering over 40 ha, have poetic names – the House of Orpheus and the House of the Nymphs, the House of the Athlete and the House of the Ephèbe and there is a noble forum, a triumphal arch to Caracalla as well as ancient oil presses. The vanished splendour of Volubilis is echoed by legendary evocations of early Islam at Moulay Idriss nearby. This most venerable pilgrimage centre, set between steep hillsides, was founded in the eighth century by one Idriss Ibn Abdallah, great-grandson of Ali and Fatima, the Prophet Mohammed's daughter. Today he is referred to as Idriss el Akbar, 'the Great'. His son, Idriss II, is buried and venerated in Fès.

Ins and outs
Getting there Moulay Idriss is 30 km north of Meknès, Volubilis a little further north. For Moulay Idriss, take a grand taxi from Rue de Yougoslavie, or from the square below Place el Hedim (a 10dh ride). There are also regular buses from below Bab Mansour. The last bus back is at 1900. Volubilis is a clearly signposted 5-km drive from Moulay Idriss, a pleasant walk on a nice day, or a short taxi ride. Alternatively, for Volubilis bargain in Meknès for a grand taxi (split cost with others, say 50dh the trip), or take a bus for Ouezzane and get dropped off near the site. If travelling by car, leave Meknès by Rue de Yougoslavie in the ville nouvelle, and follow the R410 as far as Aïn el Kerma, and from there the N13 to Moulay Idriss.

Moulay Idriss

Coming round the last bend from Meknès, Moulay Idriss is a dramatic sight, houses and mosques piled up around two rocky outcrops, with the zaouïa, or sanctuary, in between. The centre of the Jbel Zerhoun region, Moulay Idriss is a pilgrimage centre, including as it does the tomb of its namesake, Idriss Ben Abdallah Ben Hassan Ben Ali, the great-great-grandson of the prophet Mohammed. The town is an alternative to Mecca in Morocco for those unable to do the ultimate pilgrimage. Moulay Idriss came to Morocco from Arabia, after defeat at the Battle of Fakh in 786. In 788 he was accepted as imam by the Amazigh Aurora tribe at Volubilis, and continued the rest of his life in Morocco, before he was poisoned in 791, to win over the loyalty of the tribes to the Idrissid Dynasty he established, and to spread the faith of Islam. This town and Fès were two of his major legacies.

However, the town of Moulay Idriss was mainly developed in the 18th century by Sultan Moulay Ismaïl, in part using materials lifted from nearby Volubilis, which the sultan plundered without restraint. Moulay Idriss was closed to non-Muslims until 1912, and even today is primarily a Muslim sanctuary, best visited during the day as an excursion, and although not unfriendly, certainly a place to be treated with cautious respect. A religious festival, or moussem, is held here in August, when the town is transformed by an influx of pilgrims and a sea of tents.

Buses and taxis stop in the main square where there are some basic restaurants and cafés. Above it is the Zaouïa of Moulay Idriss, as well as shops for various souvenir items associated with pilgrimage: rosaries, scarves, candles, and a delicious array of nougats, candies and nuts. The sanctuary itself, with its green-tiled roofs, a succession of prayer halls, ablution areas and tombs, is closed to non-Muslims.

Looking up from the square, the médina clings to the two hills, on the left is Khiba, while Tasga is on the right. Steep paths climb through the residential areas. After the climb there is a rewarding view over the sanctuary, showing the courtyards and roofs, and the adjacent royal guesthouse. The road through the town, keeping right, leads to a Roman bath just above the stream. Further on, beyond the road, there is a ruined 18th-century palace with a good view of the town.

Volubilis

ⓘ *Below the Jbel Zerhoun and 5 km from Moulay Idriss along the N13, the site is signed from the road, has parking (10dh usually), a café and ticket office but little else. It can be viewed in a day trip. In summer start early to avoid the heat. On the way in, note the collection of mosaics and sculptures, an 'open-air museum'. 0800 to sunset. 20dh.*

Volubilis is by far the most impressive Roman site in Morocco and sits in a spectacular spot, the hills and Moulay Idriss behind, vast views over the plain below. While much has been removed to adorn other cities over the centuries, or taken to museums such as the one in Rabat, the structure of the town is largely intact, the design of the buildings clearly discernible from the ruins. Many floor mosaics remain, remarkably unaffected by the passing centuries.

◖ *The site of Volubilis was used in the filming of Martin Scorsese's The Last Temptation of Christ.*

Background Archaeological evidence points to the possibility of a Neolithic settlement at Volubilis, while tablets found show there was a third-century BC Phoenician settlement. In

AD 24 it was the western capital of the Roman kingdom of Mauretania, and from AD 45 to 285 the capital of the Roman province of Mauretania Tingitana. Under the Romans the immediate region prospered from producing olive oil. However, as Volubilis was at the southeastern extremity of the province, connected to Rome through the Atlantic ports, its weak position necessitated extensive city walls.

Under the Emperor Diocletian, Rome withdrew to the coastal areas, leaving Volubilis at the mercy of neighbouring tribes. The city survived but its Christian and Jewish population diminished in importance, becoming the Christian enclave of Oualila during the eighth century. Though proclaimed sultan in Volubilis, Moulay Idriss preferred Fès. By the 11th century, Volubilis was totally deserted. It suffered again when Moulay Ismaïl ransacked the ruins to build Meknès, and further in the earthquake of 1755. French excavations and reconstruction began in 1915. The metal tracks on the site date from this period.

The site From the ticket office the entrance to the city is by the southeastern gate. A path, with sculptures and tombstones alongside it, leads down to a bridge across the Oued Fetassa. Up on the other side the first important remains in an area of small houses and industrial units is of an **olive press complex**. The mill stones, for crushing the olives, and the tanks for collecting and separating the oil, can be seen. Olive presses can be found through much of the city, as olive oil production was as essential an element in its economy as it is in the area today. Many of the same techniques are still used.

Right of the olive press is the **House of Orpheus**, a large mansion. In this building, as in most, some areas will be clearly roped off, and it is advisable to respect this, to avoid the whistle and wrath of the otherwise very friendly guardian. The first entrance gives access to a room with an intricate dolphin mosaic, to a kitchen with a niche for religious figures, and to a paved bathroom and boiler room. Note the complex heating system. The second entrance leads to an open court with a mosaic of the goddess Amphitrite, with living rooms around it, including a dining room with an Orpheus mosaic, showing the hero playing his harp.

Roman imperial settlements, even the most provincial, had impressive arrays of public buildings to cement a general feeling of Romanity. This was architecture as identity, and Volubilis was no exception. Heading further down into the site, and then to the right, lie the **Baths of Gallienus**, public baths which are the distant ancestor of the Moroccan hammam. Beyond this, the large public square in front of the Basilica is the **Forum**. In this area are a number of monuments to leading Roman figures. The **Basilica** is one of the most impressive ruins, with a number of columns still intact. This third-century building was the court house for the city.

Beside the Basilica is the **Capitol**, also with columns. In the court in front there is an altar, and steps leading up to the **temple** dedicated to Juno, Minerva and Jupiter Optimus Maximus. This building had great state importance, being the place where the council would assemble on great occasions.

Adjacent to the Forum is the **House of the Athlete**, named after the mosaic of an athlete winning a cup. The Triumphal Arch dominates the skyline, as well as the Decumanus Maximus, the roadway leading to the Tangier Gate. This was built in AD 217 to honour Emperor Caracalla and his mother Julia Domna. Originally finished with fountains, and medallions, the arch was heavily reconstructed by French archaeologists.

Although not of the same finesse as the honorary arches surviving in the Roman cities of Tunisia and Libya, it is nevertheless impressive. The Decumanus Maximus, the main street, had a colonnade with small shops, in front of a series of large houses, some containing interesting mosaics.

Starting on the left, from just beside the Triumphal Arch, the **House of the Ephèbe** was built around a courtyard with a pool. The house is named after the bronze statue of a

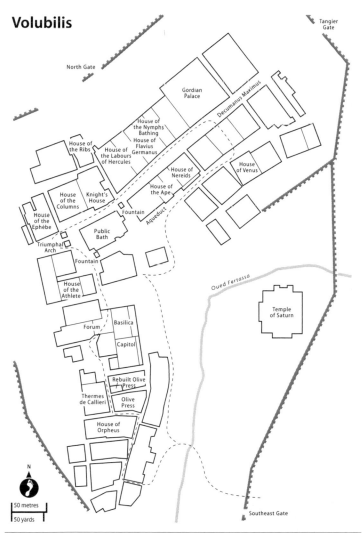

Volubilis

North Gate

Tangier Gate

Gordian Palace

Decumanus Maximus

House of the Nymphs Bathing

House of the Ribs

House of Flavius Germanus

House of the Labours of Hercules

House of Nereids

House of Venus

House of the Columns

Knight's House

House of the Ape

House of the Ephèbe

Fountain

Aqueduct

Triumphal Arch

Public Bath

Fountain

Oued Fertassa

House of the Athlete

Temple of Saturn

Forum

Basilica

Capitol

Rebuilt Olive Press

Thermes de Callieri

Olive Press

House of Orpheus

N

50 metres
50 yards

Southeast Gate

beautiful boy or ephebos found in the ruins. Adjacent is the **House of Columns** and then the **Knight's House** which has an interesting mosaic of Bacchus, good-time god of wine. In a more serious taste, the **House of the Labours of Hercules** has a mosaic with individual pictures of Hercules's life, and another of Jupiter. Further up, the **House of the Nymphs Bathing** has a mosaic showing nymphs undressing. The largest house on this side, the **Gordian Palace**, is fronted by columns, but the remains are quite plain. This may have been the governor's residence from the time of Gordian III, with both domestic quarters and offices.

On the right hand side of Decumanus Maximus from the Triumphal Arch there is a large **public bath and fountains**, fed by an aqueduct. Three houses up is the **House of Nereids** with a pool mosaic. Behind this and one up is the House of Venus, which has one of the best arrays of mosaics. The central courtyard pool has a mosaic of chariots. There are also mosaics of Bacchus, on the left, and Hylos and two nymphs, on the right. Nearby is a mosaic of Diana and the horned Actaeon. From the House of Venus cross back over the Oued Fetassa to the remains of the **Temple of Saturn**, a Phoenician temple before the Romans took it over. From here, follow the path back to the entrance, perhaps for refreshments in the café.

Meknès listings

For Sleeping and Eating price codes and other relevant information, see pages 12-20.

🛏 Sleeping

Meknès médina *p54, map p56 and p59*
At peak times, especially spring holidays, book in advance or arrive early.
€€€ Riad Safir, 1 Derb Lalla Alamia, Bab Aissi, T035-534785, riadsafir@menara.ma. Cosy, with warm reds and oranges and lots of carved wood detailing, this is a cosy little French-run guesthouse with just 3 rooms. Food is available if booked 3 hrs in advance, classical music plays and there's a roof terrace too. The owners plan to open another house nearby.
€€ Le Riad, 79 Ksar Chaacha, T035-530542, riad@iam.net.ma. Though heavily decorated (6 suites are each decorated to a theme – Sherazade, Ali Baba, Berber, etc), the rooms have no views and the courtyard is used as a restaurant. Overpriced.
€€ Riyad Bahia, 13 Tiberbarine, T035-554541, www.ryad-bahia.com. A restaurant downstairs and a riad with rooms upstairs. Bedrooms are decorated with old wooden

doors, low tables and cushions; suites have fireplaces. Beds are good and big and there are windows onto the street as well as the courtyard. There's Wi-Fi, internet terminals and a multi-levelled terrace with good views.
€ Hotel Regina, 19 Rue Dar Smen, T035-530280. Built in 1913, and always a hotel, Regina is being slowly improved, though it has some way to go still. Rooms have basins but sagging beds. The toilets are clean and it's a friendly place, with a big covered central courtyard.

Meknès ville nouvelle *p54, map p56*
There are some very reasonably priced central hotels here. Some of the older ones near the top end of Av Mohammed V and the Av des FAR, tend to be noisy as there are a number of bars here.
€€€ Hotel Transatlantique, Rue el Meriniyine, T035-525051, transat@iam. net.ma. Central, with 120 a/c rooms, 2 restaurants, bar, tennis, 2 good pools, and they accept credit cards. A fading 1930s hotel, rooms in the old wing (l'aile ancienne) have balconies with view over gardens or the

médina. The 60 rooms of the new wing, built in the 1960s, have been modernized.

€€ Akouas Hotel, 27 Rue Emir Abdelkader, T035-515967, www.hotelakouas.com. A modern hotel with a bar and a pool and mirrored reception. There are 52 rooms on 7 floors – some have balconies. The views aren't the best, but there are potted plants to lighten the concrete and there's even a nightclub.

€€ Hotel Bab Mansour, 38 Rue Emir Abdelkader, T035-525239. Plain but reliable, with 76 modern rooms, decorated in beige and white. TV, restaurant, bar and nightclub.

€€ Hotel de Nice, 10 Rue d'Accra, T035-520318. Fresh flowers in reception brighten up this good mid-range modern hotel with a restaurant and bar. Rooms have sparklingly clean bathrooms and balconies with climbing plants. Central and with safe parking.

€€ Hotel Rif, Rue d'Accra, T035-522591. Rif has 110 rooms and a courtyard with a pool. Reception has big leather chairs and huge bellows on the walls, rooms have a/c, TV, big desks and mini bars. It's comfortable without ever being stylish, though there are one or two Moroccan touches, to remind you where you are. External facing rooms can be noisy – if this worries you go for one overlooking the pool.

€ Hotel Majestic, 19 Av Mohammed V, T035-522033. An old 1930s style place with a switchboard but a hi-tech modern hot water system. There are 47 clean rooms, dark wood under layers of varnish and purple bedspreads. Excellent value, friendly staff. Rooms on street are on the noisy side, inner rooms are quieter but smaller.

€ Hotel Palace, 11 Rue de Ghana, T035-520407. Just opposite the side entrance to main post office. Has very clean, basic rooms, some with bathrooms. The bar is noisy but doesn't impinge on your sleep. Safe parking for 10dh or park in street with a warden.

€ Hotel Touring, 34 Av Allal Ben Abdallah, T035-522351. Cheap, with large rooms, but not overly concerned about their guests.

€ Youth hostel, Av Okba Ibn Nafii, near the municipal stadium and Hotel Transatlantique, T035 524698. 1000-1200, 1600-1700. This is the YHA's headquarters in Morocco and is one of the best and most friendly hostels with dormitories around a garden. Well maintained, 60 beds, 25-35dh per night, kitchen, meals available, bus 25 m, train 1200 m.

Camping

Camping Agdal, 2 km out of Meknès centre, opposite the Heri es Souani, T035-551828. Take buses 2 or 3, or better, a petit taxi. A 4-ha site with shop, café, laundry, electricity for caravans, and hot showers, clean and well organized, petrol only 2 km. Some rooms soon available, alcohol – a bit noisy near the café area, piped music. Lots of shade.

Camping Belle-Vue, on the road to Moulay Idriss some 15 km north, T068-490899. Site of 3 ha, 60dh 2 people with car and tent, small shop, showers, laundry, electricity for caravans, petrol 100 m. Loo blocks could do with some maintenance.

Moulay Idriss p62

Since the king suggested that the notion that non-Muslims couldn't stay overnight in Moulay was outdated, riad owners have started moving in on Moulay. So far what's here is rather gaudy, but expect better accommodation soon.

€€ Erroiede, 35 Derb Lamrayeh, T035-544186. A whole self-catering flat, Erroiede has a small kitchen and a terrace. Plain but central and good value.

€€ Hannaoui, 5 Rue Ben Yazgha, T035-544106, zakia_hanaoui_5@hotmail.com. Contemporary Moroccan style, this is a friendly and enthusiastic place with views over the stream and mountain. The 'hammam' is a bit like a bathroom with a big heater, but it has lots of well-labelled herbs and local plants.

€ Slimani, Derb Drazat, Quartier el Hofra, T035-544793, slimanit@yahoo.fr. 5 rooms,

including a couple of darker rooms downstairs, this is a typical Moulay guesthouse, with lots of modern Moroccan fabric. Comfortable beds, and lots of them.
€ Colombe d'Or, 21 Derb Zouak Tazgha, T035-544596, www.maisondhote-zerhoune. ma. 2 rooms on the roof terrace, 4 on the 1st floor as well as a Moroccan salon. There are ceramic doves among the clutter and there's lots of decoration. Good value.

Camping
Zerhoune Belle Vue, en route to Meknès. Also, opposite the turning to Volubilis, the proprietor of the café allows people to camp.

🅾 Eating

Meknès médina *p54, map p56 and p59*
Meknès has a small but growing range of Moroccan restaurants catering mainly to tour groups.
¶¶¶ Restaurant Zitouna, 44 Jamaâ Zitouna, T035-532083. In the style of a Moroccan palace in a médina side street near Bab Tizmi, Moroccan menu, no alcohol.
¶¶ Restaurant Collier de la Colombe, 67 Rue Driba, T035-525041. Housed in a fine 19th-century city residence, a short walk off Pl Lalla Aouda in the médina. Moroccan food for tour groups during the day. Interior is all very peach, good views over to the ville nouvelle.
¶¶ Restaurant Riad, 79 Ksar Chaacha, T035-530542 (see also Sleeping, above). A range of traditional Moroccan menus concentrate on the standards, with tagines and pastillas. You can eat inside or out, in a garden with flowers and cacti and a small, slightly grubby pool. No alcohol licence and can fill up with tour groups.
¶¶ Riad Bahia, 13 Tiberbarine, T035-554541, www.ryad-bahia.com (see also Sleeping, above). An excellent range of tagines includes lamb and aubergine and lamb and apricots. Everything is calm and very Moroccan, with pouffes and plants and carved wood.

Two sides of Place el Hédim fill up with stall selling cheap light meals with a preponderance of brochettes. There's not much to choose between them, so take a wander and see what takes your fancy.
¶ Oumnia, 8 Ain Fouki Rouamzine, T035-533938. A cosy little family-run place with a good-value fixed menu. Follow the signs off Rue Rouamzine.

Meknès ville nouvelle *map p56*
¶¶¶ Restaurant Belle Vue, in Hotel Transatlantique, Rue el Marinyen, T035-525051. Extensive international menu, good wines, excellent views over Meknès médina from its hilltop location.
¶¶ Bar Restaurant La Coupole, Av Hassan II, down the street from the Hotel Palace, T035-522483. French/Moroccan menu, plush interior, reasonable food, over-elaborate service, licensed, upmarket bar next door.
¶¶ Café Restaurant Gambrinus, Av Omar Ibn el Ass, opposite the market, off Av Hassan II, T035-520258. French, Spanish and Moroccan cuisine, kindly service and interesting wall murals.
¶¶ Le Dauphin, 5 Av Mohammed V, T035-523423. Licensed French restaurant serving seafood and with a good garden.
¶¶ Pizzeria Le Four, 1 Rue Atlas, T035-520857. A licensed place around the corner from the station with reasonable international cuisine and pizzas. Serves an interesting mix of tour groups, local businessmen, independent travellers, and local students.
¶¶ Restaurant Bar Brasserie Metropole, 12 Av Hassan II, on the corner near the Central (food) Market, T035-522576. Brochettes and chicken, licensed.
On Av Mohammed V, uphill from the Hotel Majestic, opposite the BCM, are a couple of cheap and cheerful roast chicken eateries:
¶ Coq Magique and **¶ Restaurant Sana**. Up on the Av des FAR, under the Hotel Excelsior, are more barbecue-type places. The

same area also has lots of bar-eateries indicated by Flag Spécial signs.

🍴 **Marhaba**, 23 Av Mohammed V. Serves very cheap Moroccan dishes in an atmospheric little space – sit on ragged chairs surrounded by tiles and arches.

Cafés

Meknès produces the best mint in Morocco, so don't pass up a chance to get your fix of mint tea here. Try one of the noisy cafés on Rue Dar Smen.

Cafe la Tulipe, Place Maarakat Lahri, T035-511094. A big busy place with wicker chairs outside under the trees. Cakes, ice cream in season.

Crémerie-Pâtisserie Miami, Av Mohammed V, in the ville nouvelle.

🍸 Bars and clubs

Meknès *p54, maps p56 and p59*
Bar Continental, Av Hassan II.
Hotel Transatlantique, Rue el Marinyen. An excellent place for a relaxing drink, not least because of the view over the médina.
Hotel de Nice, 10 Rue d'Accra.
La Caravelle, 6 Rue de Marseille.
La Coupole, Av Hassan II.

⛰ Activities and tours

Meknès *p54, maps p56 and p59*
Hammam
Hammam des Jardins, aka **Hammam Maha**, very handy for the ville nouvelle. Heading towards the médina on Av Hassan II, take a right between BCM and Agora salon de thé. After 25 m, drop left down some steps, then go right. Hammam, separate entrances for men and women, overlooks a semi-abandoned small park.

Hammam Sidi Omar Bou Aouada, turn right as you face Dar Jamaï museum on Pl Hedim, baths on your right about 25 m further on, unmarked.

⊖ Transport

Meknès *p54, maps p56 and p59*
Bus
Local buses No 5, 7 and 9 run between the ville nouvelle and the médina. **CTM** buses to **Rabat**, **Casablanca** and **Fès** (7 a day), **Tangier**, **Ifrane**, **Azrou**, **Ouezzane** and **Er Rachidia** (daily) leave from 47 Av Mohammed V, T035-522583/4. Private lines go from the terminal below Bab Mansour.

Car hire
Stop Car, 3 Rue Essaouira, T035-525061. **Zeit**, 4 Rue Antsirebe, T035-525918.

Taxi
Grands taxis, which are a particularly good option to both **Fès** and **Azrou**, leave from the car park below Pl el Hedim, opposite the private line buses. Ask the drivers hanging around for the destination. For **Moulay Idriss** (and then a short walk to **Volubilis**) they leave from near the Shell station on your right as Av Hassan II descends. Negotiations over prices can be long and painful, with various people hanging around to act as intermediaries and take their cut. See also the taxi rank near the Palais de la Foire. Light blue petits taxis hop between ville nouvelle and médina.

Train
The main station is some way from the centre, T035-520017/520689. Regular departures for **Rabat** and **Casablanca**, **Tangier** (with a change at Sidi Kacem), and eastwards for **Fès**, **Taza** and **Oujda**. If you are going to stay in ville nouvelle, get off at the **Meknès Amir Abdelkader** station, the first of the 2 Meknès stations as you come from Casa/Rabat. This station is just below Av Mohammed V, and closer to the centre of the ville nouvelle than the other main station.

Meknès *p54, maps p56 and p59*
Airline offices Royal Air Maroc, 7 Av
Mohammed V, T035-520963/523606. Closest
airport is at Fès. **Banks Banque du Maroc**, 33
Av Mohammed V. **BMAO**, 15 Pl 2 Septembre.
BMCE, 98 Av des Forces Armées Royales,
T035-520352. **Bureau de change** open daily
1000-1400, 1600-2000. **Credit du Maroc**, 33
Av Mohammed V. **SGMB**, Pl Al Wahda Al
Ifriquia, T035-527896. **Wafa Bank**, 11 Av
Mohammed V, T035- 521151. As usual, the
most useful. **Cultural centres Institut
Français**, zankat Farhat Hachad, Av Hassan II,
T035-524071. Organizes lectures and films,
hosts occasional concerts and plays. Closed
mid-Jul to early Sep. A bright note in Meknès'
rather sleepy cultural life. **Medical**
services **Chemists**: Pharmacie d'Urgence, Pl
Administrative, T035-523375, 0830-2030.
Depot de Nuit: Medicaments d'Urgence,
Hotel de Ville, Pl Administrative, 2030-0830.
Hospitals: Hôpital Mohammed V,
T035-521134. Hôpital Moulay Ismaïl, Av des
FAR, T035-522805. Probably the best of the
bunch is **Polyclinique Cornette-de- St-Cyr**,
22 Esplanade du Docteur Giguet,
T035-520262. **Post PTT Centrale**, Pl
Administrative, 0800-1400, 0800-2100. Also
the PTT on Rue Dar Smen, in the médina.
Useful numbers Ambulance: T15. **Fire**: T15.
Police: T19.

Middle Atlas

From Fès or Meknès there are a number of interesting towns to visit in the Middle Atlas, possible stopovers to break a journey south to Marrakech, places to escape the summer heat and do some walking in hills and cedar forests. If you already know the more major sites and towns in Morocco well, you may want to take in some of the Middle Atlas towns instead. In a week you could comfortably combine visiting Fès and Meknès (plus Volubilis and Moulay Idriss) with a circuit southwards which might include overnights in Azrou, and then Ifrane or possibly Sefrou or Immouzer du Kandar. A loop southwest of Azrou would take you down to Khénifra and back up via the Aguelmane Azizga and Oum er Rbia, Morocco's largest river which flows into the Atlantic at Azzemour. Strategically located on the imperial cities to Tafilalet road, next to magnificent mountains, Midelt at an altitude of 1525 m, looks as though it will have a good future as a base for hikers.
▸ *For listings, see pages 76-79.*

Azrou *For listings, see pages 76-79*

Azrou, 70 km south of Meknès, is a small Amazigh market town and hill resort at the heart of the Middle Atlas. The word 'azrou' means rock in Tamazight, and at the middle of the town next to the large new mosque is the eponymous rock. The town has a relaxed air and good hiking in the wooded vicinity. The ruined kasbah was built by Moulay Ismaïl.

Ins and outs
There are plenty of buses from Meknès and Fès to Azrou, which is situated at a crossroads of routes leading up from Marrakech (via Beni Mellal and Khénifra) and Er Rachidia (via Midelt). Coming from Marrakech, you will have to change at Beni Mellal if you don't get a direct bus. All buses, except those of CTM, arrive at the bus station opposite the Grand Mosque. The grand taxi station is close by, near the roundabout. Grands taxis for Khénifra are close to the rock. Azrou is a one-horse sort of place, so there are no difficulties getting around.

Background
One of Azrou's claims to fame is that under the French Protectorate, it was chosen to be home to the Collège berbère, a training school for Moroccan Berbers which was founded on the premise that Arabs and Imazighen were fundamentally different – and should be educated and ruled as such. The divide and rule policy backfired – it was in the interests of

neither Arabs nor Imazighen for a colonial regime to continue to control Morocco; in any case, loyalty to Islam and the Alaouite throne proved to be stronger than ethnic ties, a fact which somehow escaped French colonial ethnographers. After Independence, the Collège berbère became the Lycée Tarik Ibn Zayid, symbolically named for the Arab conqueror of Andalucía. In the late 1990s, Amazigh cultural movements began demanding more official recognition of their cultural identity and Morocco's handling of its large Amazigh minorities will be interesting to watch in coming years.

Sights

Azrou's traditional character, once created by the green-tiled roofs of the arcades round the market square, has taken a beating. Although there are a few good hotels and it is ideally located as a base for exploring the cedar forests, it has yet to find its place in the tourist market. It seems to function as a sort of suburb to its more upmarket neighbour Ifrane. The heart of Azrou, **Place Mohammed V**, is to the right on leaving the bus stop. There is a covered **market** near Place Mohammed V, while the **Ensemble Artisanal** ① *0830-1200, 1430-1800*, is situated off Avenue Mohammed V, with a fixed-price shop and a number of craftsmen working on the premises – look out for the Middle Atlas carpets. A large **Amazigh souk** is held just above the town on Tuesday, with vegetables, textiles and some interesting Middle Atlas carpets, as well as traditional entertainment from musicians and others. The town also has a small pool for summer use.

Excursions

If you have a car there are some very scenic routes south of Azrou where the landscapes are truly spectacular. One loop would take you up to Aïn Leuh (see below), past Lac Ouiouane and across the **Plateau des cèdres** to the source of the Oum er Rbia (Morocco's major river) and the Aguelmane Azigza to Khénifra (a possible overnight), or back up from Khénifra on the main N8 to Azrou via Mrirt (large Thursday souk).

If you have time, you should seek out the region's largest and most famous cedar, the **Cèdre de Gouraud**, still named for some half-forgotten French military commander. This is signposted to the right off the Azrou to Ifrane road, down a narrow, winding road. Barbary apes will be anxiously waiting among the trees to share the contents of your picnic.

Of more specialized interest is the abandoned **Benedictine monastery** at **Tioumliline** ① *turn right a few hundred metres up the hill after the Ifriquia petrol station above Azrou on the Midelt road*. The monastery, founded in 1920, was finally relinquished in 1963, becoming a vocational training centre, abandoned along with the dispensary in the 1980s. Low stone buildings, a cloister planted with cypress, lilac, and a Judas tree survive on this beautiful site, as does the church building and the graves of five fathers. The monastery was important as a meeting place for Moroccan intellectuals in the heady days after independence, providing a refuge to abstract painter Gharbaoui, amongst others. The location is lovely and birdwatchers may find things of interest in the mixed deciduous/cedar woodlands here.

At 19 km south of Azrou, a turning off the N8 leads to **Aïn Leuh**, an Amazigh village with a Wednesday souk important to the semi-nomadic Beni M'Guild tribe, a ruined kasbah from the reign of Moulay Ismaïl, and nearby cascades. You then follow a narrow road through cedar forest and across a plateau, past **Lac Ouiouane** and its 1930s chalets to the source of the River Oum er Rbia, 20 km away. In places, the cedar forest has been cut back to form a thick green crown on the tops of the hills. The villages here are desperately poor, there is little vehicle traffic and children will come racing out at the first sign of a passing vehicle. Many of the houses are little more than stone shelters with crude plank roofs, now partly rendered more watertight with plastic. Drive slowly as the road is narrow. Eventually, you drop down to the source of **Oum er Rbia**, clearly visible with its water works from above. There is a car park (lots of men wanting to warden your car) and steps leading to a series of concrete platforms built on the rocks where the river waters come boiling out from between the boulders. (Some of the springs are said to be sweet, others salty.) After the platforms, you can clamber on to where the water comes crashing into a small, but not actually very deep pool (no diving). After the source, you can head west on a narrow and in places much deteriorated metalled road through beautiful landscape to join the main N8 south of Mrirt. The other option is to head on south to **Aguelmane Azigza**, a crater lake surrounded by forest and ideal for swimming. The tree-lined spot has its devoted followers among Moroccan campers and is a fine location for some birdwatching. There also may be accommodation on offer in a local café. The road continues to rejoin the N8 at Khénifra.

Ifrane and the lakes ➤➤ *For listings, see pages 76-79*

Ifrane, 17 km north of Azrou and 63 km south of Fès, is a mountain resort founded by the French in 1929 which today has numerous large villas and chalets, as well as a royal palace and hunting lodge. It still manages to have something of a colonial hillstation feel to it – despite the arrival of a large new campus university housed in chalet-type buildings and vast new social housing developments on the Azrou side of town. When this is occupied by the king, the town becomes busy with staff and politicians. From the town there are good walks in the cedar forests, and a drivable excursion round the *dayats* (crater lakes). There is some skiing to be had at the nearby resort of **Mischliffen** and there is a small airport maintained for private and royal flights.

The dayat lakes
North of Ifrane, leave the N8 to the east for a tour of the dayats, seasonal limestone lakes which are a haven for wildlife, especially birds. There are four lying between the N8 and the R503: Aaoua and Ifrah are the largest but you can also visit Afourgah and Iffer. Dayat Aaoua, 12 km from Ifrane, is a scenic place to picnic if the lake is full, which is not the case in drought years, and can make the area disappointing for birdwatchers. In good circumstances, however, the dayats are home to coots, herons and egrets, look out for the black-winged stilt, and numerous reed warblers. The surrounding woodland, made up mainly of holm-oak and cedar, is alive with birds: tits, chaffinches, short-toed treecreeper, jays, greater spotted woodpeckers and raptors including black and red kite, Egyptian vulture and booted eagle. In the woodland Barbary apes can be seen and where the woodland gives way to more open plateau look out for the jackals.

Immouzer du Kandar
A small hill resort, 80 km south of Fès, and beautiful in spring with the apple blossom, Immouzer a popular excursion from Fès, from where there are regular buses and grands taxis. It is also a lively place during the Fête des Pommes in July. Market day is Monday in

the ruined kasbah. Just north of Immouzer du Kandar are the popular picnic/camping springs, **Aïn Seban** and **Aïn Chifa**, clearly signed to the west of the road. In drought conditions they are less attractive.

Khénifra and around ➨ *For listings, see pages 77.*

Khénifra, capital of the Zaïane region and 96 km southwest of Ifrane, is a relaxed (if rather dull) Middle Atlas town with a population of around 100,000. The town's men are famed for their horsemanship. It has large Wednesday and Sunday **souks** – the place perhaps to pick up an Amazigh rug. The town, with its strategic location at the heart of the Middle Atlas, was developed by Moulay Ismaïl in the late 17th century. In the late 19th century, Sultan Hassan I named local strongman Moha ou Hammou ez Zaïani as caïd. The French had considerable difficulty in bringing Khénifra under their control, and suffered a major setback there in 1914, at the hands of Moha ou Hammou. The town only came under the Protectorate's control in 1921 when he was killed in a battle with French forces. A few kilometres south of the town on the N8 is a **monument** to this resistance hero.

Khénifra still has a somewhat military feel to it. There is a main avenue with the usual buildings on stilt-legged arcades (cybercafés here). At the north end of town near the horse-monument roundabout are a large number of steep-roofed French buildings, often topped with storks' nests, while over the river is the **kasbah** area with an old bridge and one or two historic buildings drowned in a mass of new constructions. A possible place for a coffee stop might be the Café des Cascades, on a low rise between town centre and horse roundabout. There is a **tourist office** at Immeuble Lefraoui, Hay Hamou-Hassan.

A popular excursion from Khénifra is to the tree-lined lake of **Aguelmane Azigza**, about 24 km along the 3485. The road continues to the source of the Oued Oum er Rbia and **Aïn Leuh**, and then back onto the N8 just southwest of Azrou (see page 73 for further details).

Midelt ➨ *For listings, see pages 77-79.*

The rough and ready mining centre of Midelt works well as base for excursions, to the abandoned mines of Ahouli in a defile of the Oued Moulouya, or an off-road trip to the Cirque de Jaffar, a natural amphitheatre in the side of Jbel Ayyachi, paramount peak of the region (see more details in 'Around Midelt' below). For many it's a handy overnight stop about halfway between the imperial cities and the Tafilalet. Despite high unemployment, the town has a calm, friendly atmosphere and a souk on Sunday.

Those in need of some shopping therapy should think carpets in Midelt. These can be bought from the weaving school (*atelier de tissage*), the **Kasbah Meriem**, the local name for the monastery/convent of **Notre Dame de l'Atlas** ① *T035-580858,* which is run by Franciscan sisters in premises off the road to Tattiouine. There is also a tiny community of Trappist monks here who relocated from Algeria. The sisters may also be a good source of information about the region. To get there, head north out of Midelt town centre, take left turn onto the track after bridge, follow the track towards the kasbah village, where you then take a sharp right and go almost immediately left up the hill. After about 1 km, the Kasbah Meriem is signed on the left, down a dip and up again, its presence indicated by trees. The atelier is left of the large metal gate. Inside, there is a simple church with a small icon of the seven sleepers of Ephesus, symbol of a myth present both in Christianity and Islam. The Franciscan sisters do lots of good work in the region, travelling off into the countryside with mules and a dispensary tent. While the covert funding by USA churches of Protestant missionary activity has attracted criticism in the Moroccan press, the Franciscans' efforts are much appreciated by locals.

For more on **hiking** opportunites and other possible excursions in the area, head for **Aït Ayach**, halfway between Midelt and Zeïda on the N13, where the Auberge Timnay can help with vehicle hire and guides (see page 77).

Around Midelt

There are some excellent excursions from Midelt. Walkers will want to head for the mountains and the Cirque de Jaffar. For those with hire car, a good half-day adventure is to drive via Mibladene up to the abandoned mines at Ahouli. In the heart of the eastern High Atlas, Imilchil is now feasible as a long day trip on the metalled road via Rich. Note that, as elsewhere in this plateau region, the winters are very cold and the summers very hot, so the best time to visit is the spring. Here the spring is later, and May or even early June are recommended for walking.

Mines of Ahouli

This excursion north from Midelt goes along the S317 to Mibladene (10 km) and over the head of the Oued Moulouya to the abandoned mining settlement of Ahouli. The road is signed right a few metres north from the central bus station junction in Midelt. The first long straight section to Mibladene is badly potholed but it then improves slightly after Mibladene, a former mining community, to the right of the road. You then wind into spectacular gorges. The road deteriorates again after an Indiana Jones-style bridge, parts of it washed away by floods.

Ahouli must once have been a hive of activity. Copper and lead were the main products. The gorge is beautiful, with poplar, oleander and even the odd weeping willow. Mine infrastructure and housing clings to the cliffs. The community even had its own rather splendid cinema (now sanded up) and swimming pool. The lower floors of the houses had heavy metal doors, to keep out eventual flood water. There is a caretaker here, and he or his son may show you round.

After Ahouli, you can drive up out of the gorges on a well-made track, turning left to more abandoned dwellings on the plateau. Turning left, and a couple of kilometres brings you to the small village and semi-abandoned ksar of **Ouled Taïr** next to the *oued*, reached by a wobbly footbridge.

Note When driving out to Mibladene, men will try to flag the car down. Most will be selling fossils or stones of some kind. With all three mines in the region (Mibladene, Ahouli and Zaïda) now closed, there is a lot of poverty and selling stones is about the only thing left to do for many.

Jbel Ayyachi

Midelt it also the jumping-off place for treks up to Jbel Ayyachi which at 3747 m is eastern Morocco at its highest, an impressive 45 km stretch of solid mountain, unbroken by any peaks. First conquered in July 1901 by the Marquis de Segonzac, the heights can remain snow-covered well into late June. In the right conditions, on a long summer's day, the climb can be done in a day bit it's probably better to take two days and bivouac out on the mountain. To tackle the Jbel Ayyachi, head first for Tattiouine, 12 km from Midelt (grand taxi transport available). Here it should be possible to find mules and a guide. For a fit party, the climb and back should take around 12 hours. Make sure you have plenty of water. Even in summer, it can be very cold at the summit.

Impressive and seemingly impenetrable with its snow-capped heights, the Jbel Ayyachi functions as a water tower for southeastern Morocco, its melt water feeding both the Moulouya to the north and the Oued Ziz to the south. Jbel Ayyachi derives its name from the local Aït Ayyach tribe. Within living memory, caves in the cliffs were occupied by freedom fighters resisting the Makhzen and the incoming French. The last of such mountain strong points were only finally taken by the central authorities in 1932.

Cirque du Jaffar

One of Morocco's best known 4WD excursions takes intrepid off-roaders up to the Cirque de Jaffar (map NI-30-II-3), one of the natural arenas hollowed out on the north side of the Jbel Ayyachi. In fact, in a good off-road vehicle it is just about possible to travel over from Midelt, via the Oued Jaffar, to Imilchil, a distance of 160 km. The initial part through the Oued Jaffar gorges is the most scenic. The route is not to be attempted in winter, however, and certainly not risked in spring if there are April snows. Consult the Gendarmerie royale in Midelt or the people at Auberge-Restaurant Timnay on the Zeïda road (see page 79).

◉ Middle Atlas listings

For Sleeping and Eating price codes and other relevant information, see pages 12-20.

⊜ Sleeping

Azrou *p71*

€€ Hotel Panorama, T035-562010, panorama@extra.net.ma. All of the 38 rooms have a balcony or terrace and big TV. Good contemporary photographs decorate the walls and there's a good restaurant and bar. Also a view, as the name suggests. The best hotel in Azrou, and good value for money.

€ Hotel Azrou, Route de Khénifra opposite the Crédit agricole, about 600 m down from central mosque, T035-562116. Freshly painted, azrou has a bar and restaurant that may or may not be open. Rooms have single beds and en suite bathrooms but not 24-hr hot water. Private parking.

€ Hotel Beau Séjour, 45 Pl Saouika. Balconies and multicoloured lights. Cold showers.

€ Hotel des Cèdres, Pl Mohammed V, T035-562326. A clean establishment with hot water, heavy old-fashioned sheets, communal showers and a fair restaurant.

€ Hotel Salam (Chez Jamal), overlooks the square, but the entrance is around the back on the Pl Saouika off Pl Mohammed V. T035-562562. Hot shower 8dh, hot water in rooms. Nice management, rather tacky decor. Roof terrace.

€ Youth hostel, Route de Midelt, Azrou, BP147, to get to it follow the signs from Pl Mohammed V, and turn left off the road to Midelt, T035-563733. Clean and friendly, 40 beds, kitchen, overnight fee 20dh, about 1 km from town centre.

Ifrane *p73*

€€€ Grand Hotel, Av de la Marche Verte, T035- 567531. A 4-star, 1940s spa hotel with a pool that may or may not have any water in it. 15 rooms and 27 suites.

€€ Hotel Le Chamonix, T035 566028. 64 bright clean rooms, a bit overpriced. Restaurant with alcohol, better choice than the Tilleuls. Ski hire from bar.

€€ Hotel Mischliffen, BP 18, T035-566607, www.concorde-hotels.com. Big 1970s hotel with 107 rooms, restaurant, bar, and pool (full in summer), 2 conference rooms. The decaying luxury choice, no doubt built to house the royal retinue.

€€ Hotel Perce Neige, Rue des Asphodelles, T035-566210. A friendly place, 22 rooms, 5 suites, good restaurant and bar. Decor a bit stuck in the late 1970s. Best upmarket choice. Restaurant Atlas has menu for 120dh, eat à la carte for 200dh.

€ Hotel des Tilleuls. T035-566658. 39 rooms. A beige European style building with 44 rooms and a bar on the ground floor. Could do with sprucing up a little.

Camping

Camping International, signposted from the town centre, T035-566156. Very busy in the summer but open all year, 6-ha site, laundry facilities, petrol only 2 km.

Khénifra and around *p74*

€€ Hotel Hamou Azzayani Salam, in the new town, T035-586020. The top place to stay in Khénifra. 60 a/c rooms, restaurant, bar and pool. Poorly maintained.

€€ Hotel Najah, on the N8, T035-588331. Modern place, hot water, comfortable rooms. Café and restaurant attached.

€ Hotel Mlilia, close to the bus station, T035-384609. Acceptable and has reasonable restaurant.

€ Hotel-Restaurant de France, Quartier Forces Armées Royales, T035-586114. Good size rooms and a decent restaurant.

Midelt *p74*

Reservations are recommended in the spring.

€€ Hotel Ayachi, Rue d'Agadir, a few mins from the town centre, signposted behind the post office, T035-582161. Very 1930s, 30 big rooms with shower, quiet, big restaurant, nightclub, safe parking and garden. Try to reserve, as sometimes it's full with tour groups.

€€ Hotel Kasbah Asmaa, 3 km south of town, T035-583945. A neo-kasbah with 35 rooms with en suite bathrooms, nomad tents, a garden and fireplaces. They can help set up treks, there's a pool and a bar-restaurant. But the place can get overrun with tour groups and feel like a Disney Morocco experience.

€ Auberge-Restaurant Timnay, Aït Ayach, halfway between Midelt and Zeïda on the N13, 20 km from Midelt, T035-583434, timnay@iam.net.ma. This is an efficient set up, with a range of accommodation, including simple rooms, camping, nomad tents and sites for campervans. There is a restaurant, shop and pool, also 4WD rental, with guide for exploring the region. For a 4WD, you may feel that 4 people are necessary to cover costs. Possible circuits on offer include Zaouïa Sidi Hamza and the upper Taâraârt Valley (2 days, 415dh per person). There are also good day trips to Canyon de Tatrout.

€ Hotel Atlas, Rue Mohammed Amraoui, T035-582938. A small family-run hotel, the Atlas is very clean, with pale blue painted rooms, colourful bedspreads and a roof terrace with views of the mountains. Shower 10dh, besara soup 5dh. Very good value.

€ Hotel Bougafer, 7 Av Mohammed V, T035-583099. Up the hill round behind the bus station, Bougafer has good, clean rooms with en suite bathrooms and simple 3- and 4-bed rooms on the top floor. There's internet access from 2 computers on the 1st floor and the restaurant has a cinema- sized TV screen, which pulls in the locals as well as tourists.

€ Hotel Roi de la Bière, Av des FAR, T035-582625, near the southern exit. A hotel, café and restaurant, the King of the Beer has 13 rooms, 7 with shower, and is very clean.

Camping
You may be able to camp in the grounds of the Hotel Ayachi, but the Timnay (above) is really the best option.

🍴 Eating

Azrou *p71*
🍴🍴 **Hotel Panorama**, T035-562010 (see also Sleeping, above). A wood fire and a 100dh menu including mountain delicacies such as Middle Atlas trout and lapin à la moutarde.

🍴🍴 **Hotel Restaurant des Cèdres**, Pl Mohammed V, T035-562326. Behind the net curtains, there are 2 fixed menus, one 'gastronomique', one 'touristique', though you may find that you can order the same things à la carte for cheaper. Service is attentive and the fish is good.

🍴 **Café Restaurant Relais Forestier**, Pl Mohammed V. The 80dh menu is reasonable. Locals come here to watch the football on TV.

🍴 **Boulangerie Pâtisserie L'Escalade**, 5 Pl Hassan II, T035-563419. Excellent little baker with very good cakes and biscuits.

Ifrane *p73*
Ifrane is not exactly a gastronomic destination but there are some reasonable options, lots of mid-range places and a handful of cafés.

🍴🍴 **Restaurant Atlas**, in the Hotel Perce Neige. Good expensive bet where you can try Middle Atlas trout.

🍴🍴 **Restaurant La Paix**, T035-566675. Grilled meat, no alcohol.

🍴 **Café-Restaurant de la Rose**, 7 Rue des Erables, next to the Mobil station, T035-566215. Menu 70dh, no alcohol, try their truite en papillottes. You can also ask for obliging local mountain guide Izem here who knows some good routes in the local outback.

Cookie-Craque, Av des Tilleuls. Pâtisserie next to Hotel des Tilleuls.

Le Croustillant Boulangerie Pâtisserie,

does OK coffee and has a good selection of pastries in a setting reminiscent of a European cafeteria.

Midelt *p74*
🍴 **Hotel Roi de la Bière**, Av des FAR, T035-582625. Moroccan salon, free internet and lots of pink cloth in this café-restaurant, with an 80dh fixed menu.

🍴 **Le Pin**, Blvd Hassan II, T055-583550. A little café which opens up into a strange complex, complete with restaurant, shop, a dusty garden and canned music

🍴 **Restaurant de Fès**, 2 Av Mohammed, T062-05 77 54. Very good couscous, 7 different salades Marocaine, and a recommended tagine with 10 vegetables. Unusually good for vegetarians. Small, welcoming and enthusiastic, it sometimes gets filled up with groups. 3-course menu for 80dh.

There are some cheap roadside places just up from the station offering mainly tagines – try **Restaurant Lespoir or du Centre**.

🏔 Activities and tours

Ifrane *p73*
Skiing at Mischliffen Near Ifrane, the season is from Jan-Mar and the resort has good, but short, slopes, sometimes with patchy snow cover. Hire equipment from the Chamonix restaurant in Ifrane and take a taxi to the resort. This is a small area with cafés and ski lifts but little else. Ski equipment and sledges can be rented cheaply at the Chamonix. During the summer the area is popular with walkers.

Midelt *p74*
For guides and hiking options, see **Auberge-Restaurant Timnay**, page 77.

🚌 Transport

Azrou *p71*
CTM buses depart from near Pl Mohammed V, early departures for **Casablanca**, **Midelt**, and **Meknès**. There are further **CTM** and private line services from Azrou to **Rissani**, **Er**

Rachidia, **Marrakech**, **Khénifra** and **Fès**, and numerous grands taxis to **Khénifra**, **Ifrane**, **Immouzer du Kandar**, **Meknès** and **Fès**.

Ifrane *p73*

There are regular buses from Ifrane to both **Azrou** and **Fès**.

Ifrane *p73*

Directory

Azrou *p71*

Banks The Banque Populaire and the BMCE (cashpoint) are on Pl Mohammed V.

Ifrane *p73*

Internet Le Croustilant, café opposite the Mobil station, has internet access. For wines and beer, there is a débit d'alcohol next to Le Croustillant. For films and photography equipment, there is a shop next to the **Hotel Le Chamonix**.

Taza

There was a time when Taza was quite a happening place, given its strategic location controlling the easiest route from the Moroccan heartland of Fès and Meknès to the eastern plains. The town, rather quiet today, is divided into three quite separate parts: the area around the railway and bus station; the ville nouvelle around Place de l'Indépendence; and the quiet médina on the hill with its narrow streets. After the hurly-burly of Fès, low-key Taza makes a good base from which to explore up into the hills of the Jbel Tazzeka National Park. ▸▸ *For listings, see pages 86-88.*

Ins and outs

Getting there

Taza is easily accessible by public transport from Fès, 120 km to the west. Coming from eastern Morocco, you will necessarily pass through Taourirt and Guercif, a major meeting of the roads some 40 km from Taza. There are trains daily from Oujda, taking around four hours, and from Meknès, around 3½ hours and Fès, two hours. There are occasional grands taxis from Al Hoceïma and from both Al Hoceïma and Nador there are buses to Taza, via Aknoul, taking around four hours. ▸▸ *See Transport, page 87, for further details.*

Getting around

Arriving by train, bus or grand taxi, you will come into the north of the ville nouvelle. The médina is a fair 3-km trek away, and as there is only one hotel there you will probably stay in the ville nouvelle. (Go straight down Avenue de la Gare, there are three hotels on Place de l'Indépendence at the end.) There is a regular bus service from Place de l'Indépendence to Place Moulay Hassan in the médina. A light blue petit taxi will cost you around 3dh from station to Place de l'Indépendence, and 6dh from station to médina.

Background

The site was first settled in Neolithic times. Later it was developed by Meknassa Amazigh groups, eventually becoming an important but finally unsuccessful fortification against the advance of the Fatimids from the east. The Almohads under Sultan Abd el Moumen captured the city in 1141-1142, making it their second capital, and using it to attack the Almoravids. The Almohads built a mosque and expanded the fortifications.

Taza was the first city taken by the Merinids, who extended the Almohad city considerably. Its important defensive role continued under the Merinids and the Saâdians, and was again pivotal in the rise to power of the Alaouites, who further extended and fortified the city, later using it as a strong point in their defence against the threat from French-occupied Algeria to the east.

The eccentric pretender, Bou Hamra, 'the man on the she-donkey', proclaimed himself as sultan here in 1902 and controlled much of eastern Morocco until 1912, when he was caught and killed. He was known as a wandering miracle-maker, travelling Morocco on his faithful beast. Taza was occupied by the French in 1914, and became an important military centre, located on the route linking Algeria with the Atlantic plains of *le Maroc utile*, between remote mountains and plateaux of eastern Morocco and the great cities to the west. Today, with the decline in cross-border trade with Algeria, Taza, like its distant neighbour Oujda, sees far less passing traffic than it did and has a distinctly sleepy feel to it. A couple of the hotels have been upgraded, however, and you could well stay here for a couple of nights if exploring or birdwatching up in the Jbel Tazzeka National Park.

Sights

The **ville nouvelle** – for hotels, restaurants, banks and other services – is a quiet place centred around early and mid-20th-century buildings on Place de l'Indépendence. The older buildings are in the small, attractive **médina** perched on the hill 3 km away from the railway station and 2 km from the centre of the new town. From the bottom of the hill there is an interesting short cut to the **kasbah** via a flight of steps which provide remarkable views. Beyond this point, further along the main road on the right, are the **Kifane el Ghomari caves**, inhabited in Neolithic times. Note that the main historic buildings in the médina are closed to non-Muslims.

The transport hub of the old town is **Place Moulay Hassan**, just outside the main entrance to the **souk**. The focus of the old quarter is the main street, commonly called the

Taza Médina

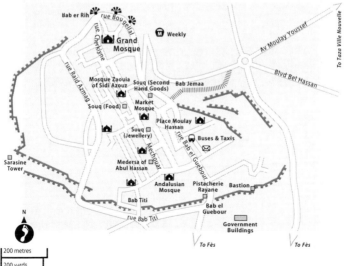

Mechouar from end to end, which runs behind Place Moulay Hassan along the entire length of the médina from the Andalucían Mosque to the Grand Mosque at the opposite end of town by the Bab er Rih gate. Between the two mosques are the various souks. Hassle is practically non existent, as there is a few articles which might be thought to interest the tourist. The fact that there is no motor traffic in the médina makes it all the more pleasant. The best thing to do is just wander – the old neighbourhoods are quite small and sooner or later you will come out on the outside road ringing the town.

Turning left just past the main gate to the souk by the Cinema Friouato is the jewellery section of the souk. From here you can turn left along a very straight and narrow section of road towards the Andalucían Mosque, or right toward the Grand Mosque. Following the latter route, the food and spice souk is off to the left, behind the broader section of the Mechouar. Further along, you may get a glimpse of the **Zaouïa of Sidi Azouz** (note its beautiful wall-basin by the door). It is difficult to gain a good view of the **Grand Mosque**, built by the Almohads in the second half of the 12th century, with further elaboration by the Merinids in the late 13th century, and the Alaouites in the 17th. In its classic proportions of 1:5, the minaret resembles that of the Koutoubia Mosque in Marrakech. Only Muslims can view the beautiful chandelier bearing 514 oil lamps which lights the mosque.

To the right of the Grand Mosque, down a steep flight of steps, you reach a section of the **ramparts**, with good views over the surrounding countryside, lower Taza, and the mountains beyond. Going left after the steps to start a rampart tour, the first section, with some steep drops, is referred to as **Bab er Rih**, 'the Gate of the Wind'. From here you have perhaps the best view of the Almohad minaret. Eventually, keeping to the outside of the town, you could look out for the the circular **Sarasine Tower**, also dating back to the Almohad times – and showing clear European influence.

At the far end of the mechouar from Bab er Rih is the **Andalucían Mosque** with its 12th-century minaret. Just before, on the right, stands the 14th-century **Medersa of Abu el Hassan**, named after a Merinid sultan. This is closed, but the exterior shows a carved lintel in cedar wood, and a porch roof overhanging the road. In a lane to the right of the mosque, Zankat Dar el Makhzen, there is the former house of Bou Hamra the pretender. The weekly **market** takes place outside the walls at this end of town, outside Bab Titi.

Jbel Tazzeka National Park

An area of fine mountain scenery, the Jbel Tazzeka National Park, south of Taza and the N6, can also be visited with your own transport on a long but rewarding day trip from Fès. The region's cork-oak forest and its undergrowth has plenty to keep ornithologists happy – look out for the rare black-shouldered kite.Scenery and kites apart, however, the main reason for doing this trip is to go intrepidly down into the Gouffre de Friouato, an immense series of hobbity caverns with scrambles, stalactites and mud aplenty.

From the plateau of old Taza, the S311 winds its way south and west, eventually linking up with the the N6 some 31 km further west. If you have parked up close to the walls of Taza, head back as though you were returning to new Taza, leaving the Préfecture on your left, and go straight ahead at the next roundabout. (Without a car you might bargain for a grand taxi to take you part of the way, from the rank by the railway station.) With no stops, a careful driver will take 1¾ hours to reach the N6. (Take water in case engine overheats.)

After a rainy winter, the **Cascades de Ras el Oued**, a few kilometres out of Taza and a popular picnic spot, might be worth a look. Next stop, some 14 km along the route, is the **Vallée des oiseaux**, which starts with a thick stand of cork oak. Nearby lies the **Dayat Chiker**, a seasonal lake. Next you will reach a fork in the road signed Maghraoua (left) and Bab Boudir (right). Go right, and 3 km further on, about 35 minutes from Taza, you will reach the turn-off right heading uphill to the Gouffre de Friouato.

Gouffre de Friouato

A descent into this magnificent cave system is not for the weak-kneed. Near the car park is a stone-built guichet building where smiling, bright-eyed Mustapha Lachhab presides over piles of biscuits, sweets, torches and batteries – everything an amateur caver could need. The officially authorized organizer of guides, he also has photocopied sheets with a cross section of the caverns. Access to the first flights of steps costs 3dh, 100dh gets you a guide to take a small group (up to four people), down the 230 m and 520 steps of the first section, through a narrow squeeze and scramble bit and into the **Salle de Lixus**, as the first main cave is rather grandly known, after the Roman site near modern Larache. Here there are stalactites, including a sort of crystal platform looking for all the world like a Renaissance pulpit, a be-turbaned individual (use your imagination) and a *hallouf* (pig). From here the caves run on at least a further 2 km, an exploration best left to the enthusiastic and well equipped. Getting down and back from the Salle de Lixus will take you about an hour. The squeeze to this section is easier coming up, by the way. If you're a real speleologist, it would definitely be worth spending time in the region as there are further caverns elsewhere. Note that, having done the descent so many times, the local

Jbel Tazzeka National Park

guides really do know how to pace a group. They now also have quite a lot of ropes and other material left behind by cavers.

After the caves, the next major stopping point, 30 km from Taza, is an unlikely *station estivale* with red-roofed houses and various seasonal eateries including the Café Bouhadli. Continue on to the Bab Taza pass from which a rough and challenging track goes north up to the Jbel Tazzeka, where there are incredible views of the surrounding mountains. After, or avoiding, the Jbel Tazzeka, the road continues through cork forest, past another signed picnic area, the **Vallée des cerfs** and then down and through the narrow gorge by the Oued Zireg and back to the N6. The map shows distances between major points and the quality of the roads. For excursions south to Immouzer du Kandar and the Dayats of Aaoua, Afourgan and Ifrah, see page 73.

East of Taza ▶ *For listings, see pages 86-88.*

Oujda Msoun
Some 20 km to the east of Taza along the N6 is the fortified farming village of Msoun. Built around 1700 in Moulay Ismael's reign to guard the approaches to the strategic Taza Gap, it is still inhabited by members of the semi-nomadic Houara tribe. The village has a shop, post office and even a teahouse. The compact, walled settlement stands isolated on a hillside, clearly visible from the main road where there is the convenient Motel-Restaurant Casbah, and a petrol station. It is possible to walk to the village from here, just 2 km.

Guercif
Guercif is an unremarkable modern agricultural town noted for its olives and shoe industry. In the 14th century, it became a stronghold of the Beni Ouattas Tribe, who later overran Taza and replaced Merinids to form the Ouattasid Dynasty. The main part of town, which lies to the south of the main road, is centred around Boulevard Mohammed V, its solid 19th-century mosque, and two adjacent squares. The railway station is reached via a driveway from the opposite side of the main road. Market day is Sunday.

Taourirt
Halfway between Taza and Oujda, Taourirt is an important commercial centre with a large **market** on Sunday. In the past the town functioned as the junction between two major trade routes: the east-west trans-Maghreb route and the route from Melilla to the Tafilalet. The centre of town is located around the junction of the N6 and the Debdou road (the ancient caravan route to the south which is packed with shops, garages, cafés and small workshops). The only tangible historic attraction is the remains of the **kasbah** on the hill 1 km to the northwest, unfortunately spoiled by electricity pylons but with excellent views.

There are several excursions around Taourirt that make it worthwhile stopping for a day or two, if you have time. The mountain village of Debdou (see below), and the **Zaâ waterfalls and gorges**. Providing there is enough water in the *oued* (unlikely between August and December), the falls make an enjoyable picnic and bathing excursion and camping is possible. To get there, turn right at the signpost 6 km along the Taza road. It is a further 9 km to the waterfalls. The track continues to Melga el Ouidane and the large

---

lake known as **Barrage Mohammed V**. There are a number of picnic spots along the route. The **Zaâ Gorges** are deep, very impressive and well worth the journey. As you leave Taourirt on the Oujda road, there is a turning off to the right. You cannot drive through the narrow defile. Leave the car where the road ends and walk from there.

Debdou

Nestling in a verdant bowl formed by the surrounding massif, Debdou, 50 km southwest of Taourirt, is an island of rural tranquillity. The fact that it's on a road to nowhere has helped to preserve its identity. The surrounding area is very scenic and provides good opportunities for walking and exploration. There is an interesting kasbah halfway up the mountainside above the main village. There are no tourist facilities, and transport links are poor.

Until the 1960s over half the population of Debdou were Jewish, and most were the descendants of Jews from Taza who fled persecution and chaos of Bou Hamra's rule (1902-08). The 'main street' branches off the main road at the entrance to the village and zig-zags for about 1 km, past store houses to a square at the top end of the village known as **Aïn Sbilia**. Overlooking the square is a balcony shaded by plane trees. A small sluice gate allows water to flow into a channel bisecting the square below which has a café. It is all very restful, the locals playing cards or backgammon and drinking mint tea.

High above the village is the still-inhabited **kasbah of Caïd Ghomriche** built by the Merinids in the 13th century and subsequently handed over to the Beni Ouattas, a related tribe, around 1350 when the Merinids ruled Morocco. Follow the signposted track (2 km) starting from the bottom end of the village. Note the colourful hammam which is still heated by a wood stove. Along the way there are pretty views of the town on the right and the waterfalls high above on the left. Just before the kasbah there is a grassy ledge with good views over the valley, and the entrance to a **cave**. The settlement is a mixture of ancient ruins, small vegetable gardens and mud houses.

At the back of the village, past the walls, and a dry moat, is a field where jagged stones stick out of the ground – the sunken headstones of tombs. Take care not to trip over them. By crossing the field and turning left for 30-40 m and then sharp right, there is a path (1 km) linking up with the main road and the source of the Oued Debdou. The same location can be reached by the main road which swings to the left just before Debdou, and runs along the mountain crest, or **Gaada de Debdou**, for 5 or 6 km. There are fantastic views from here and good walking opportunities. Beyond this the road descends from the plateau down into the arid Rekkam plain where it becomes a rough track, eventually leading to Outad Ouled el Hadj. **Market** day is Wednesday.

El Aïoun

Halfway between Taourirt and Oujda, and within easy reach of the Beni Snassen Mountains, El Aioun was founded by Moulay Ismaïl in 1679. It has a small kasbah, restored in 1876 by Sultan Moulay Hassan in response to the threat of French expansion from Algeria. To the south of the town is a **cemetery** where those who died fighting colonialism are buried. During the first half of the 20th century, El Aïoun became a centre of the Sufi Brotherhood of Sheikh Bou Amama, whose zaouïa is located here. The weekly **souk** is held on Tuesday and frequented by members of the local Ouled Sidi Sheikh tribe.

Missour

A tranquil town with many donkeys and unpaved roads, Missour comes alive for the weekly market. There is a fair medium-priced hotel here and although unaccustomed to foreigners, locals are helpful. If you are lucky enough to be here on a Wednesday, there is a large local **souk** situated on the hill by the water tower, past the new mosque. The lower part of the market is disappointing, but the top end of the main enclosure has the fruit and vegetable market, and a separate area beyond encloses the livestock market. Both enclosures have tea tents. There is a view of the town and the mountains from the adjacent hill.

Oued Moulouya

Past Missour, the road continues for about 30 km through a still bare but slightly more dramatic landscape that would make a good Western film set. After Tamdafelt, the road runs along an attractive stretch of the Oued Moulouya, with pisé villages and richly cultivated riverbanks. Two fortified kasbahs built by Moulay Ismaïl around 1690 to guard the imperial route from Fès to Sijilmassa are still inhabited: **Saida** and **Ksabi**. The inhabitants, originally forming an agglomeration of 10 ksars, are mostly descendants of Alaouite guardsmen from the Tafilalet. At over 1000 m, the freshness of the air and quality of light in this remote region are exhilarating. After Ksabi the road swings away from the river and crosses the high plain of Aftis until it joins the N13, 15 km east of Midelt.

Taza listings

For Sleeping and Eating price codes and other relevant information, see pages 12-20.

● Sleeping

Taza *p80, map p81*

€ Hotel Friouato, Av de la Gare, T035-672593. 58 rooms (with heating in winter), bar, restaurant, tennis and pool (in summer). Has seen better days but good for a drink in the large peaceful garden. Inconvenient location between the médina and the ville nouvelle: to get there turn left at the foot of the steps that climb the hill to the old town.

€ Grand Hotel du Dauphiné, at the centre of the town on junction of Av de la Gare and Pl de l'Indépendance, T035-673567. 26 rooms, renovated a few years ago and all the better for it, even though the 'period charm' has gone.

€ Hotel de la Gare, at the main crossroads near the station, T035-672448. Adequately clean, friendly owners, café, téléboutique next door. Best rooms on the 1st floor, cold

showers only. Handy for early starts with grand taxi, bus and train stations close by.

Guercif *p84*

€ Hotel Howary, Av Moulay Youssef, T035-625062. A busy small hotel on the Oujda road near the railway station. Rooms are variable, as is the plumbing. You may have to ask for clean bed linen but staff are friendly and helpful.

Taourirt *p84*

€ Hotel Mansour, on the Debdou road just off main crossroads, T036-694003. Large rooms, adequately clean, good café below. Hot water available.

● Eating

Taza *p80, map p81*

₦ Grand Hotel du Dauphiné, junction of Pl de l'Indépendance and Av de la Gare, T035-673567. Huge 1950s dining hall, good value if you don't mind a limited menu (sometimes

only steak and chips), beer available.
Hotel Salam Friouato, T035-672593. Has reasonable, unexciting meals.
Café Restaurant Majestic, Av Mohammed V, Moroccan food.
Restaurant Azzam, Av Mohammed V.
Snack Bar Youm Youm, behind Hotel de la Poste on Blvd Moulay Youssef, serving brochettes.

Cafés
Café Andalous, in the old town where terrace overlooks the animated Pl Moulay Hassan. Sit and observe the local scene.
Café des Jardins, Av Ibn Khatib. Pleasant place in the municipal gardens en route to the old town, terrace with views, closed at night.
Café el Ghissani, opposite Café Andalous by the main entrance to the souk. Popular café, again good for people-watching.
Pâtisserie des Festivités, 1 Blvd Mohammed V, just off Pl de l'Indépendence. Cosy, good for breakfast and cakes.

Guercif *p84*
The best eateries are the group of transport cafés known as 'le complexe' on the main road, the meat used for the brochettes is very fresh, direct from the in-house butcher.
Place Centrale has several snack places and grocery stores catering for travellers.
Café Nahda is a small, friendly, efficient place on the corner of Rue Mohammed V and Rue Ibn Battuta near the mosque. The café opposite is also good.

Shopping

Taza *p80, map p81*
Pistacherie Rayane, 5 Av Moulay Hassan, by the entrance to the old town. Sells factory-fresh nuts, very much cheaper than elsewhere.

Transport

Taza *p80, map p81*
Bus
CTM buses leave from their office on Pl de l'Indépendence for **Oujda** and **Fès/Meknès/Casablanca**. Other companies operate from near the railway station, turn right at the end of Av de la Gare. Regular services to **Oujda/Guercif/Taourirt** (4 hrs), **Fès** every hour (2 hrs), **Nador** (4 hrs), **Al Hoceïma** (4 hrs) and **Aknoul** (1 hr). Make sure you take a new-looking bus by a reliable company for Al Hoceïma and Nador.

Taxi
Grands taxis leave from the transport cafés by the bus station to **Oujda**, **Fès**, **Al Hoceïma** and **Nador**, amongst other places.

Train
At Taza the ONCF locomotives switch from electric to diesel, hence speed heading eastwards is slow. There are at least 3 daily departures for **Oujda** (stopping at **Guercif** and **Taourirt**). **Casablanca** is 7 hrs away, **Tangier** a good 8 hrs away, if you are lucky with the connection at **Sidi Kacem**. **Fès** is 2 hrs by train, **Meknès** 3 hrs.

Guercif *p84*
CTM bus connections to **Oujda**, **Fès**, **Midelt** and **Er Rachidia**. CTM offices are between the central square and Pl Zerkatouni. Private lines: **Taourirt/Oujda** and **Taza/Fès**, **Nador**. **Er Rachidia** departs from 'le complexe' on the main road. ONCF train services to **Taourirt/Oujda** and **Taza/Fès/Casablanca**.

Taourirt *p84*
Buses for **Oujda** (every ½ hr) and **Nador** (around 5 a day) depart from the Agip petrol station past the main crossroads.
Guercif/Taza/Fès (virtually every ½ hr during the day and hourly at night) depart from near the Shell petrol station on the same

road, as do the grands taxis that ply the N6. Grands taxis for **Debdou** leave from the rank on the Debdou road. There are trains to **Oujda** 0530, 0800, 1800, 1930 (approximate times); **Taza/Fès/Casablanca** 0830, 1045, 2030, 2230 (approximate times). Once the new Nador line opens, Taourirt's transport options will increase.

Debdou *p85*

There's an early morning and an early afternoon bus departure to **Taourirt** as well as taxis (most frequent in the morning and early evening – if you don't want to get stuck here, try to leave before 1800).

❶ Directory

Taza *p80, map p81*
Banks Banks with ATMs include the **BMCE**, near the Hotel du Dauphiné, in the new town.

Guercif *p84*
Banks **Banque Populaire**, on market square. BM and BMCE, near Shell petrol station on Oujda road. **Medical services Chemists**: **Pharmacie centrale** on the market square.

Taourirt *p84*
Banks **Banque Populaire**, on the main road. **Medical services Chemist**: Pharmacie **Echifa**, opposite the new mosque. **Petrol** At the south end of the main boulevard before the bridge.

Missour *p86*
Banks BMCE, CMD and Wafabank next to Hotel Mansour. **Medical services Chemist**: on the road out to Debdou: **Al Jabri** and **Al Qods**.

Contents

90 Tangier
- 91 Ins and outs
- 91 Background
- 96 Sights
- 101 Listings

108 North Atlantic coast
- 109 Asilah
- 110 El Utad, the stone circle at Mzoura
- 111 Larache
- 114 Listings

118 Ceuta
- 118 Ins and outs
- 119 Background
- 119 Sights
- 122 Listings

124 Tetouan
- 124 Ins and outs
- 125 Background
- 125 Sights
- 128 Beach resorts around Tetouan
- 129 Listings

132 Chefchaouen, the Rif and Al Hoceïma
- 132 Chefchaouen
- 135 Northern Rif
- 136 Ouezzane and Southern Rif
- 137 Al Hoceïma
- 139 Listings

Tangier & Northern Morocco

At a glance

⊖ **Getting around** Tangier is small enough to explore on foot, but you'll probably want to get a taxi from the station to the centre. The rest of the area is served by buses and grands taxis.

⊘ **Time required** Allow a couple of days for Tangier, then spend a week exploring the coast either side and the Rif.

⊛ **Weather** Winter in the north can be cool and wet – in January the average maximum temperature in Tangier is 16°C – and in the hills and mountains it can be downright cold, especially at night. For most of the year, however, the weather is pleasant and cooler than the rest of the country.

Tangier

Tangier is a product of its location: the gate to the Mediterranean Sea and the meeting point of Africa and Europe. The Phoenicians and Carthaginians established trading posts here. The Romans made it a capital city. It was invaded by the Vandals and Visigoths and occupied by the Arabs. The Portuguese took the town before the Spanish arrived. From 1923 to 1956, it was an international city, and its tax-free status and raffish reputation attracted European and American writers and artists. Tangier also had fame as a gay destination in the days when homosexuality attracted severe moral opprobrium in Europe. These days, Tangier is trying to bury these ghosts and reinvent itself as a modern city with a new port, stadium and business district. Arriving by sea, it may well be your first point of contact with Morocco and, despite a certain reputation for hassle, Tangier has remained popular with travellers. The kasbah, former residence of sultans, is particularly worth visiting, as is the médina, a dense maze of houses, shops and narrow, steep streets. A day is probably enough to see the main sights; two days would give you more time to take in the atmosphere and make a side trip to the Caves of Hercules on the Atlantic coast. ➦ *For listings, see pages 101-107.*

Ins and outs

Getting there

Tangier's **Ibn Batouta Airport**, T039-393720, is 15 km southwest of the city on the N1 road to Rabat. Entry formalities can be slow. Catch bus 17 or 70 from the terminal to the Grand Socco (Place du 19 Avril 1947), or take a grand taxi (160dh by day, 200dh after 2000, rates displayed on wall by customs).

The train no longer stops at Tangier Ville and Port. Rather, the terminal is at Tangier Moghougha, a 15dh petit taxi ride from the town centre, 20dh for the port, more at night. Have change ready. Taxi drivers will want to fill up their vehicles so you may have to wait.

CTM buses arrive at the terminal in Avenue des FAR, adjacent to the port gates, and the former Tangier Ville railway station. Private lines arrive at the terminal at the end of Rue de Fès. There are plenty of buses to Tangier, from Casablanca, Fès, Meknès and Rabat, as well as from local places like Asilah, Larache and Tetouan. The bus station is a short (12dh) petit taxi ride from the city centre hotels.

If you are driving into the city in the summer from the south, expect slow traffic north of Asilah after the motorway ends. The A1 from Rabat brings the driver into Tangier along Rue de Fès. The N16 from Ceuta feeds into Av Mohammed V, as does the N2 from Tetouan.

There are car/passenger ferry services from Algeciras in Spain and Gibraltar. Within the port compound, there is a rank for both kinds of taxi. Hard negotiation over prices will be probably be necessary. ▶▶ *See Transport, page 106, for further details.*

Getting around

Tangier is quite a small place but the bus station (*mahattat el kirane*) is a good way out. You will need to get a petit taxi (12dh), which ought to be metered, or a grand taxi. A trip within the city by petit taxi is 10dh. Taxis can be flagged down even when they have other passengers. If it is going in your direction, it will take you. A grand taxi ride will cost 10dh for a trip within the city. Prices go up by 50% after 2000. There are handy Boughaz minibuses and grands taxis from the Grand Socco to the bus station and the Atlantic coast sights.

Tourist information Office du Tourisme ⓘ *29 Blvd Pasteur, T039-948050, open Mon-Sat 0830-1630.* **Syndicat d'Initiative** ⓘ *11 Rue Khalid Ibn el Oualid, T039-935486.*

Background

Perhaps the oldest city in Morocco, Tangier was active as early as 1600 BC. There was a Phoenician settlement here. Roman mythology ascribes its founding to the Greek giant Antaeus, son of Poseidon, god of the Earth, and Gaia, goddess of the earth. Antaeus challenged Hercules, but the hero killed the giant and had a child by his widow, Tingis. Hercules pulled apart Spain and Africa to give this son, Sophax, a city protected by the sea. Then, out of filial piety, King Sophax named his city Tingis.

Thanks to its location on the Straits of Gibraltar, Tangier has always been important. At one point, Rome made it capital of the empire's North African provinces, its people receiving Roman citizenship in AD 38. It controlled the city until AD 429. Later, the Vandals and Byzantines struggled to control the region, then the Muslim Arabs took the

1 Tangier

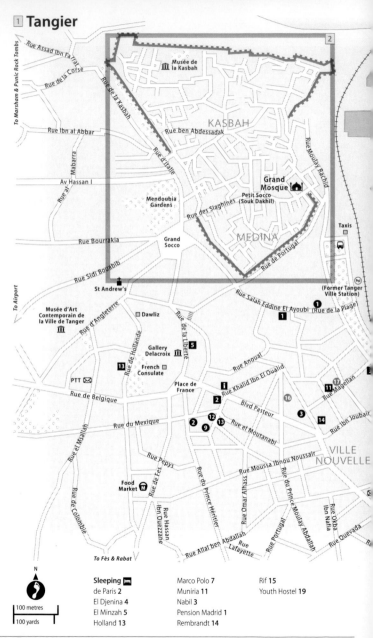

Rue Assad Ibn Fa Tral
To Marsham & Punic Rock Tombs
Rue de la Corse
Rue de la Kasbah
Rue Ibn al Abbar
Mabarra
Rue al
Av Hassan I
Rue Sidi Bouabib
Rue Bourrakia
To Airport

Musée de la Kasbah

KASBAH

Rue ben Abdessadak

Rue d'Italie

Mendoubia Gardens

Grand Mosque

Petit Socco (Souk Dakhil)

Rue des Slaghines

Grand Socco

MEDINA

Rue Moulay Rachid

Rue de Portugal

Taxis

(Former Tanger Ville Station)

Rue Salah Eddine El Ayoubi (Rue de la Plage)

St Andrew's

Musée d'Art Contemporain de la Ville de Tanger

Dawliz

Rue d'Angleterre

Gallery Delacroix

Rue de Hollande

Rue de la Liberté

French Consulate

PTT

Place de France

Rue de Belgique

Rue du Mexique

Rue et Msallah

Rue Pepys

Rue de Fès

Rue de Colombie

Food Market

Rue du Prince Héritier

Rue Hassan Ibn Ouezzane

Rue Khalid Ibn El Oualid

Rue Anoual

Blvd Pasteur

Rue et Moutanabi

Rue Moussa Ibnou Noussair

Rue du Prince Moulay Abdallah

Rue Omar Alhass

Rue Portugal

Rue Allal ben Abdallah

Rue Lafayette

To Fès & Rabat

VILLE NOUVELLE

Rue Magellan

Rue Ibn Joubair

Rue Okba Ibn Nafia

Rue Quevada

Sleeping

de Paris 2
El Djenina 4
El Minzah 5
Holland 13

Marco Polo 7
Muniria 11
Nabil 3
Pension Madrid 1
Rembrandt 14

Rif 15
Youth Hostel 19

N
100 metres
100 yards

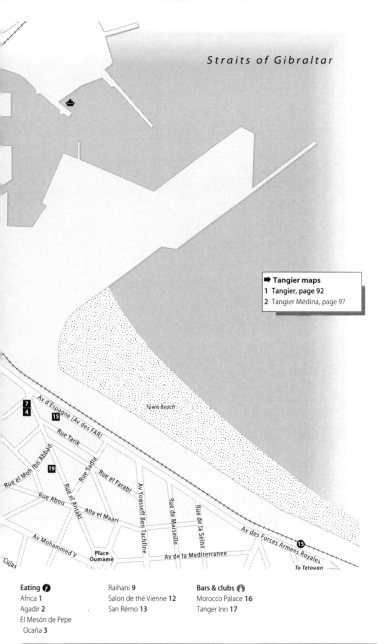

Straits of Gibraltar

➡ **Tangier maps**
1 Tangier, page 92
2 Tangier Médina, page 97

Av d'Espagne (Av des FAR)
Rue Tarik
Rue el Moh Ibn Abbad
Rue Sadia
Rue el Farabi
Rue Abou
Rue el Antaki
Alla el Maari
Av Youssef Ben Tachfine
Rue de Marseille
Rue de la Seine
Av Mohammed V
Place Oumame
Av de la Mediterranee
Av des Forces Armees Royales
Cujas
Town Beach
To Tetouan

Eating 🍴
Africa **1**
Agadir **2**
El Mesón de Pepe
Ocaña **3**

Raihani **9**
Salon de thé Vienne **12**
San Rémo **13**

Bars & clubs 🍸
Morocco Palace **16**
Tanger Inn **17**

city in AD 706. It remained a point of conflict between major Arab and Berber dynasties before achieving commercial importance in the Mediterranean during the 1300s.

Tangier was first conquered by the Portuguese in 1437, and subsequently reoccupied in 1471, became Spanish in 1578 and Portuguese again in 1640. They built fine houses, Dominican and Franciscan chapels and a cathedral and the city was part of the dowry brought by the Portuguese Catherine of Braganza when she married Charles II of England in 1661. The English succeeded in alienating the Portuguese population, forcing both religious orders and Jews out of the city, before finally departing themselves in 1684, destroying the kasbah as they left. Sultan Moulay Ismaïl rebuilt the town after they left.

In the 19th century Tangier became a popular base for European merchants and housed a large European colony. It was also the focus of political competition between expansionist European powers. In 1923 the city became a tax-free International Zone controlled by a 30-member international committee. From then until the early 1960s Tangier had its heyday – a hedonistic, decadent freeport and playground of an international demi-monde – thus reinforcing the truth of earlier descriptions of the city. St Francis had seen it as a centre of sin, while in the 17th century Samuel Pepys had described it as a latter-day Sodom.

Celebrity visitors

The streets of Tangier are full of artistic and literary memory. Among its illustrious visitors (other than Pepys and St Francis) are Camille Saint-Saëns (who drew on Issaoua trance music for his *Danse macabre*), film stars Marlene Dietrich and Errol Flynn, Oscar Wilde, author-translator Paul Bowles, Ian Fleming, Richard Hughes (*High Wind in Jamaica*) and James Leo Herlihy (*Midnight Cowboy*). Woolworth-heiress Barbara Hutton had a house here, as did the heiress to the Knoll furniture fortune, the crumbling York Castle, up in the kasbah. Winston Churchill, Ronnie Kray, and the photographer Cecil Beaton all passed through. Painters who discovered light and the Orient in Tangier include Eugène Delacroix in 1832, Henri Matisse (1912), Kees Van Dongen and more recently Francis Bacon. The city's reputation as a haven of freedom for the likes of Tennessee Williams, Truman Capote, William Burroughs, Allen Ginsberg, Jack Kerouac, Brion Gysin and Joe Orton in the 1950s and 1960s continues to draw visitors. Today backpackers relive something of those heady days by visiting the Tanger Inn, Rue Magellan (see page 105), a surviving fragment of Burroughs' Interzone.

Though many of the city's literary sites were lost in the demolition-rebuilding of the 1990s, the romantic-minded can still find something of Tangier's artistic soul. There are plenty of decaying apartment buildings, restaurants and low-life bars. The Grand-Hôtel Villa de France still survives, home to Gertrude Stein and Matisse, as does the Teatro Cervantes. Down near the port, next to the Hôtel Cecil (a favourite with Roland Barthes), is the Immeuble Renschaussen, where Burroughs and Gysin did artistic cut-ups in one of the lofts. Up at the kasbah, the Palais Menebhi was home to Gysin's 1001 Nights bar. Further west on the Montagne at the Villa Mimosa, Bowles finished *Let it Come Down*, another tale of an American adrift in the mysterious East. West of the city, the Plage Merkala was the setting for tales by M'rabet, Charhadi and other members of Bowles' coterie. And the heavily revamped Salon de thé Porte still carries a hint of a literary yesteryear.

The end of cosmopolitan Tangier

Tangier as a centre of easy money and loose morals was not to last, however, and the freeport was reunited with Morocco in October 1956 although its tax-free status was maintained until 1960. Since Independence, Tangier has declined in international economic importance and its tourism was soon overshadowed by the enormous development of the industry elsewhere in the Mediterranean. Today the city functions essentially for the Moroccan tourist and travel market. In the summer, up to two million migrant workers and their families pass through the port, and Tangier is their first contact with their homeland. In the 1980s, the green cliff tops of La Montagne, west of the city, came to be favoured by Gulf amirs as the ideal place for a holiday home. Soon, vast palaces in the neo-Kuwaiti style appeared like UFOs in the pine and eucalyptus woods around the city.

Contemporary Tangier

Tangier has always been through highs and lows, and the 1990s were in many ways the trough of a low period. A building boom, in part financed by the profits of the kif trade, meant masses of new development as profits were recycled in. Many historic buildings were torn down, replaced by blocks of concrete-brutalist ugliness. And then came the late king's 'clean up public life' campaign. Corruption scandals and court cases hit the city, various local figures disappeared behind bars or overseas, all to the good many would say. But the big change came with Mohammed VI's accession to the throne in July 1999. The new king made the Northwest the first region he visited outside the capital. Tangier was ecstatic. The long-ignored Palais Marshan was dusted down, there seemed to be some hope for a region too long forgotten by the powers that be.

A feisty local press have kept things moving along, associations have been set up to do something for street kids, to support the unemployed and illiterate, to save the kasbah and the Teatro Cervantes. A new port is being constructed, the A1 motorway link to Rabat completed, and an intellectual design set, tired of crowded and touristy Marrakech, have rediscovered the virtues of Tangier. The general environment has improved too, with new management for city services and an awareness that not everything old should be pulled down. Tangier's attraction for other creatives has also remained intact, the Cinema Rif on the Grand Socco having been renovated and reborn as the Cinémathèque de Tangier, an important centre for the arts in the heart of the city.

The future of Tangier

With a population that has quadrupled from 250,000 in 1982 to a million, Tangier continues to sprawl ever further inland, its growth fuelled by rural in-migration and high unemployment. In times of pressure, the frustration of the deprived spills over in riots in the poor areas on the city edge. But things are better than they were and many of the bidonville inhabitants are being rehoused. Work is expected to start soon on a rail tunnel between Spain and Morocco, though it is unlikely to be completed before 2025, and the city's future development will certainly be interesting to watch as Morocco moves closer to the European Union. The new royal interest is a very positive sign.

With its special history, Tangier is an endearing place, a town of past cosmopolitan glories. Some say it is best remembered from a vantage point, perhaps a cliff-top café, overlooking the Straits and the distant Iberian coast across the choppy sea, but no doubt it will remain a place of legend. As Mohammed Choukri put it, "In Tangier, any capable storyteller can invent a story and be sure to convince listeners of its truth."

Sights

Tangier is more of an atmosphere than a city with numerous unmissable sights. If you manage to avoid hasslers and hustlers, then it is a city for the flâneur, for strolling, with steep streets and stairways as well as boulevards. Yet there are minor galleries, out-of-the-way cafés and semi-sights for you to put together a wander with a purpose. The main attraction is the views: over the Straits to Spain, from ville nouvelle to the médina, down alleys which could twist on for ever or end in a sticky situation.

Of the ancient city nothing remains. Descriptions are full of 'it is possible that' and 'probably be' and the few antique pieces that have been unearthed are disappointing from a dating and workmanship point of view. The limits of the city have been defined, using the position of necropolises. It extended west to Mendoubia, south to Bou Kachkach and northwest to Marshan Plateau, where there are Punic or maybe Roman tombs hollowed out of the rock, overlooking the Straits.

● *The best view of Tangier is from the top terrace of Nord-Pinus at the very top of the kasbah. If you can't afford that, go through the arch (Bab er Raha) off the northern side of the Place de la Kasbah and appreciate the uninterrupted vista over the straits to Spain.*

Grand Socco

The Grand Socco is where the médina begins, Tangier's answer to Jemaâ el Fna in Marrakech. The square has been spruced up, apparently on suggestion of the king, and it now has fountains and seats and tiled pedestrian areas. At the top of the square the **Cinémathèque de Tanger** ① *T039-934683, www.cinemathequedetanger.com,* has become one of Morocco's most significant arts venues, showing Moroccan and international arts films and documentaries. Formerly the Cinema Rif, it is the centrepoint of a cultural renaissance in the city and stages premieres, seasons and themed cycles and also has a good café with free Wi-Fi. Note the tiled minaret of the **Sidi Bou Abid Mosque** (1917) on the corner of the Grand Socco and Rue Sidi Bou Abid.

On Thursday and Sunday Rifi Berber women sell all sorts of wares in Rue de la Plage (Rue Salah Eddine el Ayoubi). Along Rue d'Angleterre they also sell woven blankets. On the Rue Bourrakia side of the Grand Socco, the arch with Arabic on it leads into the **Mendoubia Gardens**, a quiet, tree-filled place in the heart of Tangier. These gardens were formerly part of the residence of the Mendoub and contain 30 bronze cannons, remnants of old French and British warships. The Mendoubia Palace is the former residence of the sultan's representatives on the International Commission.

Kasbah

In Tangier, the kasbah is constructed on the highest point of the médina. It was fortified back in Roman days, and it was the traditional residence in Tangier of the sultan and his harem. It was burnt to the ground by the English as they left in 1684. More recently, during the heyday of Tangier as an international city, the kasbah was considered a fashionable address for people such as the novelist Richard Hughes (who lived at 'Numéro Zero, La Kasbah, Tangier'). Today, parts of the kasbah are threatened by landslips: after particularly heavy rains, the locals hold their breath and wait to see whether a section of the cliffs will slither down towards the sea. Especially at risk is York Castle, 17th-century home of English governor, the Duke of York.

To get to the kasbah from the Grand Socco, head downhill across the square, aiming for the horseshoe-arched entrance gate and follow down Rue d'Italie and then up Rue de la Kasbah and enter by Bab el Kasbah. From the médina, follow Rue des Chrétiens from the Petit Socco, and then Rue Sidi Ben Rassouli to Bab el Assa.

Musée de la Kasbah ① *T039-932097, Sat-Mon, Wed and Thu 0900-1600, Fri 0900-1130, 1330-1600, closed Tue, 10dh*. The Musée de la Kasbah is in the former palace of the kasbah, the Dar Al Makhzen, and includes Moroccan arts and antiquities. The palace was built by the Sultan Moulay Ismaïl in the 18th century, and was used as the Sultan's palace up until

② Tangier Médina

➡ **Tangier maps**
1 Tangier, page 92
2 Tangier Médina, page 97

KASBAH

Place du Tabor Espagnol
Rue Riad Sultan
Bab er Raha
Place de la Kasbah
Bab Haha
Bab el Kasbah
Musée de la Kasbah, Museum of Moroccan Arts & Museum of Antiquities
Bab el Assa

KASBAH MGOINA
Place Oued Aherdane
Rue de la Kasbah
Rue d'Italie
Bab el Bahar
Rue Dar Baroud

Rue des Chrétiens
Rue de la Marine
Grand Mosque
Rue de la Tannerie
Petit Socco (Souk Dakhil)
Rue Siaghine
Rue de la Poste
Place de la Tannerie
Mendoubia Gardens
Bab Fahs
Spanish Cathedral
MEDINA
Rue Smarine
Rue Bourrakia
Rue Salah Eddine el Ayoubi
Old American Legation
Rue du Portugal
Rue de Cadix
Grand Socco
Sidi Bou Abid
Rue de la Liberté
Rue d'Angleterre
To Ville Nouvelle

N
50 metres
50 yards

Sleeping 🛏
Continental 1
Dar Nour 2
Mamora 3
Pensión Palace 5
Riad Tanja 9

Eating 🍴
Le Detroit 2

1912, when Sultan Moulay Hafid, exiled to Tangier, lived there. The palace is itself worth seeing, with an impressive central courtyard. A museum since 1922, it has had a recent overhaul, with projections, video, large maps and music all illuminating the exhibits from Tangier and the surrounding region. The hub of the museum is seven rooms around a large central courtyard with pale marble columns. This is truly a magnificent setting for the displays. Exhibits range from prehistoric bone tools to decorated ostrich eggs. The collection of ceramics is especially strong and there is also a mosaic from Roman Volubilis. Pick up an explanatory leaflet in English on your way in.

The garden of the palace, a beautiful mature Andalucían arrangement with fragrant plants and a marble fountain, is also worth exploring. As you leave the palace stop at Café Le Detroit if it's open, for a drink and pastries.

In front of the palace is the **Place de la Kasbah**, where criminals were once punished or executed. Note the **Grand Mosque** adjacent to the port. In the sea wall a gate leads out onto a belvedere with excellent views across to Spain. Nearby is **Villa Sidi Hosni**, former residence of Barbara Hutton, the American heiress who was famous for her parties, among other things (read all about it in Iain Finlayson's *Tangier, City of the Dream*).

Médina

Lying below the kasbah, and running from the Grand Socco (Place de 19 Avril, 1947) down to the port, the médina is focused on the Petit Socco, and is full of narrow, twisting streets and old houses, many of which are now shops, hotels or restaurants catering for tourists. It is a quarter which has captured the imagination of numerous European and American writers, the stories of Paul Bowles being among the most evocative. Tangier médina has the advantage over many others of a slope, which aids one's sense of direction a little: generally you go down to the Petit Socco and up to the kasbah. If you really don't have time to get lost, get an official guide, but avoid the advances of the unofficial ones.

Rue Siaghine, the old silversmiths' street, running from the Grand Socco to the Petit Socco, is still an important commercial area of the médina, and the easiest route by which to enter the main area of the médina. To the right of Rue Siaghine, is the **mellah**, the Jewish quarter. You also pass the **Spanish Cathedral**, now boarded up.

The **Petit Socco**, the belly of the médina, was once bigger, but now seems strangely cramped. It is surrounded by a number of famous but primitive pensiones, and the Café Central, formerly a café-bar attracting the likes of William Burroughs, Allen Ginsberg and Jack Kerouac. However, today, with no alcohol sold in the médina, it is a fairly ordinary café with a terrace from which to watch life pass by.

Below the Petit Socco, the **Grand Mosque** lies in between Rue de la Marine and Rue des Postes. This is built on the site of a Portuguese cathedral, although that had been predated by a mosque and, probably, a Roman temple. Opposite is a 14th-century medersa. Also on Rue des Postes (Rue Mokhtar Ahardan) is the Pensión Palace, where Bertolucci filmed scenes for *The Sheltering Sky*, based on the Paul Bowles novel.

The **Old American Legation** ⓘ *8 Zankat Amerika, T039-935317, www.legation. org, 0930-1200, 1600-1830,* is America's oldest diplomatic property. It was given to the US by the Moroccan sultan in 1821 and used as a Consulate until 1961. It has the distinction of being the only historical monument to have remained in US possession since the birth of the American Nation. Now a museum and study centre, on display here are a letter from George Washington to Moulay Abdallah and a collection of mirrors, as well as a good collection of prints including works by Lecouteux and Ben Ali Rbati, an early Moroccan naïve painter.

Ville nouvelle

Tangier's ville nouvelle is a veritable catalogue of late 19th and early 20th-century architectural styles. **Place de France** (Place de Faro) has a good view of the bay, with the famous Café de France alongside, where wartime agents met and made deals. Next to it is the **Terrasse des Paresseux**, where would-be emigrants can see across the Straits to Spain and shoeshine boys and Polaroid-snappers harass the tourists. **Boulevard Pasteur** (becoming Avenue Mohammed V further down) is the main shopping and business street of the new town. Find time to explore the area behind here and look out for the 1940s cinemas, have tea at Pâtisserie Porte, then drop in at the Librairie des Colonnes back on the main boulevard. You could then wander médina-wards again down Rue de la Liberté, stopping off for contemporary art, photography and video art at the **Galerie Delacroix** ⓘ *1100-1300, 1600-2030, free,* if there is an exhibition on.

Near the Grand Socco

At 50 Rue d'Angleterre, is the Anglican **Church of St Andrew's** consecrated in 1905. The churchyard gate is discrete, in a low whitewashed wall, just left of some birdsellers' stalls, at the top side of the Grand Socco. Inside, the church hides in luxuriant vegetation. The key is kept by the groundsman, who will unlock the church and give you a guided tour. Architecture and internal decoration are modelled on Moorish Granada. Note the Arabic inscriptions of the Lord's Prayer and Gloria at the altar end. Memorials and graves, both inside and outside, feature a number of important former residents of Morocco, including 19th-century British consul Sir John Drummond Hay, early 20th-century *Times* correspondent Walter Harris, Caïd Sir Harry McLean, Scottish adviser to Sultan Moulay Abd al Aziz, and Emily Keane, 19th-century wife of the Cherif of Ouezzane. Turn right out of the churchyard gate, follow the wall uphill and you will come to the former British Consulate, now the **Musée d'Art Contemporain de la Ville de Tanger** ⓘ *52 Rue d'Angleterre, T039-938436, 10dh.* Here there is a small but fine selection of late 20th-century Moroccan painters. There are a couple of wacky pictures by wild woman Chaïbia Tallal, plus early works by the likes of Farid Belkahia, founder of the Casablanca École des Beaux Arts, Saâd Hassani and others.

Marshan

Marshan is a neighbourhood of 20th-century villas up on the Marshan plateau, west of the kasbah. Café Hafa, the clifftop café, lies down a narrow street near Rue Shakespeare. Crowded at weekends with local youth, it is the place for a sticky, Polo-mint tasting tea, flavoured in season with orange-blossom. The **Punic rock tombs**, little more than large coffin-sized shapes hollowed out of the soft rock, are nearby. The closest clifftop viewing place near the poorer parts of the city, it is popular with local women and kids on weekend afternoons.

Beaches

Back in the centre, the town beach and the clubs alongside it (which still offer a range of drinking, eating and dancing opportunities) were previously an expatriate zone where anything was permissible and a good time easily available. In its heyday, this beach was said to be the third most beautiful in the world, after Rio de Janeiro and Miami. Jack Kerouac and Joe Orton were among the habitués. Roland Barthes enjoyed Las Tres Caravelas, which then gave way to the Miami. More recently, Mario Testino photographed the local wildlife. During the day, the locals are out playing football. Work is continuing to clean it up but it may still be wise to avoid the beach itself after dark. There are more relaxing, less crowded and cleaner beaches east along the coast – possibly on the stretch south of Ceuta. Nearer Tangier, there is bathing at **Playa Blanca** and **Sidi Kankouch**, also further on at **Plage Dahlia** (11 km after Ksar Es Seghir). Beaches west of Tangier such as **Plage Merkala** can be dangerous for swimming but have the advantage of being sunny until the early evening.

Atlantic coast west of Tangier

An excursion west is a rewarding experience, with a dramatic drive en route. The coast of Southern Spain can be easily seen on a clear day. From the coast road to the north of the town there is a special viewpoint. The options are to negotiate a round-trip price with a grand taxi driver in Rue d'Angleterre, take a Boughaz minibus from the port gates, or, in your own transport, follow Rue Sidi Bou Abid and Rue Sidi Amar on to the S701. This goes up into the **Montagne**, an exclusive suburb of royal palaces and villas, past discrete gates with plaques bearing names like Siddartha. In places, the road and woods would not be out of place in Devon (except for a few palm trees). You may see pines sculpted by the Chergui wind. After dense eucalyptus woods, the landscape opens up, with views of the ocean and fine stands of parasol pine.

Some 11 km from Tangier, the extreme northwestern corner of Africa is reached. Coming from Tangier, bear right for the **Cap Spartel lighthouse** with its Café-Bar Sol. Going left, rocky coastline is followed by the wild Atlantic and **Robinson Beach**. This is a dramatic place, and swimmers should exercise caution (there are drownings every year and very little the coastguard can do). In spring, there are plenty of wild flowers, while in summer, tiny temporary cafés with cane awnings spring up among the rocks above the crashing surf.

South of Cap Spartel, the **Caves of Hercules** ① *1000 to sunset, nominal charge*, are natural formations which were extended by quarries for millstones up to the 1920s. Later, prostitutes worked here and Tangier's rich and famous held parties. From a window shaped like Africa which overlooks the sea there is an impressive view.

After the Caves of Hercules take a rough farm track off the road to Roman **Cotta**, a small site centred around a factory for *garum* (anchovy paste) and the remains of a temple.

Coast east of Tangier

① *Bus 15 from Grand Socco, Tangier, serves this route, which is busy on a Sunday and very busy in summer. Out of season many places are closed.*

From Tangier, 10 km east along the S704 road around **Cap Malabata**, tourist developments, including the Hotel/Casino Mövenpick complex, numerous cafés as well as some excellent beaches are used by the people from Tangier. Cap Malabata is where the Atlantic and the Mediterranean meet and it is said the waters (with a little imagination) can be seen as two different colours. Despite this the views are magnificent. The Victorian pile on the hill is the Château Malabata, a Gothic folly inhabited by a family.

Ksar es Seghir is a small seaside town 37 km east of Tangier, dominated by the ruined Portuguese castle. The town was named Ksar Masmuda under the Almohads, and Ksar al Majaz under the Merinids, who added walls and gates in 1287. The Portuguese took the town in 1458. The floor of the town's hammam, the mosque and the intact sea gate arch should be noted. There are other cafés and restaurants, including the recommended Restaurant Caribou, Café Dakhla to the west of the town, Café Dahlia to the east and Café Lachiri on the bridge (seafood). There are possibilities for camping, and a splendid beach. Onwards, between Ksar es Seghir and Ceuta, is a string of beautiful and deserted beaches.

Tangier listings

For Sleeping and Eating price codes and other relevant information, see pages 12-20.

☺ Sleeping

There are 3 main hotel areas: off the Petit Socco; near the port entrance (ask to be dropped near Hotel Marco Polo, for example); and around the Blvd Pasteur. For the budget traveller, the hotels near the seafront are easiest to find and deal with.

Médina *p98, map p97*
The best places to stay in the médina are mostly clustered at its northwestern tip, in or near the kasbah.

€€€€ Nord-Pinus Tanger, 11 Rue Riad Sultan, La Kasbah, T061-228140, www.hotel-nord-pinus-tanger.com. Tangier's most sophisticated hotel, the beautiful Nord-Pinus has an extraordinary position at the very top of the kasbah, looking over the sea to Spain, or down into the gardens of the palace. Opened in 2007, the place already seems well lived in and exceptionally well loved by its French owner. Traditional Moroccan design elements – *zellige* tiles from Fès and rugs – are complemented by striking contemporary photographs and some nice touches such as huge shower heads and back-illuminated mirrors. Sit on the terrace reading one of the many beautiful books lying around listening to the birdsong in the palace gardens below. The restaurant (see page 103), serving high quality French and Moroccan cuisine, is also open to non-guests – ring to reserve.

€€€ Riad Tanja, Rue du Portugal, Escalier Américain, T039-333538, www.riadtanja.com. Big, stylish bedrooms have ornate wooden furniture, red rugs, large pouffes and views over the market; the couple of smaller rooms without external windows are less desirable. The restaurant (see page 103) is a popular destination in its own right.

€€ Dar Nour, 20 Rue Gourna, La Kasbah, T062-112724, www.darnour.com. Not for those partial to swinging cats, Dar Nour is nevertheless a stylish, romantic place. The merging of several houses in the narrow backstreets of the kasbah has created lots of cosy nooks and crannies. If all this makes you feel a little claustrophobic, you can escape to the roof terrace, where there's a spectacular 360-degree view. It's a quiet spot too, away from the bustle of the médina. Old furniture and fresh flowers set off the Moroccan fabrics and lights to fine effect. Traditional Moroccan meals cooked to order. Ten rooms.

€€ Hotel Continental, 36 Rue Dar Baroud, T039-931024, hcontinental@iam.net.ma. Despite being at the Eastern end of the médina, above the port, the large, old fashioned Continental has a seafront hotel feel. Rooms have double glazing, which pretty much keeps out the port noise, and some have balconies with good views. Touches such as antique radios and a grandfather clock give the place some antique gravitas. Used by Bertolucci in the filming *The Sheltering Sky*.

€€ La Tangierina, 19 Riad Sultan, La Kasbah,

T039-947731, www.latangerina.com. Lower key (and also lower price) than the Pinus next door, La Tangierina is still a very elegant place to stay. There are Moroccan and a European living rooms, both very cosy, the latter with a wood fire. Each room has a working antique radio and there's a small communal breakfast room. Bedrooms are done in pale brick, with horseshoe arches and white drapes. Bathrooms are rather small but there's a hammam and the best rooms have geranium-fringed private terraces and sea views through the sash windows.

€ Mamora Hotel, 19 Rue des Postes, (Rue Mokhtar Ahardan, T039-934105. Immaculately clean and good-value hotel in the centre of the médina and one of the best in this area. The best rooms have big views over the green-tiled roofs of the mosque to the sea beyond. The morning call to prayer will almost certainly wake you, however.

€ Pensión Palace, 2 Rue des Postes (Rue Mokhtar Ahardan), T039-936128. There's no chance of being treated like royalty here – in fact you may not even be treated much like a paying guest. But reasonable rooms around a lovely, plant-filled square courtyard make up for the disinterested service.

Seafront and ville nouvelle p99, map p92

€€€€ Dar Nilam, 28 lotissement Tingis, T039- 301146, www.darnilam.com. Lots of ornate Moroccan decoration and antique style in a small hotel 2 km along the seafront from the town centre. "We reserve you a mythical receiving", according to their website.

€€€€ Hotel el Minzah, 85 Rue de la Liberté (Zankat el Houria), T039-935885, www.elminzah.com. Big, central and luxurious, El Minzah has 100 rooms with bathrooms. Dating from the 1930s, the hotel has beautiful gardens set around an Andalucían courtyard, two restaurants, wellness centre, wine bar, coffee bar, tea room, mini-golf, tennis, and a pool. The place feels a little tired, however.

Rooms are a little ordinary for the price and even the pantalooned staff can't make it feel like value for money.

€€€ Hotel Rembrandt, Av Mohammed V, T039-937870/2. Conveniently in centre of ville nouvelle, Rembrandt has a good pool, a restaurant and a popular, modern bar with views through buildings down to the sea. The 73 rooms lack much character but are double glazed and some have good views.

€€€ Hotel Rif, 152 Av des FAR (ex-Av d'Espagne), T039-937870. A grand old landmark seafront hotel now refurbished and reopened with a swimming pool complete with waterfall and soft red and blue furnishings. Business traveller centred.

€€ Hotel de Paris, 42 Blvd Pasteur, T039-931877. Clean, central hotel with old tiled and ugly floral bedcovers. Street-facing rooms have no double glazing and can be noisy. Not bad value, especially if you can bargain them down a little.

€€ Hotel el Djenina, 8 Rue el Antaki (Rue Grotius), just off Av d'Espagne, T039-942244, eldjenina@menara.ma. 40 well renovated, airy rooms with en suite bathrooms. The hotel is clean and simple – not especially full of character or style but reliable and modern, which makes it stand out in Tangier.

€€ Hotel Marco Polo, Av d'Espagne, T039-931877. Small comfortable hotel with a surreal cave in the reception. Modern, cool and tiled, rooms have satellite TV, minibars, sea views, comfy beds, traffic noise and terrible art. Big suites would be good for families.

€€ Hotel Holland, 139 Rue de Hollande (up the hill on Av de Belgique from Pl de France, turn right, near the Dawliz multiplex), T039-937838. A rambling, badly converted villa with fairly basic rooms and safe parking. Reservations essential in summer as it's used by Moroccans on the drive home.

€ Hotel Muniria, Rue Magellan, T039-935337. A friendly, family-run little place with 8 rooms and a preponderance of blue, from the hand-painted wardrobes to the bedspreads. Former clients include William Burroughs, Kerouac and Ginsberg, though the hotel makes admirably little of the fact. Some sea views.

€ Hotel Nabil, 11 Rue Magellan, T039-375407. A large, good value hotel a block back from the seafront that can feel semi-abandoned. Rooms are basic but are a decent size, and have private balconies. There's even a roof terrace, if you can find someone to lend you the key.

€ There are also cheap and basic pensiones on Rue de la Plage, past Restaurant Africa, up the hill from the port. Prices are around 80dh. They cater to those who need no more than a place to lie down before or after catching a ferry and many do not have showers. They include **Talavera**, **Madrid**, **Le Detroit**, **Playa** and **Atou**, the last being particularly cheap, while Le Detroit is about the best.

Youth hostel, 8 Rue el Antaki, at right angles to Av d'Espagne, T039-946127. Clean and well run with 60 beds. Overnight fee 40dh, advanced booking essential. Bus 100 m.

Camping

Campsites are not much cheaper than a budget hotel and rather far from the city. Camper vans should be secure enough.
Camping Miramonte, 3 km west from city centre, not far from Marshan district, very handy for Plage Merkala, T039-937138. Well-kept site up on a hillside with lots of shade, bar/snacks, small pool, showers, laundry, petrol at 400 m.

Atlantic coast west of Tangier *p100*
€€€€ Hotel-Club Le Mirage, Cap Spartel, near the caverns, T039-333332, www.lemirage-tanger.com. Excellent service, the discretely rich rent one of the 25 'deluxe bungalow-suites' for the whole season. Piano bar and 2 restaurants.
Camping Achakar, Les Grottes d'Hercule, Cap Spartel, near the Caves of Hercules, 12 km west of town, T039-333840.

❷ Eating

Médina *p98, map p97*
¶¶¶ Nord-Pinus Tangier, 11 Rue Riad Sultan, La Kasbah, T061-228140, www.hotel-nord-pinus-tanger.com. The views alone would make the cost of eating here worthwhile, but the food is also excellent and there's a Moroccan/French wine list too. High quality French and Moroccan cuisine, with an emphasis on seafood – ring to reserve.
¶¶¶ Riad Tanja, Rue du Portugal, Escalier Américain, T039-333538, www.riadtanja.com. With red rugs, brass candlesticks and dark wood tables, this cosy place is especially beautiful as the evening light streams in. Moroccan cuisine with a twist, with dishes such as monkfish pastilla and spicy couscous.
¶ If your stomach flora has adapted to Morocco, in the médina, there are a number of cheap, basic restaurants, such as **Mauritania** and **Assalam** in Rue de la Marine, and a similar selection on Rue du Commerce.

Seafront and ville nouvelle *p99, map p92*
¶¶¶ El Erz, Hotel el Minzah, 85 Rue de la Liberté, T039-935885. Popular international hotel restaurant with a wide range of European dishes, often with music, and a terrace for eating al fresco with a view.
¶¶¶ El Khorsan, Hotel el Minzah, 85 Rue de la Liberté, T039-935885. Reservations recommended. Like El Erz, in the Hotel el Minzah. Great views across the straits and one of the country's best reputations for Moroccan cuisine.
¶¶ Anna e Paolo, 77 Av Prince Héretier, T039-944617. A bit of a schlep out of the centre, this is worth making the effort for good Italian food such as *melanzane alla parmigiana* as well as pizzas and pasta.
¶¶ Casa d'Italia, Palais des Institutions Italiennes, T039-936348. In the one-time servants quarters of the Palais Moulay Hafid, in smart Marshan (page 99), to the west of

the médina, this is an upmarket Italian place favoured by the expats who live around here. You might be able to sneak a look around the palace after your pasta.

Casa España, 11 Rue Jabha el Ouatania. The restaurant of Tangier's Spanish club is a little bit of the Iberian peninsula transferred across the Straits, upstairs on an unprepossessing street. Smart and light, with all the Spanish standards, including multiple paellas and wine.

El Mesón de Pépé Ocaña, 7 Rue Jabha el Ouatania. Easily missed, a popular and authentically dark and atmospheric tapas bar down a small street behind Hotel Rembrandt. It's a more earthy version of the nearby Casa España, but still attracts a smart, though very male, crowd. Pull up a bar stool, order a drink and the tapas will flow.

L'Marsa, 92 Av Mohammed VI. Good pizzas and pastas by the seafront, with a big outdoor seating area. It's large and modern – certainly not the most beautiful restaurant in town, but good for a quick eat. Also does salads and some traditional Moroccan food.

Populaire Saveur, 2 Escalier Waller, T039-336326. Popular by both name and nature, this little fish place on the steps up from the market to Rue de le Liberté has good set menus in a homely atmosphere.

Raihani, 10 Rue Ahmed Chaouki. Good Moroccan food as well as some French dishes, in the centre of the ville nouvelle. Was being refurbished at the time of writing.

San Rémo, 15 Rue Ahmed Chaouki, T039-938451. Closed Mon. Fresh pasta and other European dishes in a pretty little bistro-style place with tablecloths and serious service.

Agadir, 21 Rue Prince Héretier, T068-827696. A tiny fragment of the 1950s near the Blvd Pasteur, this small and simple licensed place behind net curtains serves good, freshly cooked Moroccan and French food with a smile. Excellent tagines and pastilla as well as some seafood.

Restaurant Africa, 83 Rue de la Plage (Rue Salah Eddine el Ayoubi), T039-935436. At the bottom of the hill by the port, this is the first place many people come to, and though it's hardly an amazing first taste of Africa, it's not bad either for a light meal. Watch out for innacuracies in the bill.

Cafés and pâtisseries

Café Central, in the Petit Socco. The former artistic rendezvous where William Burroughs and Tennessee Williams used to hang out. It's lost most of its magic but it's still a good place to watch the crowds go by.

Café de France, 1 Pl de France, has a history as a meeting place for artists and intellectuals. Mixed clientele of local notables, tourists and *passeurs* looking out for potential emigrants to hustle across the Straits.

Café Hafa, see page 99.

Pâtisserie La Española, Rue de la Liberté. Posh pâtisserie and salon du thé.

Salon de thé/Restaurant le Detroit, T039-938080. Pricey for food, but good for tea, coffee, pastries and a panoramic view of the Straits.

Salon de thé Vienne, corner of Rue du Mexique and Rue Moutanabi. Large and showy.

Zoco Chico, Petit Socco. A gringo-centric place, this is a contemporary little café with a few tiled tables right on the Petit Socco. It sells couscous, fallafel and tabouleh as well as good coffees.

Atlantic coast west of Tangier *p100*
Le Mirage, out at Cap Spartel, T039-333331. International cuisine with a loyal following in a spectacular setting.

🍸 Bars and clubs

Tangier *p90, maps p92 and p97*
Tangier is not what it once was – most of the famously seedy bars of the past are gone. There is, however, a new generation of beach bars. See also the Eating section for tapas bars.

Caïd's Piano Bar, Hotel el Minzah, 85 Rue de la Liberté, T039-33 34 44. Moroccan decoration and expensive drinks in an atmospheric bar.

Morocco Palace, 11 Rue du Prince Moulay Abdallah, T039-938614. An Oriental-disco mix with floorshow including performance by a singing dwarf. A Fellini film set.

Pasarela, Av Mohammed VI, T039-945246. Beachside complex with bars, a pool, and occasional live music.

Patio Wine Bar, Hotel el Minzah, 85 Rue de la Liberté, T039-935885. A wine bar in which to explore the wines of Morocco and overseas, a little pricey and rather uneven in service and quality.

The Pub, 4 Rue Sorolla, T039-934789. Food, beer and other drinks in a pseudo- pub atmosphere.

Régine, 8 Rue Mansour Eddahbi, T039-340238. Where the serious local money goes dancing.

Scotts, Rue Moutanabi. Gay, but not exclusively so, the highlight is the paintings of Rif boys in Highland gear by local decorator, Stuart Church.

Tanger Inn, 1 Rue Magellan, T039-935337. Small bar popular with those reliving the Beat experience. The first stage on a long Tangerine night out.

😊 Entertainment

Tangier p90, maps p92 and p97
Art galleries **Galerie Delacroix**, Rue de la Liberté. **Tanjah Flandria Art Gallery**, Rue Ibn Rochd, behind the Hotel Flandria, T039-933000. **Cultural and language centres Institut Français**, Rue de la Liberté, easily identified by the Galerie Delacroix sign. Good temporary exhibitions.

😊 Festivals and events

Tangier p90, maps p92 and p97
Late May/early Jun The annual **Jazz Festival**, www.tanjazz.com, is popular so try to book accommodation in advance when it's

on. There are street parades and free concerts on the Grand Socco, paying concerts in the Mendoubia gardens.

🔘 Shopping

Tangier p90, maps p92 and p97
Food
There is a market between Rue d'Angleterre and Rue Sidi Bou Abid and numerous fruit sellers along Rue de la Plage and its side streets. On Rue el Oualili, is another food market.

Handicrafts and antiques
Tangier is not the best place to buy handicrafts, for although shops have a large selection, production tends to be in Marrakech and the pressure to buy in Tangier can be intense, with bazaarists and hawkers used to gullible day trippers from Spain. The cheapest shops and stalls, with the most flexible prices, will be found in the médina. Shops in the ville nouvelle may claim fixed prices but in most cases you will be able to bargain.

Coopartim, Ensemble Artisanal, Rue de Belgique, T039-931589, a government controlled fixed-price craft centre with a number of workshops is a good place to start. In the médina, try **Marrakech la Rouge**, 50 Rue es Siaghin. For crafts and antiques see **Galerie Tindouf**, 64 Rue de la Liberté, T039-931525. For kitting out your villa on the Montagne with Indian antiques, try **Adolfo de Velasco**, down on Av Mohammed V on the opposite side to the Post Office. **Laure Welfling**, 3 Pl de la Kasbah, T039-932083 is a cut above most of Tangiers' shops – aimed at the interior design set, it has good ceramics.

Newspapers and books
Foreign newspapers can be bought from shops in Rue de la Liberté or outside the post office in Av Mohammed V. For books in French, Spanish and a few in other languages, go to **Librairie des Colonnes**, 54 Blvd Pasteur, T039-936955.

Tangier *p90, maps p92 and p97*

Bicycle and motorcycle hire
Mesbahi, 7 Rue Ibn Tachfine, just off Av des
FAR, T039-940974. Renting bicycles, 50cc and
125cc motorbikes, deposit required for 3 days
or more.

Birdwatching
Without doubt this is the best place in North
Africa to watch the migrations to and from
Europe. Over 250 different species have been
counted crossing this narrow strip of water,
and while the main movements are from
Mar-May and Aug-Oct, early and late movers
ensure that there are always some birds to
observe. The stretch of coast from Cap Spartel
in the west to Punta Ceres in the east and the
advantage of height gained by Jbel Kebir and
Jbel Moussa provide ample viewing spots.
The massive migration of large raptors is very
impressive. Flocks of white stork can be
spotted too. Smaller birds including warblers
and wheatears, swallows, larks and finches
also take this route.

Tour operators
Holiday Service, 84 Av Mohammed V, T039-
933362. **Wagons-Lit Tourisme**, Rue de la
Liberté. **Limadet Ferry**, Av du Prince Moulay
Abdallah, T039-932649. **Comanav Ferries**,
43 Rue Abou Alaâ el Maâri, T039-932649.
Transtour Ferries, 4 Rue el Jabha al Outania,
T039-934004.

Tangier *p90, maps p92 and p97*
Air
Tangier's **Ibn Batouta Airport**, T039-393720,
is 15 km southwest of the city on the N1 road
to Rabat. Catch bus 17 or 70 from Grand
Socco or a grand taxi. Arrive 1-2 hrs early.
EasyJet (www.easyjet.com) fly here from
Madrid and Atlas Blue
(www.atlas-blue.com) fly from **London**

Heathrow. There are also direct flights to
other European cities including: **Amsterdam**,
Barcelona, **Brussels**, **Frankfurt** and **Paris**.
Internal direct flights to: **Agadir**, **Al
Hoceïma** and **Casablanca**.
Airline offices: Air France, 20 Blvd
Pasteur. **British Airways**, 83 Rue de la
Liberté, T039- 935877. **Iberia**, 35 Blvd
Pasteur, T039-936177. **Royal Air Maroc**, Pl
de France, T039-935501/2.

Boat
At the port avoid all touts selling embarkation
cards – these are free from the officials.
Ferry tickets to **Algeciras** can be bought at
travel agents in Blvd Pasteur, or at the ferry
terminal. **Trasmediterranea**
(www.trasmediterranea.es) run a car and
passenger service about 10 times a day on
high speed (1 hr) and standard ferries (2½
hrs). Passengers from €42, cars from €160.
Check in at least 1 hr early, to allow time to
collect an embarkation card, complete a
departure card, and have your passport
stamped.
There are departures every 2 hrs from
Tangier to **Tarifa** with FRS (www.frs.es), a
mere 35-min journey. Passengers €39, car
€99, with a free bus transfer to **Algeciras**.
Tickets to **Sete**, in the South of France,
can be bought from **Voyages Comanav**, 43
Rue Abou el Alaâ el Maâri, T039-934096,
www.comanav.ma. There is a ferry every 2-4
days. Passenger tickets from €40. Car and 2
passengers from €205.
There are also less frequent ferry services
to **Gibraltar**, and **Genoa**.

Bus
Bus station on Av Jami' al Duwal al Arabia,
T039-946682, information, T039-932415.
Tangier is fairly small and thus it is unlikely
that you will want to use local buses. If you do
they can be picked up in the Grand Socco or
in Av des FAR outside the port gates.
Boughaz minibuses, from just outside the

port gate, may be useful to get to the private bus station, or on excursions from Tangier westwards.

CTM buses depart from the ticket office near the entrance to the port in Av des FAR. Departures include: **Kénitra**, **Rabat** and **Casablanca**; **Larache** and **Asilah**; **Meknès** and **Fès**; **Agadir** and **Tiznit**.

Private buses, running from the terminal at the end of Rue de Fès, go to most destinations and are generally cheaper. **Tetouan** every 15 mins (1 hr); **Asilah** 3 daily (30 mins); **Larache** every hour (1½ hrs); **Meknès** 4 daily (5 hrs); **Fès** 2 daily (6 hrs); **Chefchaouen** 6 daily (2½ hrs); **Ceuta** 3 daily (2 hrs); **Ouezzane** 0900, 1400 (4 hrs). To get to the terminal take a petit taxi.

Car hire
Avis, 54 Blvd Pasteur, T039-938960, and at the airport. **Budget**, 7 Av du Prince Moulay Abdallah, T039-937994, and at the airport. **Europcar**, 87 Av Mohammed V, T039-938271. **Hertz**, 36 Av Mohammed V, T039-933322, and at the airport. **Leasing Cars**, 24 Rue Henri Regnault, and at the airport, a little cheaper.

Taxi
Grands taxis Can be picked up from the Gare du Routier or in front of Tangier Ville railway station, to destinations within or outside of the city. You will need to set a fare with the driver. To **Tetouan** and **Ceuta** this is a quick, practical and not too expensive option. For excursions from Tangier to the Caves of Hercules or Cap Malabata negotiate for a grand taxi in Rue de Hollande.
Petits taxis Turquoise with yellow stripe, may be cheaper, although that will depend on your skill as the meters are not always operated. For a taxi, call T039-935517.

Train
Information T090 20 30 40. The former port station on Av des FAR is firmly closed. Trains now arrive/depart from the suburban Moughougha station, a 20dh taxi ride out in the new suburbs. Departure times change: in general there are 3-4 a day, including a 2230 overnight train with couchettes for **Marrakech**. Other departures include: **Rabat**, **Casablanca** and **Marrakech**. **Meknès**, **Fès** and **Oujda** can be reached by making a connection at **Sidi Kacem**. All trains stop at **Asilah**.

Directory

Tangier *p90, maps p92 and p97*
Banks All the usual banks with ATMs are on Blvd Pasteur/Av Mohammed V. The **Crédit du Maroc**, on the ground floor of the Tanja Flandria Hotel, has a bureau de change, as does the **BMCI**, down the street opposite the Terrasse des paresseux, next to the Café de France. The **Wafa Bank** (ATM) is further down the slope, on your left just before the PTT. Banks are open 0830-1130 and 1430-1630.
American Express: c/o **Voyages Schwartz**, 54 Blvd Pasteur, T039-933459, open Mon-Fri 0900-1230, 1500-1900, Sat 0900-1230.
Internet Plenty of internet places around town for about 10dh per hr. Try **Cyber Pasteur**, 61 Bld Pasteur, or **Fun Clic**, 66 Bld Mohammed V. **Library** Tangier Book Club, Old American Legation, 8 Rue d'Amerique, the médina, T039-935317. Open Tue-Sat 0900-1200. **Medical services Ambulance**: T15. **Chemists**: Pharmacie de Garde, 26 Rue de Fès, T039-932616. **Hospital**: Emergencies: T039-930856, also try T039-934242.
Post PTT, 33 Av Mohammed V, T039-935657, Mon-Fri 0830-1200, 1430-1800, Sat 0830-1200. **Telephone** International phone (24 hrs) far right of post office. Also telephone from the PTT at the junction of Rue el Msala and Rue de Belgique. There are also the usual téléboutiques. **Useful addresses Fire**: T15. **Garage**: Tanjah Auto, 2 Av de Rabat. **Police**: (general) Rue Ibn Toumert, T19; (traffic) T177.

North Atlantic coast

With none of the hassle of Tangier, yet some of its European sophistication, it's not surprising that coastal Asilah has become a firm fixture on many tourists' itineraries. Beautifully whitewashed, its old fortified Portuguese centre makes a good spot for a peaceful couple of days by the sea. Further south, Larache is much less discovered but has some of the same architectural attractions in the winding streets of its médina, and, across the estuary, some evocative ancient Roman remains at Lixus.

» For listings, see pages 114-117.

Asilah

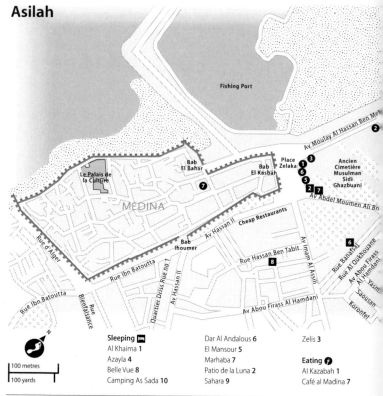

Sleeping		
Al Khaima **1**	Dar Al Andalous **6**	Zelis **3**
Azayla **4**	El Mansour **5**	
Belle Vue **8**	Marhaba **7**	**Eating**
Camping As Sada **10**	Patio de la Luna **2**	Al Kazabah **1**
	Sahara **9**	Café al Madina **7**

Asilah ⟫ *For listings, see pages 114-117.*

Asilah, 40 km south of Tangier (and also referred to as Arzila), is a striking fishing port and coastal town of white and blue houses, surrounded by ramparts and lying alongside an extensive beach. It is the northernmost of the former Portuguese outposts (the others include Azemmour, El Jadida and Safi). A small place with a Mediterranean feel, Asilah might provide a pleasant introduction to Morocco, in spite of the extent to which tourism dominates. If you turn up in August you'll coincide with the annual influx of people for the International Festival of Asilah, which usually includes jazz and Moroccan music, and exhibitions by contemporary Moroccan artists.

Ins and outs

Asilah lies off the main N1 Tangier to Rabat road. It is accessible both by road (buses and grands taxis take 60 minutes from Tangier) and by rail (50 minutes from Tangier). The rail station is some 2 km north of the town, and there aren't very many taxis in Asilah. Buses and taxis stop at the Pl Mohammed V, close to the old town. There are buses from Larache, too, taking about one hour. ⟫ *See Transport, page 117, for further details.*

Background

Modern Asilah stands on the site of the Phoenician town of Silis, or perhaps Zilis. The area was subsequently settled by Romans in Anthony's reign and the Byzantines. In 966, the town was rebuilt by El Hakim II, ruler of Cordoba. It was the last stronghold of the Idrissid dynasty. The Portuguese occupied Asilah from 1471, and built the town's fortifications, and in 1578 King Sebastian landed there on his way to defeat at what was to become known as the Battle of the Three Kings. This defeat led to the Spanish absorption of Portugal, and thus of Asilah, but the Portuguese influence on the town is still quite discernible.

The Moroccans recovered Asilah in 1691, under Moulay Ismaïl. In 1826 Austria bombarded Asilah, then a base of piracy, as did the Spanish in 1860. In the late 19th and early 20th century Ahmed al Rasouli, the bandit chief who terrorized much of northwestern Morocco, was based in the town, as described by his one-time hostage and later friend, Walter Harris, in *Morocco That Was*. Al Rasouli built his palace in the

Casa Garcia 2
El Espigou 4
La Place 3
La Symphonie des
  Douceurs II 6

Le Pont 4
Oceano Casa Pepe 5

médina, and from it exercised power over much of the region, being for a time its governor. The Spanish took Asilah in 1911, as part of their Protectorate of northern Morocco.

In more recent years, Asilah has played host to an international summer arts festival and the old neighbourhoods are squeaky clean and home to weekend retreats for wealthy Casablancans. The result is pretty and whitewashed and there are some excellent fish restaurants.

Sights
The médina is the main interest of Asilah, a quarter of predominately white and blue buildings, reflecting in their design the influence of the Portuguese. Note the modern murals on some of the houses in the médina, painted by artists during the festival. The ramparts were built by the Portuguese in the 15th century, and are set with a number of important gates, including Bab el Kasbah, Bab el Bahar ('the sea gate'), Bab Ihoumar, a structure topped with the eroded Portuguese coat of arms, as well as Bab el Jbel ('the mountain gate') and Bab Ihoumer. At points it is possible to climb the fortifications for views of the town and along the coast. Within the médina, **Le Palais de la Culture** is a cultural centre converted from the former residence of the brigand Ahmed al Rasouli, built in 1909 right beside the sea. It is difficult to gain access except during the festival, but it is possible to visualize those who incurred al Rasouli's wrath being made to walk the plank from the palace windows over the cliff front.

The souk has a Thursday **market** attracting farmers from the surrounding area. In addition to the sale of the usual fruit, spices and vegetables, handicrafts distinctive of the Rif region are also on display.

The **beach** is often windy (but at times can be beautifully calm) and frequented by bathers, men touting camel rides and fishermen. It stretches beyond the building works to the north and south of the town.

El Utad, the stone circle at Mzoura

The stone circle at Mzoura makes a good excursion from Rabat or Tangier for those with plenty of time and a car. Though there are numerous prehistoric rock art sites in the High Atlas and Djebel Beni, the barrow at Mzoura is the only one of its kind in the country. The best time to visit Mzoura is in late summer when the vegetation has died back. After a rainy winter, the countryside will be at its best. This is also a good trip for birdwatchers, giving them a focus point in a rolling landscape of open fields, stands of eucalyptus and occasional corrugated-iron roofed homesteads but unspoiled by industrial agriculture. It also gives you a glimpse into the living conditions in the countryside.

The first trace of prehistoric occupation you meet are three great menhirs, lying on the ground. Look out for the scooped-out 'bowls' in one of the stones, referred to as 'cup and circle' by English archaeologists and testimony to some obscure cult after the stones had fallen. Further on, to your right, the stones of the circle once ringed a high barrow, heavily excavated by the Spanish. Most stones are only 1.5 m high, and within them lies a sort of stone walkway – possibly the original base of the barrow. The most spectacular feature is a stone standing 4.5 m high. You can also locate a lintel in the circle, once the entrance to the barrow.

Getting there On the N1 north of Larache – a winding, busy road – there is a major roundabout near Sidi Tnine el Yamani where you should branch off for Tetouan (R417). Just under 4 km from the roundabout, turn left at the Somepi garage and head up the recently widened road for Sidi Yamani. After about 3 km, in the village, you reach a Y-junction, where you need to take the left-hand fork. About 6.5 km after the village, after passing a large abandoned Spanish building on your left, you should turn off right onto a sandy track that comes after a minor cutting, with the road running slightly downhill. (If in doubt, ask a local for 'el utad', the funerary monument.) Once you turn off, the track doubles back sharply taking you the 2.5 km to the hamlet where the circle is located. When you get to the hamlet, keep left; the track to the circle runs between the bramble hedges of the farmsteads, eventually veering round to the left.

Larache ➤ For listings, see pages 115-117.

Bigger than Asilah, and rather less bijou, Larache is a relaxed, faded seaside town, with a good beach and not too many tourists. A halfway house between Spanish and Moroccan urban life, it is a sleepy sort of place, with views over the ocean and the Loukkos estuary, plus the evocatively named, 16th-century Château de la Cigogne, the Fortress of the Stork. It was at Larache that Jean Genet was to find a haven, writing his last novel here.

Background

Larache (El Arayis in Arabic) is named for the vine arbours of the Beni Arous, a local tribe. The area has one of the longest histories of human occupation in Morocco, going back to Phoenician, Carthaginian and Roman times at the settlement of nearby Lixus. Larache was occupied by the Spanish during 1610-1689 and as part of their Protectorate, from 1911. At that time, the harbour was added and the new town was developed. Larache became the principal port of the Spanish northern zone. Today, the town draws its livelihood from the agro-food industry and fishing, although it has lost its status as a major port. Revenues from migrant workers and the building industry are important, too. Tourism may get a boost here soon as a large resort complex is planned on the Atlantic beach north of the river.

Sights

On the very edge of the old town of Larache is a large piece of Renaissance military engineering, with the usual pointy bastions, dating from the 16th century. The isolated structure, now housing the local museum of antiquities, is the **Château de la Cigogne** ① *T039-912091, Wed-Sun 0900-1200, 1500-1730.* Also called Castillo de las Cigueñas or Al Fath, the museum contains a small amount of material from Lixus.

The Avenue Mohammed V is the main street of the new town. At the eastern end, heading for the central plaza, there are the fortifications and then the post office on the right and the **Iglesia de Nuestra Señora del Pilar** on the left. The circular **Place de la Libération**, with a fountain, is the heart of the town; the entrance to the médina, an arched gate, Bab el Khemis, is on the north side.

Exploring further, on the clifftop overlooking ocean and estuary, the 16th-century **Kebibat Fortress** was used by the Spanish as a hospital. Shamefully, it has been left to fall into ruin. The Spanish Consulate occupies a fine art deco building, and you will also easily locate the Neo-Moorish style central **market**, recognisable by its towers.

The médina is a poor quarter of steep and narrow streets and high walls best viewed from below or the north side of the estuary. Just inside is the Spanish-built market square. There are a number of souks, notably **Socco de la Alcaiceria**, the cloth market.

The main beach is an extensive strip of fine (though littered, in season) **beach**, with a number of cafés nearby. To get there, see Ancient Lixus, below.

One final port of call in Larache is the tomb of writer **Jean Genet** (1910-1986) out in the old Christian cemetery near the lighthouse and prison. The cemetery has been cleaned up, part of the works currently being financed by the regional government of Andalusía. With the views over the ocean, Genet could hardly have chosen a better final resting place.

Larache

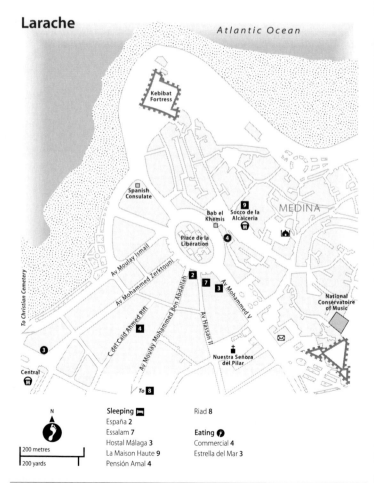

Sleeping 🛏
España **2**
Essalam **7**
Hostal Málaga **3**
La Maison Haute **9**
Pensión Amal **4**

Riad **8**

Eating 🍴
Commercial **4**
Estrella del Mar **3**

Excursion to Ancient Lixus

ⓘ *The site is just over the Oued Loukkos, on a hillside to the west of the N1. Without a car, you may have to walk or take a petit taxi (30dh) and wait by the roadside for a grand taxi with a space in order to get back again. Best option is to get the bus No 2 (3dh) which runs from the port to the beach, Plage Rimmel. Open daylight hours. The east side of the site next to the N1 is fenced in by green railings. A small site map on a metal plaque can be found next to the locked entrance gate. After a recent incident of armed robbery here, you will be accompanied on your visit by a guard with a large wooden truncheon, which may or may not make you feel safer.*

Located on a spectacular site on the right bank of the Oued Loukkos about 4 km from the sea, Ancient Lixus is the second most important Roman site in Morocco after Volubilis. Heathland butterflies and the occasional raptor are added bonuses of a visit to the site.

Tchemich Hill, on which the town is located, 50 m above sea level, was obviously an excellent location for defensive reasons and the views from here are beautiful, especially in the early evening, when the sun is going down over the meanders of the estuary. For some ancient writers Lixus was the location of the Garden of Hesperides, where Hercules harvested golden apples to gain his place on Mount Olympus. The first traces of settlement date from the seventh to sixth century BC and in pre-Roman inscriptions the future Lixus is referred to as Semes. The oldest evidence of building goes back to the fourth century BC. There was a seventh-century Phoenician and later a Carthaginian settlement here. Rome annexed the town in 40 BC. Coins with Latin and neo-Punic inscriptions suggest the inhabitants had a dual culture, as was the case in so much of Roman North Africa. The town became a colony under the Emperor Claudius I, when salt,

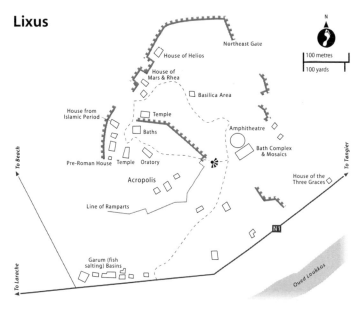

Lixus

olives and fish were the main exports. Eventually reaching an area of 62 ha, Lixus prospered until the late third century AD, in part because of its strategic position on the road from Tingis (Tangier) to Sala Colonia (Rabat). It remained active and was occupied until the fifth century AD and in Arabic historiography, re-emerges as Tohemmis. This remained a Muslim settlement until Larache was founded in the 14th century. Recent archaeological finds in the region will shed further light on the town's history.

Getting around the site The easiest way up into the site is via the track near the gate, generally closed, at the north end of the garum (fish salting) basins behind the railings on the N1 (just nip around the railings). Head uphill to find the **amphitheatre**, excavated in 1964 and, with its its quality stonework, probably the most impressive ruin. Spectators would have been able to enjoy a play and superb views of the flood plain beyond at the same time. Just beyond the theatre is a small **bath complex**. There are some mosaics still in situ in the hall area, although the central mosaic of Neptune has been removed. In the circular caldarium are traces of painted plaster. Clear evidence of demolition/rebuild can be seen from the column drums inserted into a wall. After the amphitheatre, either follow the track uphill to discover the remains of **apsed temple** (crumbling half-tower) or cut across left (west) and scramble up to visit the **acropolis** area. Look out for the impressive vaulted cisterns. It is possible to make out an oratory, a small open space with a stubby column in the middle and twin semicircular niches. The layout of the colonnaded **forum** can also be seen. Dominating the highest point of the site is a rectangular, vaulted chamber some 4 m high, probably a **cistern** for feeding the nearby bath complex.

Beyond Lixus the road leads onto the **beach**, where there is a car park and camping areas. In summer, there are lifeguards and organized beach activities for the local children.

North Atlantic coast listings

For Sleeping and Eating price codes and other relevant information, see pages 12-20.

☺ Sleeping

Asilah *p109, map p108*
Asilah is a good place to rent a private house. Try the Spanish site www.elbaraka.net.
€€ Hotel Al Khaima, Km 2 Route de Tangier, BP 101, T039-417428. A large hotel with 113 rooms by the beach, 2 km outside town. Reasonable size rooms, restaurant, disco, bar, tennis courts and pool. Can be noisy though, and you don't get any of the style of Asilah.
€€ Hotel Azayla, 20 Av Ibn Rochd, T039-416717, h.azayla@menara.ma. A modern hotel just outside the médina, Azayla is decorated with art and black and white photos and spacious rooms have wicker

chairs, pine furniture, a/c and double glazing.
€€ Hotel Mansour, 49 Av Mohammed V, T039-917390, www.hotelmansour.fr.fm. Decorated with faded photographs of scantily clad ladies in a forest with swans, Hotel Mansour doesn't go for minimalistic good taste. However the bedrooms are simple and clean. Much better value out of season.
€€ Hotel Patio de la Luna, 12 Pl Zelaka, T039-416074, hotelpatiodelaluna@yahoo.es. Charming and whitewashed, the Patio de la Luna is Asilah's most attractive hotel. Spanish owned, it has blue shutters and a solar-powered water heater on the roof. There's a peaceful patio with candle lamps and views over the town from the little roof terrace. Comfortable and stylish rooms have good beds. Reservations essential in summer.

€€ Hotel Zelis, 10 Av Mansour Eddahabi, T039-417069. With 61 rooms (3rd floor ones are best) and a pool, Zelis is modern in a 1980s sort of way. The bright red carpets might make your eyes water but there are sea views and minibars to compensate. Exercise machines on the roof terrace facing the sea.

€ Dar Al Andalous, 30 Rue Banafsaj, T039-417840. If you can put up with the plastic plants and garish attempts at traditional Moroccan style, this is a clean and comfortable option along a street off the main square. Some rooms sleep 4.

€ Hotel Belle Vue, Rue Hassan Ben Tabit, T039-417747. Sometimes referred to as the 'Belle Vue Zilis', this is not to be confused with the Hotel Zelis. There's some damp and certainly no *belle vue*, but it's a good deal for the price all the same. Reasonably big rooms, decent shared showers, a sunny rooftop terrace.

€ Hotel Marhaba, 9 Rue Zallaka, T077-326841. Overlooking a green space not far from the médina, red brick Marhaba has turquoise shutters and adequate rooms, the best of which have balconies at the front. Avoid the darker rooms, which are poor value. Showers are 5dh and are not always hot.

€ Hotel Sahara, 9 Rue Tarfaya, T039-917185. With old tiled corridors and well tended plants, the Sahara is a model budget hotel. Simple clean rooms have art and a lamp and a bed and nothing more. Some lack windows but the whole hotel is absolutely spotless and it's very friendly too. All the rooms face onto a central sunny tiled courtyard and the 5dh shared showers are good. At this price you'll struggle to find better accommodation in all Morocco.

Camping

There are numerous camping sites just north of the town along the road to Asilah.
Camping As Sada, on the Tangier road, 300 m out of town, T039-917317. Overlooks the ocean and also has some chalet-type accommodation. Wash-block not great.
Camping International, site of 1 ha, 50 m to beach, showers, laundry, petrol 300 m, electricity for caravans.
Camping Atlas, 100 m to beach, snacks, showers, laundry, grocery, first aid, electricity for caravans.

Larache *p111, map p112*
Reserve in summer when the town is busy.
€€€ Dar Zuina, Dchar el Hommar, T071-273629 or T061-243809, www.darzuina.com. 7 km outside Asilah, Dar Zuina is a colourful, peaceful guest-house in the countryside. Attractive gardens, and some rooms have a private terrace.

€€ La Maison Haute, 6 Derb ben Thami, www.lamaisonhaute.com. Stylish and colourful, the Maison Haute is a guesthouse in a great spot in the médina, on the corner of Socco de Alcaiceria, just behind the Place de la Libération. There are 6 rooms and a suite, the best of which have good views, as does the roof terrace. Book in advance.

€€ Hotel Riad, Rue (or Calle or Zankat) Moulay Mohammed Ben Abdallah, signed from Av Mohamed V, T039-912626. The converted former residence of the Duchess of Guise has 24 rooms with big tiles, coloured glass and worn, loose old carpet. There's a restaurant but no bar and a small pool. The place has some vaguely stylish wrought-iron furniture, but it could do with sprucing up. In summer, karaoké in the garden may keep you awake.

€ Hotel Cervantes, 3 Rue Tarik Ibn Ziad, close to Pl de la Libération, T039-910874, ali621@caramail.com. Bright, spacious rooms with sea views and some character. Bathrooms are none too clean but it's friendly.

€ Hotel Essalam, 9 Av Hassan II, T039-916822. Clean, central and bright, nice reception, all new bathrooms and big roof terrace. Perhaps the best cheap option.

€ **Hotel España**, 6 Av Hassan II, T039-913195, hotelespana2@yahoo.fr. Once a grand place in an outpost of Spanish provincial life, it's now a little worn and the corridors are musty. Bathrooms are modern, tiled and clean, though, it's central and there are some views over the square or onto a colourful terrace with potted plants.

€ **Hostal Málaga**, Rue de Salé, T039-911868. 25 rooms, many of which are small and a little stale with tiny bathrooms. Larger rooms are lighter and some have balconies. Friendly.

€ **Pensión Amal**, 10 Rue Abdallah Ben Yassine, T039-912788. The closest to bus and grand taxi stations. 14 rooms, clean, quiet and better than the other cheapies.

❷ Eating

Asilah *p109, map p108*
Asilah has 2 main restaurant areas: near the old ramparts on Av Hassan II there are plenty of cheap places with seating areas under the walls, selling Moroccan food and pizzas. The more upmarket seafood restaurants are in Pl Zallaka and onto Av Moulay Al Hassan Ben Mehdi. In some of the more expensive restaurants, you will be shown a great dish of fresh fish to choose from. Your chosen fish is then weighed, and you are charged by the 100g. If this is the case, make sure you know how much you will be charged. In the cheaper restaurants, go for grilled rather than fried fish, as the oil is sometimes used far more than it should be.

††† **Al Kazaba**, T039-417012, A restaurant and salon de thé, Al Kasaba has a good reputation for seafood. It's smart, with white tablecloths and incongruous all-year tinsel. The menu includes French and Moroccan cuisine – if fish isn't your thing, try the brochettes.

††† **Casa Garcia**, Av Moulay Al Hassan Ben Mehdi, T039-417465. The most feted of Asilah's restaurants, Garcia's fills up quickly with well-off Europeans. There's nothing very Moroccan about it, but the food is good enough that at least one person regularly flies in from France for the day just to eat here. The decor, like the food, is fishy – crabs and lobsters suspended in nets. Turn up early or reserve, especially for the outdoor tables.

†† **La Place**, 7 Av Moulay Al Hassan Ben Mehdi, T039-417326. Simpler than most of its neigh- bours, has a couple of tables outside, tagines for 50dh as well as fish dishes by weight.

†† **Le Pont**, 24 Av Moulay Al Hassan Ben Mehdi, T067-987116. Straightforward Moroccan place, 4 plastic-covered tables facing the sea, serves seafood pastilla, couscous, tagines, as fish dishes, such as swordfish steak. An excellent place to try Asilah's seafood without any pretentions.

†† **Oceano Casa Pepe**, Pl Zallaka, T039-417395. Just outside the médina walls, popular Pepe's has tables outside and smart white jacketed waiters. Inside there are wooden beams and fake candle lamps. Good, varied seafood menu.

†† **Restaurant el Espigon**, Av Moulay Hassan, T039-417157. Famous for its paella, which must be ordered a day in advance. The roasted tomato and pepper salad is also recommended.

† **La Symphonie des Douceurs II**, 26 Pl Zellaka, T039-416633. Long thin café with 3-D art and some pastries. Ice cream in season.

† **Café al Madina**, just inside the médina. A good place to sit, with seats facing the square and walls. Coffee and pastries as well as snacks and Moroccan standards.

† For the best value eating, wander along the line of restaurants along Av Hassan II and let the waiters tempt you in to the Calairis, which does pizzas, or Rabie, Yalis or Ali. They're all of a similar ilk and have good value menus for 30dh.

Larache *p111, map p112*
†† **Restaurant Estrella del Mar**, 68 Calle Mohammed Zerktouni, T039-911052. The town's best restaurant is opposite the fish market and has a suitably fishy menu. It's

nicely decorated, with a carved ceiling, tablecloths and a wooden boat. Raciones downstairs, a bit smarter upstairs.

†† Restaurant Larache, 18 Av Moulay Mohammed Ben Abdallah, T039-913641. Tagines and fish – try the mixed fried seafood – in a simple place with a blackboard.

† Try the fish grills down by the port for cheap fresh-out-of-the-sea seafood.

† Restaurant Commercial, Pl de la Libération. Very cheap fish dishes served under the arches just to the right of the gate into the médina.

🏵 Festivals and events

Asilah p109, map p108
Aug The International Festival of Asilah is a cultural festival which has taken place in Asilah since 1978 and involves performers and artists from all over the world. Events throughout the town attract many spectators.

🚌 Transport

Asilah p109, map p108
The bus station is on Av de la Liberté, T039-987354. There are regular bus links with **Tangier, Ouezzane, Tetouan, Meknès,** **Rabat** and **Casablanca**. Grands taxis, particularly convenient for **Tangier**, leave from Pl Mohammed V. Asilah train station, T039- 987320, is a pleasant 30-min walk outside the town alongside the N1 to Tangier and can be reached by local bus or by either petit or grand taxi from Pl Mohammed V. There are 6 trains daily to **Tangier**, 4 daily to **Meknès**, **Fès** and **Oujda** and 2 daily to **Rabat** and **Casablanca**.

Larache p111, map p112
Town is easily reached by the N1 from Tangier or Rabat. The bus station is just off Av Hassan II. Buses from **Asilah** (1 hr), **Ksar el Kebir**, **Rabat** (3½ hrs) and **Meknès** (5½ hrs). There are grands taxis from **Rabat, Asilah** and **Tangier**.

🅾 Directory

Asilah p109, map p108
Banks Banque populaire, Pl Mohammed V, has ATMs. **Police** Av de la Liberté, T19 or T039-917089. **Post** PTT, Pl des Nations Unies. **Medical services** **Chemist**: Pharmacie Loukili, Av de la Liberté, T039-917278. **Hospital**: Av du 2 Mars, T039-917318.

Ceuta

Ceuta is an odd sort of place, an enclave of provincial Spain, an African equivalent of Great Britain's Gibraltar. However, unlike Gibraltar, Ceuta has not established itself as a minor tourist attraction. Instead, it gives the impression that it would like to be a Mediterranean Hong Kong: it has the right sort of location, between two continents, developed Europe and upcoming Africa. But the Gibraltar-Spain frontier was opened in 1985, and in many ways Ceuta has been sidelined into becoming a passenger transit port. The chaotic Ceuta-Fnideq frontier may well be your first or last point of contact with Morocco. ▸▸ *For listings, see pages 122-123.*

Ins and outs ▸▸ *Phone code: (+34) 956.*

Getting there
There are frequent ferries from Algeciras to Ceuta, and the journey is rather quicker than Algeciras to Tangier, though the advantage of Tangier is that you are at the start of the Moroccan rail network. It's best to arrive early in Ceuta, so you have plenty of time to clear the frontier and move on to Tetouan or Tangier. Coming from Morocco, the Fnideq-Ceuta frontier is reached most easily from Tetouan by grand taxi. The taxis leave Tetouan from opposite the main bus station, expect to pay around 25dh a place. There are also occasional buses from Tetouan to Fnideq. Note that on the frontier formalities can be slow. Passports have to be checked and stamped by Moroccan officials both ways. Vehicles have to be registered and papers, including insurance, registration and licence, checked. Cash can be exchanged on the Moroccan side of the frontier at the Banque populaire booth. Driving up to Ceuta from Tetouan you can take the direct route or take the scenic route via Martil, which takes around 45 mins. ▸▸ *See Transport, page 123, for further details.*

Getting around
Unless you intend to stay the night, you will need to get from port to Moroccan border at Fnideq, 3 km away. There is a bus from Ceuta city centre, leaving from Plaza de la Constitución. To get there, turn left as you leave the ferry terminal, and follow round along Paseo de las Palmeras (a 15-minute walk, maximum). You can spend both pesetas and dirhams in Ceuta in restaurants and shops. Like mainland Spain, the enclave has a long afternoon siesta with shops closed 1300-1600. Sunday is very much a day of rest.

Tourist information Patronata Municipal de Turismo ① *at the exit to the ferry port, Mon-Fri 0830-2030 , Sat ans Sun 1000-2000.* Helpful and has maps and leaflets. See also www.ceuta.es.

Background

Ceuta (Sebta in Arabic) is a Spanish enclave on the Moroccan coast, which since 1995 has had the status of 'autonomous town', putting it somewhere between the Spanish autonomous regions and the municipalities. Ceuta has an excellent strategic position on the Strait of Gibraltar and was occupied by the Carthaginians, Greeks and Romans. After being taken in the Arab conquest, the site was captured by the Portuguese in 1415 but on the union of Spain and Portugal was transferred to Spain in 1581, under whose control it has remained ever since as little more than a military prison. Its later fame arose from its importance as a supplying fortress for Spanish forces during a series of 19th-century sieges of the northern *presidios*. Fighting near Ceuta in 1859 nearly led to the total loss of the enclave. In 1860 a Spanish military force invaded Morocco from Ceuta. In the 20th century Spain once again became embroiled in a bloody war in northern Morocco in which it badly lost important battles at Anoual in 1921 and in the Chefchaouen-Tetouan campaign in late 1924. Ceuta ultimately survived this episode thanks largely to Abdelkarim's internal political difficulties and the improved Spanish generalship under Franco. And it was from Ceuta that the future *caudillo* launched his forces to impose his form of law and order on mainland Spain in 1936.

Ceuta, along with Melilla to the east, remain potential friction points between Morocco and Spain. Morocco regards both as occupied territory and in 2002 things came to a head when Moroccan soldiers occupied a tiny rocky islet, Isla Perejil, just northwest of Ceuta. Though the island was inhabited only by goats at the time, the action was called the first military invasion of Western European soil since the Second World War. Spain eventually reclaimed the island (though it's not entirely clear that anyone had actually taken enough notice of it before to know whether it was in fact part of Morocco or Spain) and relations between the two countries have since improved. Indeed, both would seem to have much more to lose by hostility than by a maintenance of the mutually advantageous status quo.

Sights

Ceuta harbour lies tucked into a bay on the north of the peninsula with the town largely packed onto a narrow isthmus lying between Monte Hacho (204 m) in the east and the Sierra Cimera hills adjacent to the frontier with Morocco in the west. The town is Spanish in character with a heavy military presence – armed forces occupy most of the larger and older buildings including the fortress areas. The shopping streets such as Paseo del Revellin and Calle Real concentrate heavily on duty-free luxury goods and electronic equipment. To the east of the town is a tree-covered hill, which is a pleasant place for a stroll. At the far eastern edge is an old Portuguese fort, or stop off at the Ermitada de San Antonio, a convent rebuilt in the 1960s and from where these is a good view of the town.

Plaza de Africa

A visit to Ceuta should probably start on **Plaza de Africa**, home to two large Catholic places of worship. The **Cathedral Museum** ① *south of Plaza de Africa, open afternoons only*, is situated in the side wall of the cathedral itself off Plaza de Africa and has ecclesiastical items in its collection including the highly decorated montage of the Virgen

Capitana. The Cathedral stands on the site of a pre-Muslim church and a mosque from the Arab period. The present building dates principally from the 17th century, though there were large-scale renovations in 1949-1958. The **Sanctuario de Nuestra Señora de África** (Church of Our Lady of Africa) dates from the 15th century with many later additions, the largest in the 18th century, and is also on the site of a former mosque. Long seen as important as a great Christian monument in Islamic North Africa, it has a spectacular baroque altarpiece. The **Palacio Municipal** (town hall) is an interesting modern building dating from 1926 and containing some fine panelling and frescoes by Bertucci. The centre of the Plaza de Africa is taken up with a large monument to those Spaniards who fell in the country's African wars (1859-60). Note the bronze reliefs of battle scenes by Susillo. The

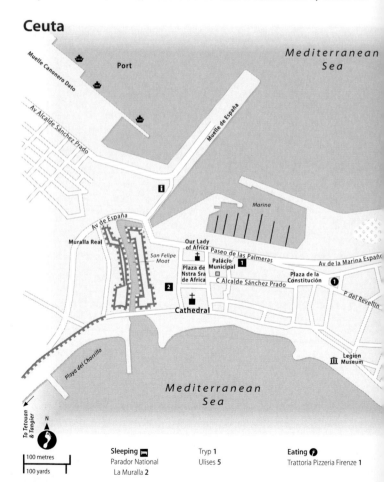

Ceuta

Sleeping 🛏
Parador National
La Muralla **2**

Tryp **1**
Ulises **5**

Eating 🍴
Trattoria Pizzeria Firenze **1**

Church of San Francisco stands in Plaza de los Reyes, which reputedly contains the bones of the Portuguese King Sebastian.

Museo de Ceuta (Archeology section)
ⓘ *30 Paseo del Revellin, Mon-Sat 1000-1400 and 1700-2000 (1000-1400 and 1900-2100 Jun-Sep), Sun 1000-1400, free.*

The Municipal Museum on Paseo del Revellin is well laid out and attractive. Rooms I and II have some fine Punic and Roman amphorae and display the activities of Ceuta and the sea including the salt-making pans on the ancient site of what is now the Parador and the Plaza de Africa. Room III has items relating to underwater archaeology with some well-preserved and decorated amphorae and pots, a corn-grinding wheel and a lead depth sounder. Other rooms (IV and V) display medieval crafts of Hispanic-Islamic origins. Rooms VII and VIII are given over to scenes, artefacts and written sources of the Spanish-Moroccan war (1859-1860).

Legion Museum
ⓘ *Avenida Dean Navarro Acuña 6, Mon-Sat 0900-1300, free.*

Celebrating the founding and activities of the Spanish special forces Legion force, there is a variety of armaments, uniforms and military memorabilia on display here.

City walls
Forming an impressive ring around the city, these Portuguese-built fortifications are at their best adjacent to the San Felipe moat and the Muralla Real. The exterior fortifications are also impressive – **Fort Desnarigado** and **Fortaleza del Hacho** (the latter, still occupied by the military, is closed to the public). Fortaleza del Hacho is probably Byzantine in origin but strengthened under the Ommayyad dynasty. It was reconstructed by the Portuguese and redeveloped by the Spanish in the 18th and 19th centuries. In the west of the town above the Ramparts Pedro La Mata are the impressive **Merinid Walls**, a 14th-century construction on earlier buildings. Of the original 2 km of walls, there now remains only a 500-m section, interesting nevertheless, including the old **Fès Gate**. Adjacent to Plaza de la Paz on

Paseo Marina are the ruins of the **Arab baths**, heavily reconstructed but accessible and a useful reminder of the high urban forms of the Arab period.

Museo de Ceuta (Fine Arts section)

ⓘ *Revellín de San Ignaciao courtyard, Mon-Sat 1000-1400 and 1700-2000 (Jun-Sep 1000-1400 and 1900-2100), Sun 1000-1400, free.*

Inside the city walls, the city museum's fine arts space is an excellent contemporary art space with white angular walls and some interesting temporary exhibitions of Spanish art.

Ceuta listings

For Sleeping and Eating price codes and other relevant information, see pages 12-20.

⊖ Sleeping

Ceuta *p118, map p120*

If you will arrive late in the day, make sure that you reserve your hotel room in advance.

€€€ Tryp, 3 Alcalde Sánchez Prados, T(+34) 956-511200, www.solmelia.com. A glass fronted exterior opens up into the huge white lobby of this contemporary hotel. 121 sleek rooms in muted tones have designer lighting, a/c, mini-bar and Wi-Fi, and there's an open-air pool with comfy chairs.

€€€ Parador National Hotel la Muralla, Pl Virgen de Africa 15, opposite the Cathedral, T(+34) 956-514940. Pan pipes playing in the lobby further underline the 1970s feel of this large, business-centred hotel. There's a pool, and plenty of modern facilities but they're not enough to make the place feel very inviting. May require a two-night stay in high season.

€€ Tryp, 3 Alcalde Sánchez Prados, T(+34) 956-511200, www.solmelia.com. A glass fronted exterior opens up into the huge white lobby of this contemporary hotel. 121 sleek rooms in muted tones have designer lighting, a/c, mini-bar and Wi-Fi, and there's an open-air pool with comfy chairs. **Hostal Plaza Ruiz**, 3 Pl Teniente Ruiz, T(+34) 956-516733, hostalesceuta@hotmail. com. One of Ceuta's more desirable small hotels, Plaza Ruiz has 17 a/c rooms with small bathrooms and pine furniture on a little square just off main street.

€€ Bohemia, Calle Cameons, T(+34) 956-510615. A central place with a degree of old style, Bohemia has good rooms, 3 of which have balconies. Shared bathrooms, plants, and lots of photos of Marilyn Monroe.

€€ Hostal Real, 1 Calle Real, T(+34) 956-511449, www.hostalreal.net. Bang in the centre of town, a good budget option, with clean if not overly bright rooms. Book ahead.

€€ Hotel Ulises, 5 Calle Camoens, T(+34) 956 514540, www.hotelulises.com. Once Ulises' lengthy refurbishment is finished in 2010 it will become the swishest hotel in Ceuta. Until then, work may disrupt the stylish feel of its 124 rooms. Rooms have dark wood furniture and floors. Black and white photos decorate the walls and there are flat screen TVs too. There's Wi-Fi on the first floor but the top floor rooms have the best views. Pool also.

⊘ Eating

Ceuta *p118, map p120*

❙❙ **Gran Muralla**, Pl de la Constitución, T(+34) 956-517625. A proper Chinese restaurant overlooking the square with views, a long Chinese menu and an interior genuine enough to make it seem like a Chinese enclave in a Spanish enclave.

❙❙ **La Marina**, 4 Alférez Bayton, T(+34) 956-514 007. Posh but friendly, Marina does paella and a wide range of other fish dishes. Popular.

❙❙ **Trattoria Pizzeria Firenze**, 3 Alférez Bayton, T(+34) 956-512088. Closed Mon night and Tues. Genuine Italian food – try the ravioli or tagliatelle with egg, spinach and porcini mushrooms or good pizzas.

₩ Ulises Café, next to the hotel of the same name. A chic and bijou place for a fine glass of wine or a bar snack.

₩ Café Central, 2 Millan Astray. Sophisticated café bar used by Ceuta's young professionals with low lighting and hanging glass lamps.

₩ El Quijote, 5 Pedro de Meneses. A small, friendly tapas bar on a pedestrian street.

₩ La Bodeguilla, Calle Millán Astray. Buzzing tapas bar with a good range of tostadas.

₩ La Jota, 6 Méndez Núñez, T(+34) 956-515365. Sandwiches, cakes, ice cream and hanging legs of ham.

The so-called 'fisherman's village' (actually a modern area where nobody seems to live) just to the east of the marina, has several restaurants. If they're open, try: **Riad Ahlam**, **La Peña** and **La Cantina**.

○ Shopping

Ceuta *p118, map p120*

There are numerous shops selling duty-free electronic goods, though nothing seems cheaper than a web search would turn up in Europe. Spirits and fuel are cheaper here than in Morocco, or Spain, come to that, given Ceuta's tax status. If you've been in Morocco for a while, you might appreciate the European high street shops, including a massive branch of Zara. For travellers heading on to Morocco, stock up on Spanish cheese and wine from the local supermarkets as well as excellent fresh seafood.

▲ Activities and tours

Ceuta *p118, map p120*

The marina, T(+34) 956-513753, has capacity for 300 vessels. The waters around here are said to have the most interesting diving in the Mediterranean. Check www.ceutabuceo.com.

Tour operators

Most of the agencies are on Muelle Cañonero Dato. Try **Viajes Dato**, Marina Club, T(+34) 956-509582 or **Viajes Flandria**, Calle de la Independencia 1, T(+34) 956-512074.

⊖ Transport

Ceuta *p118, map p120*
Air
Transportes Aereos del Sur, T902-404704, www.aena.es, have helicopter flights from Ceuta to **Jerez** and **Málaga**.

Car hire
Africa Car, through Flandria Travel Agents, Independencia 1, T(+34) 956-512 074.

Taxi
T(+34) 956-515 406. Between the frontier and Fnideq there are grand taxis, costing 5dh.

Bus
There are some long-distance Spanish buses, from the bus station on the south coast road in Ceuta, to **Casablanca**, **Al Hoceïma** and **Nador**. Tetouan is a better option for finding bus services. There are bus and grand taxi services between Fnideq and **Tetouan**, and between Fnideq and **Tangier**. On the Spanish side, buses take euros only, though you can usually persuade taxi drivers to take dirhams (€3, or around 35dh).

Boat
The **Algeciras-Ceuta** high-speed ferries are cheaper and quicker than those between Algeciras and Tangier, with passengers from 450dh and cars from 1500dh, taking 80 mins. There are normally 20 services a day, generally with refreshments available. Tickets can be bought in the port building, online (www.trasmediterranea.es or www.euroferrys.com) or from the numerous travel agents around the town centre.

❶ Directory

Ceuta *p118, map p120*
Banks Banco de España, Pl de España. Banco Popular Español, 1 Paseo del Revellin.

Tetouan

Set between the Rif and the Mediterranean Sea, Tetouan has a dramatic beauty, the white buildings of the médina contrasting with the backdrop of the mountains. There's some impressive colonial architecture in the Spanish town and the médina has been made a UNESCO Heritage Site. The city is an interesting place to explore, albeit with more noise and hassle than Chefchaouen to the south. Tetouan's main sites can be covered in a rather rushed half day; a full day would give you time to explore the city pretty thoroughly. Between Ceuta and Tetouan, and also further round the coast, there are a number of resorts – some fashionable, others with a more downbeat appeal – which can be visited en route or as an excursion from the city. ›› *For listings, see pages 129-131.*

Ins and outs

Getting there

Tetouan is easily visited as a day trip from Tangier, if you don't want to stop over. There are buses in from Chefchaouen, Fès, Meknès, Ouezzane and of course Tangier, operated by both the CTM and private companies. There is also a bus from Casablanca (seven hours). Chefchaouen to Tetouan takes around one hour, Tangier to Tetouan 1½ hours. There is also a daily bus from Al Hoceïma (five hours). Coming from Ceuta, it's best to get a grand taxi from the frontier.

Tetouan is about 70 minutes from Tangier through beautiful hilly country. Note that there are police checkpoints at all major junctions, so keep your speed down. Watch out too for hair-brained overtaking on the seemingly fast, winding sections of the road. On the last stretch into Tetouan, the road becomes triple lane as it goes up and over a high ridge. The middle lane is for overtaking, for Tetouan-bound traffic on the northwest side, for Tangier-bound traffic on the southeast side. You run into Tetouan through its sprawling suburbs, past a turn-off right onto the main route for Chefchaouen and Fès.
›› *See Transport, page 131, for further details.*

Getting around

Taxis from Tangier and Tetouan arrive in the new town, close to the bus station, about 10 minutes' walk from the médina. (From the bus station, to get to the médina, head up Rue Sidi Mandri and turn third right down Avenue Mohammed V, which will bring you to Place Hassan II.) In summer, if you want to go to Martil or Cabo Negro, buses go from Avenue Massira, near the old train station, instead of from the main bus station. To get there, take Avenue Hassan II, to the right of the main bus station, which meets Avenue Massira after the Ensemble Artisanal on the right.

Note When visiting Tetouan watch out for the various seedy characters and con artists with a keen eye for tired backpackers stumbling off a late bus from Fès. If you are arriving by bus, you are at your most vulnerable at the main bus station. Pay attention to your belongings and avoid having any dealings with faux guides. The tourist office (below) can arrange for an official guide, should you want one, for 120dh for a half day.

Tourist information Office du Tourisme (ONMT) ① *30 Rue Mohammed V, T039-961915, Mon-Fri 0830-1630.*

Background

Tetouan was founded in the third century BC as Tamuda, but was destroyed by the Romans in AD 42. The Merinid ruler Sultan Abou Thabit built a kasbah at Tetouan in 1307. Sacked by Henry III of Castille in 1399 to disperse the corsairs based there, Tetouan was neglected until it was taken over by Muslims expelled from Granada in 1484. They were to bring with them the distinctive forms and traditions of Andalucían Islamic architecture, still observable in the médinas of Granada and Cordoba. Many of the Andalucíans worked as corsairs, continuing the tradition. A Jewish community was established here in the 17th century which gave the impetus to open up trade with Europe. Trade with the West continued to boom in the 18th century during the reign of Moulay Ismaïl. In 1913 Tetouan was chosen as the capital of the Spanish Protectorate over northern Morocco. The Spanish created the new town, which has remained an important regional centre in independent Morocco.

Sights

Ville nouvelle
Place Hassan II, the focal point of the city and a former market, is the best place for a stroll or a sit in a café terrace of an evening. It is dominated by the **Royal Palace**, with its gleaming white walls and green tiled roof. Dating from the 17th-century it was completely transformed under Hassan II. Looking onto the square is the **Pasha Mosque** with its distinctive green door and green and brown tiled minaret. **Bab er Rouah** has also had a facelift. The other major focus point in the ville nouvelle is Place Moulay el Mehdi, along Boulevard Mohammed V from Place Hassan II. Here there is an impressive golden-yellow cathedral and a large fountain in the middle. **Instituto Cervantes** ① *3 Calle Mohamed Torres, T039-967056, tetuan. cervantes.es,* has good exhibitions and documentaries.

Médina
Bab er Rouah, in the corner of Place Hassan II, leads into the médina where Andalucían influence is still apparent in the whitewashed walls and delicate wrought- iron decorations on the balconies. A typically confusing maze of streets and souks, it is well worth exploring, although perhaps with the assistance of an official guide. In the souks look out for artefacts in Tetouan's favoured red colour. Rue Terrafin is a good route through the médina, and leads into Rue Torres and Rue Sidi el Yousti, and out at Bab el Okla. North of Rue Sidi el Yousti is an area with some of the larger and more impressive houses.

Souks **Souk el Hout**, with pottery, meat and fish is to the left of Rue Terrafin behind the palace. Here there is a delightful leafy square, pleasant surroundings for admiring the wares. Behind the souk is a small 15th-century fortress, the **Alcazaba**, now taken over by a cooperative. Take the left hand of the two north-bound lanes from the Souk el Hout and on the right is **Guersa el Kebir**, a textile souk selling the striped, woven blankets worn by Rifi women. The red, white and blue of the fabric is particularly striking and it's sold by women

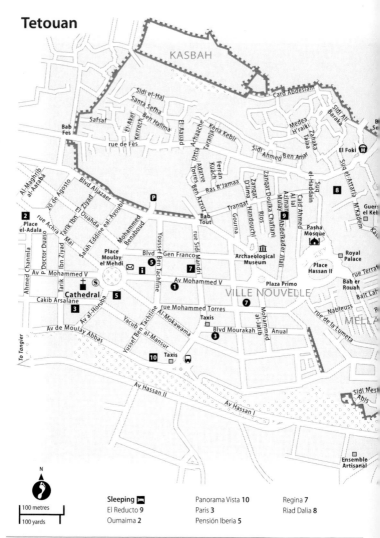

Tetouan

KASBAH

Sidi el-Hal
Santa Sefha
Safsaf   El-Akel   Ben Halima
Kerretch
Bab   rue de Fès   El-Aujad
Fes

Card Abdeslam

Sidi Ali
Baraka

Medea   Zahaba
H'raiki   Talaa
Kena Kebir
Sidi Ahmed Ben Amar   El Foki

Archouin   Tarianja
Pittu   Adarve Torres ben Azzuz
Ferran   Ras R'Jamaa
Kuach
Zangat Douka Chafani   Azimati   Muluy Abdelkader Jilali   Caid Ahmed   Suq el-Haddadin

Suq el-Attaria
M'Kaden

Al-Maghrib
al-Araba   Blvd Aljazaer
20 de Agosto
rue Achra   El Ouahda   Salah Eddine eal-Ayoubi
Place   Tarik Ibn Ziyad   Mohammed
el-Adala   Tarik Ibn Ziyad   Benaboud
P   Bab Tout
Tarangat
Dlima Handouchi
Gourna   Rios

Guersa
el Keb

Ahmed Chanmla
Av P. Doctor Duaso
Place   Blvd   Gen Franco
Moulay   Youssef Ben Tachfine
el Mehdi   Av Mohammed V   Archaeological   Pasha
Museum   Mosque   Royal
Palace
Av Mohammed V   Place
Hassan II
Cathedral   Plaza Primo
Cakib Arsalane   VILLE NOUVELLE   Bab er   rue Terra
Rouah
Av al-Honba   rue Mohammed Torres   Bait Lah
Taxis   Nableuss
Av de Moulay Abbas   Yacub Ben Tachtine   Al-Mokawama   MELLA
Youssef Ben al-Mansur   Blvd Mourakah   Anual   rue de la Lumeta
Mohammed al-Jatib
To Tangier   Taxis
Av Hassan II
Av Hassan I

Sidi Mes
Abis

Ensemble
Artisanal

N
100 metres
100 yards

Sleeping 🛏
El Reducto **9**
Oumaima **2**
Panorama Vista **10**
Paris **3**
Pensión Iberia **5**
Regina **7**
Riad Dalia **8**

dressed in the same colours. **El Foki** market can be found by following your nose – the smell of the traditional, flat, round loaves is impossible to miss. Look out too for the **L'Usaa Square**, with its white houses around a mosaic fountain and a rose garden.

Further on from this souk, leading up to Bab Sebta, are a number of specialist craft souks and shops. Running between Bab Sebta and Bab Fès is **Rue de Fès**, a more general commercial area, although with a number of souks around. From Bab Sebta the road out of the city passes through a large cemetery. Above the médina is the crumbling **kasbah** (closed to visitors), and nearby a vantage point providing stunning views over the city.

Jewish quarter On Place Hassan II, the first alleyway south of Bab er Rouah leads onto the main street of the mellah, the 19th-century Jewish quarter, where there are a number of abandoned synagogues. The original Jewish population has all but disappeared. The earliest mellah was near the Grand Mosque.

Archaeological Museum ① *Blvd Aljazaer, near Pl Hassan II, T039-967103. Mon-Fri 0830-1630. 10dh.* Built in 1943, this museum contains a small archaeological collection from the prehistoric and pre-Islamic sites of the northern region of Morocco, plus some pieces from the once-Spanish Saharan provinces and a large library. Of most interest, however, are the Roman statues and mosaics found at ancient Lixus near Larache. The most notable mosaic portrays the Three Graces of Roman mythology – there's been some modern conservation to fill in the gaps, but it's sensitively done. Other rooms display prehistoric tools, bronzes and pottery. Of note here is the Sumerian ex-voto statuette found close to Asilah. Most of the small figures date from the first century AD. Other highlights include a scale model of the stone circle of Mzoura (see page 110), 15th-century Portugese tiles and a Latin inscription from Tamuda telling of a Roman victory over the Berbers.

Eating 🍴
La Restinga **1**
Pâtisserie Rahmouni **5**
Pizzeria Roma **7**
Sandwich Ali Baba **3**

Musée d'Art Marocain/Musée Ethnographique ⓘ *T039-970505. Mon-Fri 0830-1200 and 1430-1730, Sat 0830-1200.* Housed in Bab el Okla and renovated in 2002, this small museum is definitely worth a visit. There are samples of local textiles and dress, weapons and musical instruments, plus a small Andalucían garden at the back. There is also a display of traditional tiles. Note that the technique for making tiles in Tetouan was different from the more mainstream Moroccan or Fassi *zellige* technique. The latter is a mosaic technique involving the assembling of thousands of tiny coloured ceramic pieces. The artisans of Tetouan produced tiles imitating the *zellige* mosaics using the *cuerda seca* ('dry cord') technique, by which the different coloured glazes were separated by a pattern of geometric lines.

École de Métiers Just outside the médina, across the road from Bab el Okla, is the École de Métiers (craft school), built by the Spanish. Here craftsmen and students work on tiles, leatherwork, carpentry and pottery. The school, generally closed for holidays in August, may be open to visitors.

Tamuda
The remains of ancient Tamuda lie to the south of the N2 road running west out of Tetouan. It was founded in the third-second centuries BC. Later, during the Roman period, in the third century AD, the original settlement disappeared under a Roman camp. So far only remains of dwellings have been excavated, no public buildings or religious buildings. Finds from Tamuda are in the Archaeological Museum in Tetouan.

Beach resorts around Tetouan

Restinga Smir
From Fnideq to Tetouan, the N13 passes through a flat strip of beaches and marshes, and a number of tourist developments. Restinga Smir, 22 km from Tetouan, has a long beach and a correspondingly long line of holiday complexes, hotels, bars, restaurants, bungalows and camping areas. Until recently it was still a small fishing village frequented only by a small number of local visitors. Now it enjoys an international reputation. There is, however, sufficient space on the vast beaches for the activities on offer which include horse riding, mini-golf, tennis, underwater fishing and windsurfing. There's also the small marina/pleasure port of Marina Smir.

Mdiq
After Restinga Smir the road passes through Kabila, another beach and marina, to Mdiq, a small fishing port with some traditional boat construction. Mdiq shares the same coastline (and clientele) as Cabo Negro (below) and there is a sense of competition between the two. Mdiq is a well-established resort offering a range of modern hotels and restaurants (mainly fish of course), nightclubs, swimming pools and the usual selection of watersports on the beach. This is certainly a popular family resort which is spreading to the north.

Cabo Negro
After Mdiq turn for Cabo Negro (also known as Taifor or Ras Tarf) which is 3.5 km off the N13. Here the beach is more rugged with the low hills which overlook the sea dotted with

small houses. This is a slightly less commercialized region, though the number of discos and nightclubs is growing. Riding is very popular here with horses for hire by the hour and day. The roads through the town follow the contours and rise at various levels up the hill.

Martil

Martil, Tetouan's former port, and one-time pirate base, stands at the mouth of the Oued Martil. It is now another popular resort, with over 10 km of sandy beach. Once it was the resort of people from Tetouan who established holiday homes here on the coast but now Martil welcomes visitors from far afield. Buses from Tetouan to Martil, Cabo Negro and Mdiq leave from Avenue Massira, near the old railway station.

Oued Laou and the coastal road south of Tetouan

Oued Laou is 44 km southeast of Tetouan, along the spectacular coastal road, the S608. It is a relaxed fishing village with an excellent beach but only basic facilities. The road continues along the coast through the villages of Targa, Steha, Bou Hamed, and Dar M'Ter. Possibly a more convenient place to stop is the fishing village, El Jebha (souk Tuesday). It is served by buses from Tetouan and Chefchaouen. A tortuous mountain road, the 8500, takes the intrepid traveller to meet the N2 west of Ketama.

Tetouan listings

For Sleeping and Eating price codes and other relevant information, see pages 12-20.

🛏 Sleeping

Tetouan *p124, map p126*
Budget hotels in and near the médina and Pl Hassan II, are often primitive and unhygienic.
€€€ El Reducto, Zanqat Zawya 38, T039-968120, www.riadtetouan.com. This little riad, well signposted just off the Plaza at the end of Mohammed V, used to belong to the Prime Minister under the Spanish protectorate and has been given a thorough overhaul by its current Spanish owner, who may be able to get you a good guide to the médina. Set around a rectangular courtyard, the 4 rooms range from the fairly small to one huge space with spectacular carved wood and an enormous bath. All have luxurious fabrics, drapes and antique tiles. Price includes breakfast. Half-board also available.
€€ Hotel Chams, Av Abdelkhalak Torres, 2.5 km east towards Martil, T039-990901. 76 rooms, 4 suites, all with bath and TV. There's a small pool, a restaurant and a bar.

Comfortable, if rather old fashioned rooms.
€€ Panorama Vista, Av My el Abbas, T039-964970. Far and away Tetouan's best mid-range option, the aptly (and tautologically) named Panorama Vista has enormous views across the valley from the Rif mountains. Rooms are modern and comfortable with TVs and good bathrooms. There's a popular café downstairs for breakfast too.
€€ Riad Dalia, 25 Rue Ouessaa, Souika, T039- 964318, www.riad-dalia.com. At the heart of the médina (call when you arrive and they'll come and meet you), the Dalia offers a Moroccan version of the riad experience at bargain prices. The cheapest rooms are small and dark, but still atmospheric, and there are stunning 360-degree views from the roof terrace. Popular with students and young Spaniards who canoodle in dark corners and smoke the hookah pipes. The building was once the house of the Dutch Consul, whose bedroom was in what is now the café on the top floor. The other guest rooms were apparently used by his several wives.
€ Hotel Oumaima, Av 10 Mai, T039-963473.

Pale yellow rooms with decent wooden beds and ok bathrooms, though you may want to use your own towel. Busy and noisy café downstairs.

€ Hotel Regina, 8 Rue Sidi Mandri, T039-962113. The 1970s decor may give you a headache and the reception is not overly friendly, but the formica and wrinkled Alpine scenes on the walls have a certain retro style. Best rooms have balconies overlooking street.

€ Paris Hotel, 11 Rue Cakib Arsalane, T039-966750. Friendly but not especially competent staff, rather small rooms. Parking.

€ Pensión Iberia, 3rd floor, above the BMCE, Pl Moulay el Mehdi, T039-963676. Small and cheap with occasional hot water. You may not get any French or Spanish out of the staff, but it's very friendly and best rooms have views over the square. No lift.

Camping

There are a number of campsites at the resorts along the coast (see below).

Beach resorts around Tetouan *p128*
Restinga Smir

€€ Hotel Karabo, T039-977070. 117 rooms, bar, restaurant, pool, tennis and disco. There are many good campsites, including **Al Fraia** and **Camping Andalus**.

Mdiq

€€€ Hotel Golden Beach, T039-975077. 87 rooms, on beachside opposite bus station.

€€€ Kabila Hotel, T039-975013. 96 rooms and a campsite.

Cabo Negro

€€ Hotel Petit Merou, T039-978115/6. 22 rooms, restaurant, bar, disco.

Camping Ch'bar, Martil Rd.

Martil

€€ Hacienda, T039-68 86 68, www.hacienda martil.com. A good 3-star with modern rooms and a pool.

€ Hotel Nuzha, Rue Miramar.

Camping Martil, by the river, or **Camping Oued La Malah**, signed further out of town.

Camping Tetouan, site of 6 ha, beach only 200 m, bar/snacks, restaurant, shop, showers, laundry, electricity for caravans, petrol at 200 m.

Municipal Camping at Martil Beach, T039-979435, site of 3 ha, beach, showers, laundry, electricity for caravans, petrol at 600 m.

Oued Laou

EE **Hotel-Restaurant Oued Laou**, T039-670854; also a campsite with a couple of chalets.

Eating

Tetouan *p124, map p126*

₮₮ El Reducto, Zanqat Zawya 38, T039-968120. In a great setting (see Sleeping, above), El Reducto does very reasonable food, mainly traditional Moroccan, but with a few Spanish touches, such as a decent gazpacho. The quality of the food doesn't quite match that of the rarefied surroundings but there's some good wine.

₮₮ La Restinga, 21 Rue Mohammed V, T039-963576. On the main street, this is a traditional place offering well-priced Moroccan food with good tagines. The restaurant has an alcohol licence.

₮ Pâtisserie Rahmouni, 10 Rue Youssef Ben Tachfine, T039-702975. Whether you like your pastries creamy, nutty or flaky you'll find an enormous selection here. There's a good savoury counter at the back and they serve excellent coffee too.

₮ Pizzeria Roma, Rue Mohammed Torres. Decent pizzas with generous quantities of cheese. It's modern rather than atmospheric – entertainment comes courtesy of rock music and a TV – but a good spot for a quick lunch.

₮ Sandwich Ali Baba, Rue Mourakah Anual, a popular place for cheap local food. Also try the places around Rue Luneta and Bab er Rouah.

⊖ Transport

Tetouan *p124, map p126*

Bus

The bus station, at the corner of Av Hassan I and Rue Sidi Mandri, T039-966263, has both **CTM** and private line services to most major destinations. Services to **Fnideq** (for Ceuta, 30 mins), **Chefchaouen** (1 hr), **Tangier** (1 hr), **Meknès** (8 hrs) and **Fès** (6 hrs). **Supratours** also operates a coach service to link up with the rail network at **Tnine Sidi Lyamani**. Through tickets can be bought from the office on Av 10 Mai (T039-967579), where 2 coaches depart each day. Buses to **Martil**, **Cabo Negro** and **Mdiq** leave from near the old railway station on Av Massira, those for **Oued Laou** from the main bus station.

Car hire

Amin Car, Av Mohammed V, T039-964407.
Zeite, Yacoub el Mansour.

Taxi

Grands taxis to **Tangier**, **Fnideq** (15dh, for Ceuta), **Chefchaouen** (30dh), the beaches and other places, leave from Blvd Maarakah Annoual or nearby.

⊖ Directory

Tetouan *p124, map p126*
Banks Banque Marocaine, Pl Moulay el Mehdi. **BMCE**, 11 Av Mohammed Ibn Aboud (Mon-Fri 0800-2000, Sat-Sun 0900-1300, 1500-2000). **BMCI**, 18 Rue Sidi el Mandri, T039-963090. **Post** Pl Moulay el Mehdi, T039-966798. **Medical services Chemist**: 24-hr, Rue al Wahda, T039-966777. **Useful addresses Police**: Blvd General Franco, T19.

Chefchaouen, the Rif and Al Hoceïma

East of Tangier and Ceuta, along Morocco's northern coast, the Rif mountains rise steeply out of the Mediterranean, making access less easy and meaning that this is one of the country's less visited areas, despite its closeness to Europe. Chefchaouen is an exception to this rule – a popular traveller hangout, with good reason, it epitomizes the area's easy-going charms, not always disconnected with the region's kif (marijuana) production. ›› *For listings, see pages 139-143.*

Chefchaouen ›› *For listings, see pages 139-143.*

The blue- and whitewashed town of Chefchaouen, sometimes called Chaouen, and even spelt Xaouen (the Spanish version), is an exceptionally photogenic Andalucían town in the Rif, 60 km south of Tetouan, set above the Oued Laou valley and just below the twin peaks of the Jbel ech Chefchaouen, the 'Horned Mountain'. The town itself could be explored in a day, but with a room in the right hotel, you might want to stay to relax in one of its many cafés or explore the surrounding countryside. At 600 m up in the hills, it makes a good centre for walking and many who come for a quick visit end up staying much longer. The town also has many sanctuaries for pilgrims and each year thousands of visitors are attracted to pay homage to the memory of Sidi Ben Alil, Sidi Abdallah Habti and Sidi el Hadj Cherif.

Ins and outs

Getting there By bus and grand taxi, Chefchaouen is within easy travelling distance of Tetouan (one hour), Ouezzane (1¼ hours) and Tangier (two hours). The journeys from Meknès (five hours) and Fès (seven hours) will require early morning starts. Driving your own car, you might take the N13/N2 which runs close to Chefchaouen from Ouezzane to the south to Tetouan. Note that as Chefchaouen is midway between central Moroccan towns and Tangier/Tetouan, buses often arrive full. ›› *See Transport, page 143, for further details.*

Getting around Chefchaouen's bus station is a 20-minute walk out of the town centre, or a short petit taxi journey. Coming in by grand taxi, you arrive close to the old town on Avenue Allal Ben Abdallah. Once you're in the old town, everything is accessible on foot.

Tourist information Chaouen Rural ① *Rue Machichi, T039-987267, www.chaouen rural.org, daily 0900-1900.* A Spanish-funded organization working with local communities and cooperatives, Chaouen Rural organize trips into the countryside around Chefchaouen and can also provide information on the town itself.

Note The selling of kif is big business here, the main production regions being to the east. Suitably persistent refusal should rid you of unwanted attentions, though these are almost always of the friendly-but-stoned variety, rather than aggressive.

Background

Set in the Djeballa region, Chefchaouen was founded in 1471 by Cherif Moulay Ali Ben Rachid, a follower of Moulay Abd es Salam Ben Mchich, the patron saint of the area, in order to halt the southwards expansion of the Spanish and Portuguese. The city's population was later supplemented by Muslims and Jews expelled from Spain, particularly from Granada, and for a time the rulers of Chefchaouen controlled much of northern Morocco. The town also grew in importance as a pilgrimage centre.

From 1576 Chefchaouen was in conflict with, and isolated from, the surrounding area, the gates being locked each night. Prior to 1920 only three Christians had braved its forbidding walls: the Vicomte de Foucauld disguised as a rabbi in 1883; Walter Harris, *Times* correspondent and author of *Morocco That Was*, in 1889; and the American William Summers, poisoned in Chefchaouen in 1892. They found Jews still speaking 15th-century Andalucían Spanish. In 1920 the town was taken over by the Spanish as part of their protectorate. They were thrown out from 1924 to 1926, by Abd el Karim's Rif resistance movement but returned to stay until Independence in 1956.

Chefchaouen

N
200 metres
200 yards

Sleeping 🛏
Andaluz 1
Mouritania 7
Parador 9
Pensión Ibn Batouta 5

Pensión La Castellana 4
Rif 10
Salam 11
Youth Hostel
& Camping 13

Modern Chefchaouen has extended across the hillsides, and the old town is now ringed by a suburb of the usual three-storey family apartment buildings. Though it is now well established on tourist itineraries, both mainstream and backpacker, Chefchaouen manages to retain a village feel. Here you may have your first sighting of the distinctive garments of the women of the Rif, the red and white striped *fouta* or overskirt and the large conical straw hat with woollen bobbles.

Sights
There are few major sites. The centre is Place Mohammed V, with its small Andalucían garden. Avenue Hassan II leads to Bab el Aïn and the médina. The market is down some steps from Avenue Hassan II, on Avenue Al Khattabi. Normally a food market, there is a local souk on Monday and Thursday.

Médina
The médina of Chefchaouen is an exceptionally photogenic place and rewarding to explore. Sufficiently small not to get lost, it has intricate Andalucían architecture, arches, arcades and porches, white- or blue-washed houses with ochre-tiled roofs and clean, quiet cobbled streets. In the maze of these narrow streets you run into water points, small open squares with shops and the solid ramparts of the kasbah. If driving, park the car in Place el Makhzen and explore the rest on foot. Approaching the médina on foot, enter by Bab el Aïn. From Bab el Aïn a small road leads through to Place Outa el Hammam. This is the main square, lively at night, and surrounded by a number of stalls and café-restaurants, popular with kif smokers.

The square is dominated by the terracotta coloured 15th-century kasbah, now the **Musée de Chefchaouen** ① *T039-986761, 0900-1300 and 1500-1830, closed Tue, 0900-1700 in Ramadan, 10dh*. As a prison it housed the Rifi leader Abd al Karim from 1926 and you can visit the suitably dark and forbidding dungeon. The museum itself is not that special – it has an exhibition of local costumes, some with very delicate embroidery, tools, musical instruments, pottery, weapons and a collection of decorated wooden caskets. More interesting is the building itself, and you can climb to the top of the tower for a good view of the town from the roof. There is also a peaceful Andalucían style courtyard garden, filled with flowers and birds.

The beautiful **Grand Mosque**, with its octagonal minaret, beside the kasbah, dates from the 15th century, but was restored in the 17th and 18th. Next door is a 16th-century medersa, unfortunately closed. Opposite the Restaurant Kasbah, at No 34, is an old caravanserai. Further on, **Place el Makhzen**, the second square, has stalls along the top side, the Ensemble Artisanal at the end.

Hillwalking
Chefchaouen has some good hillwalking, with spectacular scenery and plentiful animal and birdlife. Don't be too surprised, however, if you experience suspicious questioning from the military involved in cracking down on kif cultivation, and be prepared for a long and strenuous day. Taking a guide (could set you back around 100dh) is worth considering. Look out for the natural spring **Ras el Maa** 3 km out of town in the direction of Jbel Tisouka (2122 m). You are within striking distance of the **Parc Naturel de Talassemtane**, still basically undiscovered by tourists. **El Malha**, **Beni Ahmed** and other

isolated villages in this park are reached by landrover taxi from Bab Taza, 25 km to the southeast of Chefchaouen on the N2 road to Ketama (Issaguen).

Northern Rif ↠ *For listings, see page 141.*

The N2, the 'route of the crests' from Chefchaouen to Al Hoceïma, is one of Morocco's most dramatic journeys, a road running through a succession of small villages with stunning views over the remote valleys and towards the snow-capped Rif Mountains. Care must be taken on this narrow, hill-top road which may be closed by snow in winter.

Ketama
Ketama (officially called Issaguen, but referred to by just about everyone as Ketama, confusingly also the name of the area) has long had a sulphurous reputation for being Morocco's capital of cannabis, a reputation not entirely undeserved. Although much money is made from kif, it doesn't really seem to have found its way into this particular town, although there is, as everywhere in Morocco, some new building. Ketama could perhaps become a centre for summer hillwalking, being at the heart of a region where the mountains are covered in cedar trees, but for the moment there is little infrastructure, and few visitors stop here. The town can sometimes be snowbound in winter. The main point of interest in the area is the nearby Jbel Tidghine, the highest mountain in the Rif at 2448 m.

If you settle for a couple of minutes in a café in Ketama, someone is certain to approach you with an offer of cannabis. But the Gendarmerie royale are watching, so avoid making any purchases.

Excursion up Jbel Tidghine (Tidiquin)
For Jbel Tidghine, you need to head for the village of Azila, about 5 km from Ketama. If driving, take the road south out of Ketama and turn left at the new, low angular building. Alternatively take a local taxi from outside the Hotel Saâda. The houses of Azila are scattered around a valley below Jbel Tidghine. Follow the road through to the open 'football field' where the odd taxi parks up, or before this, turn off right by some trees on a dirt track to come out just above the mosque. Hopefully, a local kid will volunteer to show you the way across the valley. You will dip down through the village, over a rough plank bridge under the walnut trees. Then passing some quite large, concrete houses, you reach the bracken and first cedars of Tidghine's lower slopes. For the climb, there are two options: either wind slowly up the old forestry department piste, or cut straight up to intersect with the forestry track further up – a good option if with a local. It is said that strong 4WDs can get to within 30 minutes of the summit. Climbing time should be about 2¼ hours, the descent 1¾ hours. Remember to bring a water bottle – there is a spring where you can refill it.

The forest is truly beautiful, with butterflies in late summer, but it's under threat from locals in need of more sources of income than livestock and the barely profitable cannabis cultivation. To bring the great trees down, the practice is to light the needles under the trees in summer. The resinous trunks burn easily, weakening the whole tree, which is then easy to fell in winter when the forestry wardens are less likely to make tours of inspection.

The last stretch up the mountain is shaley scree, quite easy to deal with but slow going. At the top, the views are magnificent. There are two, stone-built, corrugated-iron roofed huts where you could stay the night if you have a warm sleeping bag.

Route de l'Unité

The R505 runs southwards from Ketama (Issaguen) to Taounate, Aïn Aicha and Fès with views of deep valleys and forested slopes. This road, the Route de l'Unité, was built just after Independence by voluntary labour battalions, to link the Spanish Protectorate of the north with the former French areas. The whole region is untouched by tourism, despite its cedar woods and mountainous terrain. If driving in this region in summer, note that car accidents are frequent. Returning migrant workers out to impress in powerful cars may fail to appreciate the dangers of the winding roads.

Ouezzane and the Southern Rif ▸ For listings, page 139.

Ouezzane is now a good sized town, rumoured to be the centre of cannabis-resin trading since the clean-up in Tangier in the late 1990s. It is also a centre for the production of olive oil and, because of its Thursday souk, is a draw for local farmers and tradesmen. For visitors, there is little to see, though perched on the north-facing slopes of Jbel Ben Hellal, it has a dramatic hillside location. A track from the town (3 km) leads up to the peak (609 m) and gives a splendid view across towards the Rif. Just 9 km north of the town is Azjem, burial place of an important Rabbi, Amram Ben Djouane, who came from Andalucía in the 18th century. Here again are impressive views of the rugged Rif Mountains and the verdant valleys between.

Ins and outs

Getting there Ouezzane lies 60 km (1¼ hours) from Chefchaouen down the N13/N2 road (look out for the Pont de Loukkos, which used to mark the border between the two Protectorates). There are grands taxis from Chefchaouen and Souk el Arba, as well as buses from Fès (five hours), Meknès (four hours) and Chefchaouen.

Getting around The bus and taxi terminals are close to Place de l'Indépendance, with budget hotels close by. Note that travelling on from Ouezzane can be awkward by bus, as a lot of buses are through services, which arrive full.

Background

Ouezzane, today an important regional centre with a population of 41,000, was founded in 1727 by Moulay Abdallah Cherif founder of the Tabiya Islamic order. This brotherhood achieved great national prominence from the 18th century, when the zaouïa in Ouezzane became the focus of extensive pilgrimage activity. Ouezzane had close links with the sultan's court, which was often dependent on the zaouïa and its followers for support.

A mid-19th-century cherif of Ouezzane married an Englishwoman, Emily Keane, in 1877 in an Anglican service – they had met at the house of the American consul where Keane was governess – although she later separated from him to live out her dotage in Tangier, where she is now buried in the Anglican Church (see page 99).

Sights

Ouezzane's **médina** has some of the most interesting architecture in the Rif, with the picturesque tiled-roof houses along winding cobbled streets. The focus of the town is the 18th-century **zaouïa**, on Rue de la Zaouïa, a distinctive green-tiled building with an octagonal minaret. Non-Muslims should not approach too close. Nearby are old lodgings for the pilgrims and the decaying cherifian palace.

Place de l'Indépendance, the centre of the médina, is busiest during the town souk on Thursday. To get to the craft souks, centred around **Place Bir Inzarane**, follow Rue Abdallah Ibn Lamlih up from Place de l'Indépendance. Ouezzane is known for woollen carpets woven in the weavers' souk at the top of the town. The blacksmiths' souk is along Rue Haddadine. There is a **Centre Artisanal** ① *Place de l'Indépendance, 0800-1900*, and another on Avenue Hassan II.

Al Hoceïma ⤵ *For listings, page 141-143.*

Al Hoceïma has one of the most beautiful natural sites on the Moroccan Mediterranean coast. Although the town, a Spanish creation of the 1920s and 1950s, has no great monuments, there is compensation in the form of nearby beaches. Despite these coastal attractions and greenery of the surrounding hills, the difficulty of getting to Al Hoceïma by road reduces the flow of casual visitors. There is an airport, however, bringing in a few package tourists. In summer there are huge numbers of migrant workers and their families back from Europe, while the winter is very quiet. East of the town is a fertile plain enclosed on three sides by hills. And off the Plage de Sfiha, also to the east of Al Hoceïma, is an intriguing group of islands, the Peñon de Alhucemas, Spanish territory since 1673, and once disputed by the French and English for their strategic position.

Ins and outs
Getting there Al Hoceïma is possibly the most isolated resort town in Morocco. You can fly there from Casablanca (in summer), or, given the distances, take an early morning bus from Chefchaouen, Fès, Nador, Tangier, or Taza. There are grands taxis, especially from Nador (three hours) and more rarely from Taza and Fès. ⤵ *See Transport, page 143, for further details.*

Getting around Al Hoceïma is not a big place. However, you might want to take a beige-and-blue petit taxi out to one of the beaches. The beaches at Torres de Alcalá and Kalah Iris, some 60 km away to the west, can also easily be reached by public transport. Ketama and Jbel Tidghine are a feasible day trip by grand taxi from Al Hoceïma.

Tourist information Délégation Régionale du Tourisme ① *Imme*uble Cabalo, Rue Tarik Ibn Ziad off Pl de la Marche Verte, T039-982830, 0830-1200 and 1400-1800.

Background
The character of the town centre of modern Al Hoceïma is distinctly Spanish, reflecting the Protectorate years. Established by the Spanish in 1926 as Villa Sanjurjo, it was built as a garrison to control the Beni Ouriaghel tribe, of which Abd al Karim was the chief, immediately after the Rif rebellion. (For those interested in colonial place names, the town was originally named Villa Sanjurjo, after one General Sanjurjo who led Spanish troops ashore here. The old part of town is still sometimes referred to by this name.) To the east of Al Hoceïma is the long and less busy beach of the Alhucemas bay, while offshore is the Peñon de Alhucemas, a remarkable idiosyncrasy of history. This small

island is owned and occupied by Spain and apparently used as a prison. It is completely dependent on Melilla for supplies and even water, and has no contact with the Moroccan mainland, off which it sits like a ship at anchor.

Today Al Hoceïma has a population of some 60,000. Off season, it has an isolated feel: Tangier lies 300 km away to the west, Melilla is 170 km to the east, Oujda some 250 km away. The image in the holiday brochures is of a villageish sort of place with low, whitewashed houses atop a cliff, surrounding a few colonial buildings. In fact, modern Al Hoceïma has streets and streets of three- and four-storey blocks, sprawling across the hillsides. This is where migrant workers put their savings. So Al Hoceïma is turning into a big town, but one without any industry or major official functions.

Nador and Al Hoceïma are the key towns for the Ta'rifit speaking region, and Arabic-speaking outsiders are not all that much appreciated here. Newsagents sell badges and stickers with the image of Abd el Karim, hero of the Rif War against the Spanish. Yet some cultural resistance aside, Al Hoceïma is very sleepy outside the summer season when the migrants from the Netherlands and Belgium pour in.

Sights
Buses and taxis pull into the neighbourhood of the Place du Rif. You should thread your way over to the Avenue Mohammed V (banks and cafés) which leads down to the wide expanse of **Place Mohammed VI**. (At the time of writing the newly renamed square was a building site but expect a pleasant new place with open views down to the sea.) The well maintained colonial building at the bottom is the Spanish school. The cafés on your right as you head down are worth a pause with their views over the horseshoe bay. At the Hotel Mohamed V, the road curves down to the main beach. The **port** is worth a look if you have time, and there are a handful of restaurants here. A stroll round the town will reveal various other remnants of Spanish times.

Just before the Hotel Mohamed V, there is a steep flight of steps that leads down to the Hotel Quemado complex and the **beach**. This gets pretty crowded in summer, although the sand is cleaned and raked every morning. There are pedalos and rowing boats for hire and jet skis. There is a rock to swim out to, and lots of enthusiastic playing of beach tennis.

Beaches east of town
Kalah Bonita beach is just within the urban area (campsite, café-restaurant, and crowds in summer, also sewage smells from the creek around the cliff). Further east are Isri, Sfiha, Souani, and Tayda. The beach at **Isri** has gravelly sand and, being below a brick factory, receives a certain amount of rubble. The left turn-off for Isri beach, coming from town, is 50 m after the Centre de visite technique, a large white building. The gravelly beach also has the rock where Abd el Karim el Khattabi made a famous speech in 1926, urging his resistance fighters to give up their arms and accept a form of autonomous government under Spanish rule. The tribes rejected this proposal and subsequently took a pounding from the Spanish airforce. Note that city taxis do not run this far out.

The beach at **Souani** ('the orchards') is rather better. The turn-off left is signed. There is a 2-km drive down to the car park next to the beach. Take care on the looping road, and don't get distracted by the superb views over to Peñon de Alhucemas. (Without a car, Souani is accessible by grand taxi, 7dh a place, and get out at Sfiha. Then walk along the beach.) The sand is dark and fine, and there are few seasonal beach cafés, showers and the

Restaurant Yasmine. In summer, for a modicum of quiet, you will need to walk along the beach towards the forest and **Tayda**, where there is an exclusive Club Med.

Excursions
There are some good day trips to the tiny fishing communities west of Al Hoceïma, namely Torres de Alcalá, Kalah Iris, and rather remote Badis. Without your own transport, the easiest approach is to take a grand taxi from Al Hoceïma to Beni Boufrah, via Imzouren. Beni Boufrah is a small rural community about 7 km from Torres. Here you change for a local share taxi. (There is also occasional transport from Beni Boufrah to Targuist.)

Torres de Alcalá has a pebbly beach and seasonal café. Just behind the beach is a campsite among the eucalyptus trees (practically no facilities). Up on the hill are the remains of a fortress, which gives the village its name, 'the towers of the citadel', Alcalá being a Spanish word derived from the Arabic for citadel.

More interesting than Torres is **Badis**, a tiny fishing settlement about 90 minutes' walk along a good piste to the east. The track starts just behind the two-storey houses of Torres village. You could drive (and there is another, more direct, piste off the Imzouren to Beni Boufrah road), but note that in summer Badis is off-limits to all outside vehicles as there is a royal campsite here. Princess Lalla Amina, Hassan II's sister, takes her annual holidays on the beach at Badis, which is unofficially off-limits to all but locals. The track runs along the clifftop and makes a good walk. You have to scramble down the last 100 m or so to reach the beach. Behind the beach, a wide valley runs inland. There is no accommodation. You can buy a few basic things at the tiny shop in the settlement about 300 m from the sea, behind the royal camping area. In summer, one of the royal security guards will probably come and have a chat.

You could make the long scramble up to what is said to be a ruined windmill high above the beach, and have a look at the tiny shrine to Abou Yacoub al Badis, born around 1260, hidden in the trees. As the Mediterranean port for Fès, Badis was once an important settlement. It was destroyed by earthquake in 1564. The Spanish-held Peñón de Velez de la Gomera, generally described in the press as an islet but in fact attached to the beach at Badis by a pebbly spit, may have some fortifications which go back to Merinid times.

Kalah Iris, 60 km west of Al Hoceïma and 9 km from Beni Boufrah, has an attractive beach. Sometimes fishermen can be persuaded to run trips out to see the impressive cliffs.

⊙ Chefchaouen, the Rif and Al Hoceïma listings

For Sleeping and Eating price codes and other relevant information, see pages 12-20.

🛏 Sleeping

Chefchaouen *p132, map p133*
Chefchaouen is a popular place for budget travellers as it has a good supply of clean cheap hotels. However, note that it gets pretty cold here in winter. Light sleepers will be awakened by the heavily amplified call to prayer from the numerous mosques.

€€€ Atlas Chaouen, T039-986265, www.achaouen@hotelsatlas.com. It's a big climb up the hill to the ugly and incongruous Atlas Chaouen – a modern building with 63 rooms that rather overshadows the town. Once you're there, the views are good and there's a small swimming pool a nightclub and a big restaurant but it all feels out of keeping with the rest of Chefchaouen.
€€€ Casa Hassan, Rue Targui-Chaouen, T039-986153, www.casahassan.com. A

sophisticated place, with *tadelakt* bathrooms and big beds. Arches, painted wood ceilings, decorated chests and wood fires add interest and there's the advantage of a/c. The place has an authentic feel, a big yellow and red hammam and a great roof terrace with views over the mountains.

€€ Barcelona, 12 Rue Al Andalous, T039-988506. Rough wooden doors and good, simple rooms, 2 of which have a/c. Roof terrace with views and tables undercover. Coloured glass, old tiles, lots of blankets.

€€ Dar Mounir, T039-988253, www.hotel-darmounir.com. Opened in 2007, Dar Mounir has 11 rooms, most of which are big, and *tadelakt* bathrooms with horseshoe arches. Windows are high in the walls, which means there's not much of a view but it's all very comfortable, with good new beds, sofas and open fires.

€€ Dar Rass el Maa, Rue Rass el Maa, T039-988080, www.chefchaouen.ch. A grand guesthouse across the stream under the mountain, overlooking the valley, Rass el Mar is good value for money. The garden is verdant, bedrooms are bright, bathrooms have colourful *tadelakt* and an excellent breakfast is served on the pretty terrace.

€€ Dar Terrae, Av Hassan I, T039-987598, www.darterrae.com. Italian-run, Dar Terae is a riad with style at a very reasonable price. Rooms are quite small, and not all have en suite bathrooms, but the beds are comfortable and there is an excellent multi-levelled roof terrace, where you can have breakfast or relax with a mint tea. Rooms have open fires for winter and it's also one of the friendliest places in town.

€€ Hotel Madrid, Av Hassan II, T039- 987496. Beds come with drapes in this reliable, if slightly old-fashioned hotel. Rooms have safes, TVs and showers and at the time of writing refurbishment work was being done.

€€ Hotel Parador, Pl el Makhzen, T039-986324. The Parador feels a little dated, with its pistachio and peach corridors, and there's

not a whole lot of space. However, many of the 37 rooms have good views, there is a pool and rooms have a/c and telephones. Safe parking, bar and restaurant.

€ Andaluz, 1 Rue Sidi Salem, T039-986034. Simple rooms are arranged around an old tiled courtyard. Single beds are on the small side but there's a wood fire downstairs and a library. Showers included.

€ Cordoba, Av Gharnata Qu Rif Andalousse, T064-430044 (mob). Simple rooms with small beds and views of kasbah walls. Rectangular courtyard with some slightly garish Moroccan fabrics. Some rooms good for 3/4 people.

€ Hotel Ahrazem, 76 Av Sidi Abdelhamid, T039-987384. 150dh with shower and loo. Friendly, blue-painted, courtyard, simple rooms just outside Bab el Souk.

€ Hostal Gernika, 49 Onsaar, T039-987434. Immaculately decorated in riad style, with tiles and arches, Gernika is a cosy hotel with a wood-burning stove and a bright seating area. Rooms have plain white walls, white curtains, good wooden furniture and views. The rooms at the top of the building have no bathroom but open up onto the three-part roof terrace. Friendly and well-run.

€ Hotel Koutoubia, T039-988433, T068-115358 (mob), hotelkoutoubia@hotmail.fr. Opened in 2007, Koutoubia is a fresh place with warm orange and red fabrics in the bedrooms and modern blue and white bathrooms. Rooms are on the small side but have nice Moroccan touches. The view from the private terrace of the suite is great, as it is from the roof terrace, where you can have breakfast if you wish. Good English spoken.

€ Hotel Rif, 29 Rue Tarik Ibn Ziad, T039-986982. Friendly hotel, bar and restaurant with good views from higher rooms over the valley. A good place to get information on walking and the local area. Traveller-friendly – drummers are encouraged, you can do your own laundry and guests are welcome to drink on the roof terrace.

€ Hotel Salam, 38 Rue Tarik Ibn Ziad, T039-

986239. Just below the médina, Salam has 10 plain rooms and a bright salon. Rooms are clean but a little damp in places.

€ Mouritania, 15 Calle Kadi Alami, T039-986184. The bedrooms are a bit dim but the beds are good and big with mirrors and clean white walls. Rooms without showers are even cheaper. If full, Souika next door is very similar.

€ Pensión La Castellana, 4 Calle Sidi Ahmad el Bouhali, T039-986295. Signposted just off the main square, La Castellana claims to be the oldest hotel in Chefchaouen. Good, hot, shared showers and bright rooms with blue walls and lots of beds. The roof terrace has good views of the médina and the hotel will happily look after bikes.

€ Pensión Ibn Batouta, 31 Rue Abie Khancha, T039-986044. Just off the road between Bab el Aïn and Pl Outa el Hammam, Ibn Batouta is clean and quiet with good value, comfortable rooms. If you want to save even more pennies, you can sleep on the roof terrace for 20dh.

Youth hostel and camping
Next to each other, 2 km from centre near the Hotel Atlas Chaouen. Follow the signs from the road in from Tetouan, or walk (carefully) through the cemetery above the médina.

Youth hostel, T039-986031, m.sarhan@ hotmail.fr. 30 beds, meals available, kitchen, overnight fee 25dh, 20dh with a youth hostelling card. The dorms might be worth reserving for groups but otherwise you're better off in a cheap hotel.

Camping Municipal, T039-986979. Small café, shop, simple toilets and showers, tents among the pine trees, good view of the valley. 20dh per person, 15-25dh per tent, or there are bungalows for 130dh.

Ketama *p135*
€ Café-Hotel Saâda, on the main drag and easily identified by its shaded terrace, about 100 m on from the Hotel Tidghine, T039-813061. An acceptable option.

Ouezzane *p136*
Ouezzane is very limited for hotels, and is perhaps best visited in passing or as an excursion from Chefchaouen. Budget hotels include **€ Marhaba**, **€ Horloge**, and **€ El Elam**, on Pl de l'Indépendance, or the more basic **€ Grand Hotel** on Av Mohammed V, although none of these is an attractive option.

Al Hoceïma *p137*
Be aware that it can be difficult to get a quiet night's sleep in Al Hoceïma in summer and that practically no street names are shown.

€€€€ Hotel Mohamed V, T039-923314. Just off Pl Mohammed VI, above the beach, all 30 rooms have sea views and balconies, as well as baths and tiled bathrooms. Quite plain for the money, but there is a bar and a restaurant.

€€ Hotel Khouzama, T039-985669. Linking rooms for families, nice café. Yellow curtains and nasty art but not a bad choice. Same owner as the Hotel Étoile du Rif.

€€ Hotel Maghreb el Jadid, 56 Av Mohammed V, T039-982504. 42 good-sized rooms, a yellow and peach old-fashioned place that will win no interior decoration prizes but is nevertheless a decent option in the town centre. Traffic noise can be a problem.

€€ National, 23 Rue Tetouan, T039-982141. Good sized rooms with TVs and old carpets. Clean, modern bathrooms.

€ Hotel du Rif, 13 Rue Moulay Youssef, T039-982268. Basic but OK. Rooms have basins; showers cost 10dh.

€ Hotel Étoile du Rif, 40 Pl du Rif (Sahat Rif), T039-840847. A stylish pink and white Spanish building, once the town's casino, dominates the main square. Above a busy café-restaurant, it's friendly and clean and the best rooms overlook the square. Handy for bus station.

€ Hotel Nekor, 20 Rue Tahnaoute, T039-983065. Just off Place du Rif, Nekor has a café downstairs and is handily placed for making an early-morning getaway in a petit taxi, though the regular cries of "Nador, Nador, Nador" may wake you.

Camping

El Jamil, also referred to as **Camping Cala Bonita**, T039-982009. East of the town, crowded in summer as close to the beach. Awful wash-blocks.

Club Méditerranée, T039-982222, is 10 km from Al Hoceima. Watersports and riding. Best booked through Club Med in your home country, but you could perhaps ring up.

🍴 Eating

Chefchaouen p132, map p133

🍴🍴 **Casa Aladin/La Lampe Magique**, 26 Rue Targui, T065-406464. Though it can't seem to quite make up its mind about what it's called, this is a good restaurant, where the best tables overlook the end of the square. The covered roof terrace has geraniums, while downstairs it's cosier, with elaborate window frames and red curtains. The food is reliably good Moroccan fare

🍴🍴 **Restaurant al Kasbah**, just off the square. Al Kasbah has lots of carved wood and cushions. There's a big chouce of tagines and couscous.

🍴🍴 **Tissemkal**, 22 Rue Targui, T039-986153. Chefchaouen's best restaurant is an atmospheric place offering warm bread, occasional free appetizers, great salads and excellent Moroccan main dishes in a peaceful and sophisticated courtyard setting. There are comfortable seats, candles, an open fire and big metal lamps.

🍴 **Café Snack Mounir**, at the end of the square. Mounir offers a range of light meals, including an unusually good vegetarian selection, as well as Chefchaouen's best coffee. A good spot to sit and watch the world go by, and better than the other options in the square.

🍴 **Café Tunssi**, Bab Ansar. Just outside the médina on the slope above the stream, café Tunssi has good views across to Jemaâ Buzafar, the mosque on the opposite hill from its three terraced levels.

🍴 **Chez Fouad**, Rue Adarve Chabu. Metal tables, blue and white tiles, tagines and fried fish and couscous and 'pitza'. Small and cheap.

🍴 **Jardin Ziryab**. Flowery gardens with tables above the far side of the stream from the centre of the town. Tea and live music and snacks and if you really like it here, you can even stay in one of the rooms here.

🍴 **Restaurant Rincón Andaluz**, just off Plaza Bab Souk. Couscous and fried fish for bargain prices at little tables on a blue-painted alleyway just outside Bab el Souk.

Ouezzane p136, map p

Eat at the basic café-restaurants on Pl de l'Indépendance. If you are driving, **Café Africa**, 10 km north of the town, is a good place to stop for a drink.

Al Hoceïma p137

There aren't many good options in Al Hoceïma. Try any of the cafés off Pl Mohammed VI overlooking the Playa Quemado. Café el Nejma and La Belle Vue, next to each other at the end of Rue Mohammed V, both have far-end terraces with views out over the bay.

🍴🍴 **La Dolce Pizza**, Pl du Rif, opposite Hotel Étoile du Rif. Relatively speaking, a surprisingly atmospheric little restaurant serving up lasagne as well as pizzas.

🍴🍴 **Club Náutico**, fishing port, T039-981641. A down-to-earth licensed place in the port with lots of men sitting round plastic covered tables watching football on TV. The food is probably Al Hoceïma's best, however – splash out on an excellent mixed plate of fried fish and don't miss the torchlit sale of the day's catch outside.

🍴 **Snack Maghreb el Jadid**, Av Mohammed V.

A friendly little snack bar next to the hotel of the same name that will rustle up brochettes or a sandwich at any hour of the day.

⚠ Activities and tours

Chefchaouen *p132, map p133*
The manager of the Casa Hassan (see Sleeping above) may be able to advise on mountain walking.

⊙ Transport

Chefchaouen *p132, map p133*
Try to reserve your bus seat in advance when you want to move on.
Bus: the bus station is down the hill out of town. Buses are often through services and can thus be full. There are several buses a day for **Ouezzane**, 3 daily for **Meknès** (5 hrs), 10 daily for **Fès** (7 hrs), 4 a day for **Tetouan** and Tangier, 2 daily for **Al Hoceïma** (8 hrs). Grands taxis: leave from the bus station on Av Allal Ben Abdallah to most of the above destinations.

Al Hoceïma *p137*
Air
The airport, **Aéroport Côte du Rif**, T039-982005, is at Charif al Idrissi, 17 km southeast from Al Hoceïma on the Nador road, with flights to **Amsterdam** (2 a week) and **Brussels** (1 a week), and **Casablanca** (2 a week) in season. **RAM**, T039-982063.

Bus
Buses leave from Pl du Rif, which has ticket booths for the different companies. Most leave early in the morning. **CTM** (T039-982273) to **Nador** (0400, 0530, 1230, 7 hrs), **Tetouan** (1330, 2100 and 2200), **Rabat** (2000) and **Tangier** (2200). There are many private bus companies. **Nejme Chamal** (Étoile du Nord) and **Trans-Ghazala** are recommended.

Taxi
Grands taxis for **Nador** and **Taza** leave from just off Pl du Rif. For destinations west of Al Hoceïma, they leave from Calle al Raya al Maghrebiya, off top of Av Mohamed V, between Mobil and Total garages and opposite the BMCI.

⊙ Directory

Chefchaouen *p132, map p133*
Banks **Banque populaire**, Av Hassan II; **BMCE**, Av Hassan II; **Crédit agricole**, Pl Outa el Hammam. **Post** PTT, Av Hassan II. **Medical services** **Chemist** beside Hotel Magou.

Al Hoceïma *p137*
Banks All on or around Av Mohamed V, most have ATMs. **Internet** **Cyberclub**, Av Mohamed V, above the Méditel shop near the turn-off for Hotel Khozama. **Internet Bades**, Av Tarik Ibn Ziad, next to BCM, on left as you come from Pl de la Marche verte. **Medical services** **Hôpital Mohammed V**, Av Hassan II. Pharmacies on Av Mohamed V.

Contents

146 Language in Morocco

150 Index

Footnotes

Language in Morocco

Moroccan Arabic

For the English speaker, some of the sounds of Moroccan Arabic are totally alien. There is a strong glottal stop (as in the word 'bottle' when pronounced in Cockney English), generally represented by an apostrophe, and a rasping sound written here as 'kh', rather like the 'ch' of the Scots 'loch' or the Greek 'drachma'. And there is a glottal 'k' sound, which luckily often gets pronounced as the English hard 'g', and a very strongly aspirated 'h' in addition to the weak 'h'. The French 'r' sound is generally transcribed as 'gh'. Anyway, worry ye not. Moroccan acquaintances will have a fun time correcting your attempts at pronouncing Arabic.

Polite requests and saying thank you
excuse me, please – *'afek* (for calling attention politely) – عفاك

please – *min fadhlek* – من فضلك

one minute, please – *billatí* – بلاتي

(to call the the waiter) – *esh-sheríf* or *ya ma'alem* – الشريف / يامعلم

thank you – *teberkallah alík/Allah yekhallík* – تبرك الله عليك

thank you – *shukran* – شكرا

Saying hello (and goodbye)
Good morning – *sabaH el-khír* – صباح الخير

How's things? – *kí yedirkí dayir?* – كي داير ؟ كي يدير

Everything's fine – *el Hamdou lillah* (lit Praise be to God) – الحمد لله

Everything's fine – *kull shay la bas* – كل شيئ لاباس

Congratulations – *mabrouk* – مبروك

Goodbye – *bisslema* – بسلامة

Goodbye – *Allah ya'wnek* – الله يعاونك

Handy adjectives and adverbs
Like French, Moroccan Arabic has adjectives (and nouns) with feminine and masculine forms. To get the masculine form, simply knock off the final 'a'.

good – *mezyena* – مزيان

happy – *farhana* – فرحانة

beautiful – *jmíla, zwína* – جميلة

new – *jdída* – جديدة

old – *qdíma* – قديمة

cheap – *rkhíssa* – رخيسة

clean – *naqía* – نقية

full – *'amra* – عامرة

in a hurry – *zarbana* – زربانة

quickly – *dghiya dghiya* – دغية دغية

it doesn't matter – *belesh* – بلاش

Quantities
a lot – *bezaf* – بزاف

a little – *shwíya* – شوية

half – *nesf* – نصف

Numerals

Days of the week
Monday – *nhar el itnayn* – نهار الاثنين

Tuesday – *nhar ettlata* – نهار الثلاثاء

one – *wahed*	nineteen – *ts'atash*
two – *zouj* or *tnine*	twenty – *'ashrine*
three – *tlata*	twenty-one – *wahed ou 'ashrine*
four – *arba'*	twenty-two – *tnine ou 'ashrine*
five – *khamsa*	twenty-three – *tlata ou 'ashrine*
six – *setta*	twenty-four – *'arba ou 'ashrine*
seven – *saba'*	thirty – *tlatine*
eight – *tmaniya*	forty – *'arba'ine*
nine – *ts'oud*	fifty – *khamsine*
ten – *ashra*	sixty – *sittine*
eleven – *hedash*	seventy – *saba'ine*
twelve – *t'nash*	eighty – *temenine*
thirteen – *t'latash*	ninety – *t'issine*
fourteen – *rb'atash*	one hundred – *miya*
fifteen – *kh'msatash*	two hundred – *miyatayn*
sixteen – *settash*	three hundred – *tlata miya*
seventeen – *sb'atash*	thousand – *alf*
eighteen – *t'mentash*	two thousand – *alfayn*

Wednesday – *nhar el arba* – نهار الاربعاء

Thursday – *nhar el khemís* – نهار الخميس

Friday – *nhar el jema'* – نهار الجمعة

Saturday – *nhar essebt* – نهار السبت

Sunday – *nhar el had* – نهار الحد

A few expressions of time
today – *el yawm* – اليومة

yesterday – *el-bareh* – البارح

tomorrow – *ghedda* – غدة

day after tomorrow – *ba'da ghedda* – بعد غدة

day – *nhar* – النهار

morning – *sbah* – الصباح

midday – *letnash* – لاتناش

evening – *ashíya* – العشية

tonight/night – *el-lila/lil* – الليلة / الليل

hour – *sa'a* – ساعة
half an hour – *nes sa'a* – نصف ساعة

Miscellaneous expressions
Watch out! (as a mule comes careering down the street) – *balak! balak!*
No problem – *ma ka'in mushkil*
How much? – *bayshhal? aysh-hal ettaman?*
Free (of charge) – *fabor*
Look – *shouf* (pl *shoufou*)
OK, that's fine – *wakha*
Good luck! – *fursa sa'ída*

At the café
tea – *ettay* – التاي
weak milky coffee – *un crème* – قهوة بالحليب
half espresso, half milk – *nes nes* – نص نص
a small bottle – *gara' sghíra* – قرعة صغيرة
a large bottle – *gara' kbíra* – قرعة كبيرة
a bottle of still mineral water – *gara' Sidi Ali/Sidi Harazem* – قرعة سيدي علي
a bottle of fizzy mineral water – *gara' Oulmes/Bonacqua* – قرعة اولماس
ashtray – *dfeya, cendrier* – طفاية
do you have change? – *'indak sarf/vous avez de la monnaie?* – عندك الصرف

At the restaurant
bill – *l'hseb* – لحساب
fork – *foursheta, lamtíqa* – فورشتة / لمتيقة
knife – *mous, mis* – موس
spoon – *mu'allaka* – معلقة / عاشق
glass – *ka's* (pl *kísan*) – كاس / كيسان
bowl – *zellafa* – زلافة
plate – *tobsil* – تبصيل
could you bring us some more bread – *afak tzídna khubz* – عفاك تزيدنا الخبز

Food and drink
bananas – *mouz* – موز
beef – *lham bagri* – لحم بقري
butter – *zebda* – زبدة
bread – *khobz* – خبز
chicken – *djaj* – دجاج
chips – *btata maklya, frites* – بطاطة مقلية
egg – *bíd* (sing *bída*) – بيض / بيضة
fruit – *fekiha* – فواكه
mandarins – *tchína* – تشينة
mutton – *lham ghenmí* – لحم غنمي
milk – *hlíb* – حليب
olive oil – *zít zítoun* – زيت زيتون

oranges – *límoun* – ليمون

rice – *rouz* – روز

tomatoes – *ma'tísha* – مطيشة

vegetables – *khudra* – خضرة

water – *ma* – ماء

At the hotel

room – *el-bít/la chambre* – البيت

bed – *tliq, farsh* – تليق / فراش

mattress – *talmíta* – طلميتة

shower – *douche* – دوش

without shower – *bila douche, sans douche* – بلا دوش

key – *es sarrout/la clef* – السروت

blanket – *ghta'/couverture* – غطاء

sheet – *izar/le drap* – أزار

corridor – *couloir* – كولوار

noise – *sda'* – صداع

At the hotel – a few requests and complaints

Can I see the room, please? – *Afak, mumkin nshouf el bít* – عفاك ممكن نشوف البيت

The water's off – *El ma maktou'a* – الماء مقطوع

There's no hot water – *El-ma skhoun ma ka'insh* – الماء سخون ماكاينش

Excuse me, are there any towels? – *Afak ka'in foutet* – عفاك كاين فوطاط

Could you bring us some towels? – *Mumkin tjíbilna foutet* – ممكن تجيب النا فوطاط

The washbasin's blocked – *El lavabo makhnouk* – الأفابو مخنوقة

The window doesn't close – *Esh sherajim ma yetsidoush* – الشراجم مايتسدوش

Can you change the light bulb? – *Mumkin tebedil el bawla* – ممكن تبدل البولة

The toilet flush doesn't work – *La chasse ma tekhdemsh* – لاشاس ماخدامش

There's a lot of noise – *Ka'in sda' bezef* – كاين صداع بزاف

Can I change rooms? – *Mumkin nebedil el bít* – ممكن نبدل البيت

On the road

Where is the bus station? – *Fayn kayin maHata diyal kíran?* – فين كاين المحطة ديال الكران

Where is the CTM bus station? – *Fayn kayin mHata diyal Saytayem?* – فين كاين المحطة ديال الستيام

road – *tríq* – طريق

street – *zanqa* – زنقة

neighbourhood, also street – *derb* – درب

bridge – *qantra* – قنطرة

straight ahead – *níshan* – نيشان

to the right/left – *ila l-yemin/sh-shimal* – الى اليمن / الى اليسر

turn at the corner – *dour fil-qent* – دور في القنت

wheel – *rwída* – رويدة

Index

A

accident and emergency 21
accommodation 12
accommodation price codes 13
Aguelmane Azigza 73, 74
Ahouli 75
Aïn Chifa 74
Aïn Leuh 72, 74
Aïn Sbilia 85
Aïn Seban 74
air
    airlines 7
    airport tax 6
    international 6
    See also under individual towns
Aït Ayach 75
Al Hoceïma 132, 137
    listings 141
alcohol 18
Arabic language 22
arts festivals 19
Asilah 109
Asiliah
    listings 114
Atlas Mountains
    Middle Atlas 71
Azrou 71
    listings 76

B

Bab Taza 135
Badis 139
banks 23
Beni Ahmed 134
Berber language 22
Bhalil 42
birdwatching
    Tangier 106

C

Cabo Negro 128
    listings 130
camping 14
Cap Malabata 100
Cap Spartel 100

car hire 8
Caves of Hercules 100
Cèdre de Gouraud 72
Ceuta 118
    background 119
    ins and outs 118
    listings 122
    sights 119
    transport 123
Chaouen 132
Chefchaouen 132
    listings 139
Cirque du Jaffar 76
clothing 21
cost of living 24
Cotta 100
currency 22

D

Dayat lakes 73
Debdou 85
dress 21
drink 18
drugs 133

E

eating 14
El Aïoun 85
El Jebha 129
El Malha 134
El Utad 110

F

Fès 28
    background 29
    Fès El Bali 32, 38
    Fès el Jedid 40
    ins and outs 28
    listings 45
    sights 32
    transport 52
festivals 19
food
    See eating

G

Genet, Jean 112
Gouffre de Friouato 83
Grand Mosque, Tangier 98
Guercif 84
    listings 86
guesthouses 12

H

hammams 39
holidays 19
hotels 12

I

Ifrane 73
    listings 77
Immouzer du Kandar 73
Isri 138
Issaguen 135

J

Jbel Ayyachi 75
Jbel Ben Hellal 136
Jbel Tazzeka National Park 82
Jbel Tidghine 135
Jbel Tidiquin 135

K

Kalah Bonita 138
Kalah Iris 139
Ketama 135
    listings 141
Khénifra 74
    listings 77
kif 133
Ksabi 86
Ksar es Seghir 101

L

language 22
Larache 111
    listings 115
Lixus 113